Risk and Foreign Direct Investment

Also by Colin White

RUSSIA AND AMERICA: THE ROOTS OF ECONOMIC DIVERGENCE

MASTERING RISK: ENVIRONMENTS, MARKETS AND POLITICS IN AUSTRALIAN ECONOMIC HISTORY

COMING FULL CIRCLE: AN ECONOMIC HISTORY OF THE PACIFIC RIM (*with E. L. Jones and L. Frost*)

STRATEGIC MANAGEMENT

Risk and Foreign Direct Investment

By Colin White and Miao Fan

First published 2006 by
PALGRAVE MACMILLAN
Houndmills, Basingstoke, Hampshire RG21 6XS and
175 Fifth Avenue, New York, N. Y. 10010
Companies and representatives throughout the world

PALGRAVE MACMILLAN is the global academic imprint of the Palgrave Macmillan division of St. Martin's Press, LLC and of Palgrave Macmillan Ltd. Macmillan® is a registered trademark in the United States, United Kingdom and other countries. Palgrave is a registered trademark in the European Union and other countries.

ISBN-13: 978–1–4039–4564–8   hardback
ISBN-10: 1–4039–4564–0   hardback

This book is printed on paper suitable for recycling and made from fully managed and sustained forest sources.

A catalogue record for this book is available from the British Library.

Library of Congress Cataloging-in-Publication Data
White, Colin (Colin M.)
     Risk and foreign direct investment / by Colin White and Miao Fan.
         p. cm.
     Includes bibliographical references and index.
     ISBN 1–4039–4564–0 (cloth)
     1. Investments, Foreign. 2. Country risk. 3. Risk. I. Fan, Miao, 1976– II. Title.
HG4538.W4145 2006
332.67′3–dc22   2005052283

10	9	8	7	6	5	4	3	2	1
15	14	13	12	11	10	09	08	07	06

Printed and bound in Great Britain by
Antony Rowe Ltd, Chippenham and Eastbourne

To our families

Contents

List of Tables

List of Figures

Preface

The present book is the result of an interest of one of the authors which has persisted throughout his career in different forms, Colin White, an interest in risk – its identification and measurement and even more its role in the historical development of different economies. All of his previous work has reflected this interest, but to a varying degree. The views expressed therefore are a distillation of what wisdom the author has acquired over a long career teaching and writing about such topics. The second author, Miao Fan, completed in 2004 a PhD thesis at Swinburne University of Technology, entitled Country Risk and its Impact on the FDI Decision-making Process from an Australian Perspective, Swinburne University of Technology 2004, which had at its core a survey of Australian managers and their attitude to country and other types of risk. She has just started a career in a bank pursuing the more practical side of risk management. She has worked over the last few years with her co-author on a number of conference papers which have progressively set out the main outline of the book.

Both authors would like to give their thanks to those whose help, whether academic or otherwise, has made such an enterprise possible. As the dedication shows, this is most of all the families of the two authors. We live in a risky world, but families reduce that risk. A life of reflection and writing is initiated with the help of parents and made very much easier by the assistance of loving partners. Colleagues are often there to discuss an interesting point and to provide the reality test to which all ideas must at some time be exposed. Universities provide the facilities critical to research, the preparation and giving of papers at conferences and the whole-hearted commitment of time and effort to the completion of a text. To all responsible for the necessary inputs many thanks.

1
Introduction

> The aim is to establish a structure for decision-making that produces good decisions, or improved decisions, defined in a suitable way, based on a realistic view of how people can act in practice.
>
> (Aven 2003: 96)

This book is an exploration of the way in which risk influences the process of decision making relating to foreign direct investment. Its initial premise is that country risk is, and should be, a major deterrent to such investment. Since FDI is of increasing significance for the promotion of economic development in countries with a low level of economic development and for the maintenance of continuing growth in developed countries, it is important to understand how risk of various types constrains the flow of such investment. FDI is much more important than trade in delivering goods and services abroad (UNCTAD 2003: xvi). In 2002 global sales by multilateral enterprises reached $US18 trillion, as compared with world exports of $US8 trillion. In the same year the value added by foreign affiliates of multinational companies reached $US3.4 trillion, about one tenth of world GDP, twice the level of 1982. Because risk is a significant determinant of foreign investment there is a need for the relevant decision makers to identify, estimate and assess the relevant risk and to respond to it (Baird and Thomas 1985: 234).

There are several books which have had an important influence on the authors. Hull, as early as 1980, anticipated most of the relevant issues. Moosa (2002) provides the conventional view about the use of present value for appraisal of international investment projects. Broader in its scope than Moosa's text, since it incorporates the real options approach, is a book by Buckley (1996), which claims to be the first book on international capital budgeting (Buckley 1996: vii). The main innovation since the publication of Hull's book has been the application of a valuation of real options to investment appraisal. A pioneering book is that by Dixit and Pindyck (1994). Probably the best introduction is a set of essays edited by Schwartz and Trigeorgis (2001). This literature has the virtue of building into an investment appraisal both uncertainties concerning future performance and interdependencies between investment projects over time.

The book is neither solely an instructional manual on how to make an international investment decision in conditions of risk, as Hull's book (1980) might be regarded, nor solely a research monograph, as the book by Dowd (1998), on the concept of value at risk, might be viewed. It is more like the book by Moosa (2002), which is intermediate between a primer and a review of existing theory. It goes much further than Moosa in considering the problem of valuation of investment, in particular how uncertainty affects that valuation. The book is therefore similar to both a review of theory, one with a critical slant, and a primer, an updating of Hull's approach to FDI, with strong indications of how an investment decision should be made. It is also like a research monograph in that it develops a treatment which brings together ideas not previously combined.

It is easy to see the elegance of the financial theory used in the 'hard' risk literature but to realise its limitations (Bernstein 1996). In this theory, there is a clear prescription on how to effect an investment appraisal, which needs to be examined. However, it is also easy to see the importance of good strategy making to the success of an individual project and to the overall performance of the relevant enterprise. All successful enterprises have good strategies, which include appropriate procedures for making decisions on which projects to run with, procedures which take full account of any interdependencies between projects of a different timing. An appropriate approach clearly requires the insights of both the financial theorist and the strategist. In an important sense, to be developed in the book, strategy should have precedence over capital budgeting, but it is always sensible to base strategy on sound quantitative foundations, where this is possible. The book does this.

The first section of this book is introductory, including three chapters which establish the context for the main arguments. In sequence they discuss and critique the existing theory relevant to risk control, explore the general nature of risk and indicate the tendency of FDI flows to be lower than expected, that is the existence of a pronounced home country bias. The second section introduces the present value formula for appraising investment projects, initially in conditions of certainty but then under uncertainty or risk. It tackles the appraisal of investment projects from three different perspectives – the financial, the strategic and the organisational. There are chapters devoted to each of these perspectives. The third section concentrates on the identification and measurement of risk, particularly country risk. It includes three chapters which deal in sequence with types of systematic risk other than country risk, country risk itself and the risk specific to an enterprise or a project. The final section comprises two chapters, showing how risk should be incorporated into an investment appraisal and how the response to risk has clearly kept aggregate FDI flows much lower than might be anticipated.

Part I

Risk and Home Country Bias

> It is hardly surprising that less investment occurs in countries
> that managers perceive to be risky ... this finding tells us
> nothing about the fundamental sources of risk.
>
> (Henisch 2002: 9)

The aim of the introductory section is twofold, to indicate the importance of risk in economic decision making, notably investment decisions, and to emphasise the prevalence throughout the world of a home country bias in the location of investment: the link between the two is a major focus of the book.

There are three chapters. The first explores the conventional treatment of risk and investment. The second considers in more detail the nature and role of risk, including country risk, in decision making relating to investment. The third considers the level of FDI in the contemporary economy, particularly how to judge whether it is large or small. This chapter shows that there is considerable evidence of a pronounced home country bias in the location of investment, as of other economic activities.

Part I
Risk and Home Country Bias

2

A Review of Theory Concerning Risk and the Foreign Investment Decision

> Possibly one of the biggest reasons for the failure of manage-
> ment science models in business is the management scientist's
> tendency to want to make his model as 'sophisticated' and as
> 'realistic' as possible without taking due account of how it will
> fit into this company's decision-making processes at their
> current stage of evolution.
>
> (Hull 1980: 134)

This chapter considers the platform of existing theory on which an acceptable treatment of risk and FDI can be built.[1] It is appropriate to consider at some length the way in which risk is treated in the financial literature and to show its limited relevance to the appraisal of foreign direct investment. It is also necessary to place the FDI decision in the context of the investment decision-making process in general.

There are five sections to this chapter:

- In the first section there is a review of the different approaches to risk.
- The second provides a statement and critique of the 'hard' risk approach.
- The third section analyses how risk is usually measured, notably as variance and as the impact of extreme events.
- Section four offers a critique of this approach in the context of the foreign direct investment decision.
- Section five considers the distinguishing characteristics of foreign direct investment and how they influence the treatment of risk.

Different approaches to risk

It is possible to conceptualise risk in different ways. There are three main approaches (Culp 2001: chapter 1).

- according to its multifarious sources, focusing on the incidence of specific unanticipated risk-generating events or behavioural changes;
- according to the impact of risky events on a key performance indicator, distinguishing risk which is systematic in its impact, affecting all the members of a defined group, and risk which is idiosyncratic and non-systematic, that is specific to an enterprise or a project;
- according to a distinction between risk and uncertainty, or more broadly between financial and business risk, the former amenable to estimation of the relevant probabilities of relevant outcomes, the latter not so and requiring a specialised knowledge to be manageable at all.

The conventional 'hard' risk literature argues:

- that the first approach is irrelevant to risk management – the sources of risk are of no significance, since it is the impact on a key performance indicator such as profit or the value of the relevant enterprise, which is important,
- that the central focus of any risk control is systematic market risk but this is conditional on a stable degree of vulnerability to market risk for any particular enterprise,
- that the third approach is unnecessary since there is only risk and no uncertainty – all probabilities are already known or can be derived from subjective assessments.

Most analysis of risk in the 'hard' literature short-circuits both the need to consider the source of risk and to make a clear and consistent distinction between risk and uncertainty, and therefore between financial and business risk. Such analysis avoids tracing the sequence of events which results in risk for the enterprise, concentrating on performance outcomes without considering the causative chains which produce those outcomes. It assumes that all possible outcomes can be measured as probabilities, albeit subjective probabilities, and that only risk is under analysis, not uncertainty.

For our analysis the source of risk is important since understanding that source allows risk to be mitigated as well as managed. In this book, risk control Is seen as consisting of both risk mitigation – actions to reduce the risk level to which the decision makers are exposed, and risk management – actions to redistribute at least some of the risk to others, whether commercially through insurance or hedging, through voluntary sharing in strategic alliances or through involuntary sharing imposed by government. Financial theory fails to put enough emphasis on the need for the mitigation of risk. In practice, sensible managers devote far more time and effort to risk mitigation than risk management, the former being strategically more important to the retention of competitive advantage than the latter.

There is a simple rule put forward by economists on how much mitigation should be undertaken in any particular situation. The commitment of resources should be taken to the point at which the marginal benefit of the action taken is equal to its marginal cost. Beyond this point additional costs are not worth incurring. The benefit consists in the reduction of risk, which in its turn can be represented by a notional increase in the present value of the investment.

The second distinction is important but is less useful for our analysis than usually assumed. Financial theory argues – surprisingly to anyone not versed in the financial theory literature – that managers should not be concerned with risk management, because the owners of an enterprise, its shareholders, have a much better opportunity to diversify risk through their choice and adjustment of a full portfolio of financial assets than managers have (see for example Doherty 2000 or Culp 2001). They are in a much better position to choose the risk/return combination they desire and to realise that choice. Most financial risk is unsystematic, accounting for something like 70% of the variability in the price of an individual share (Buckley 1996: 27). Because unsystematic risk can be diversified away it allegedly has no influence on the behaviour of financial investors. Systematic market risk is the prerogative of financial investors. In practice, most managers find such a suggestion unacceptable since any risk of a project failure threatens their own position. Moreover, the distinction does not seem useful for the present analysis. There is risk which is systematic, but it is systematic by country or by industry. There is a sense in which at the enterprise or project level all risk is unsystematic.

The third approach raises the issue of the difference between business risk and finance risk. On one account (Buckley 1996: 33–34), financial risk is reflected in the premium added when an enterprise has debt, which rises with the level of its gearing ratio. Business risk is the risk characterising the overall situation of an enterprise. This is not a helpful use of the terminology. Financial risk is better seen as the risk which arises from the operation of financial markets and the uncertain movement of prices within those markets, business risk that which arises from the core activities of the business itself. All enterprises are identified by their core activities and assets, and are expert in those areas of activity in which they have core competencies. Such competencies rest upon an advantage in access to information which yields them a competitive advantage over their competitors, one which allows them to earn an above-normal or monopoly profit. The insider is always privileged, having information not accessible to others. In areas of expertise, the risk managers can mitigate risk in a significant way. All enterprises have as one of their core competencies risk control in the core area(s) of activity, so-called business risk. Their ability to make an above normal profit partly reflects this source of competitive advantage, the ability to control core risk. The competitive advantage of any enterprise consists largely in an ability to leverage an informational advantage in the area of core activity by mitigating, rather than managing, that risk.

The distinction between core and incidental risk is critical (Doherty 2000: 223–225), the former being part of normal business activity (Culp 2001: chap. 1). There is no point in trying to hedge away the raison d'etre of entrepreneurship, that is, the core risk. It is wise to hedge only incidental risk such as the foreign exchange risk which arises from changes in the relative values of currencies. With perfect markets for risk, it would be possible to cover all risks, both core and incidental, but in such a world all enterprises earn only a normal rate of return.

The three approaches are different perspectives on the same problem, complementary rather than contradictory; each is important but not in the way often argued by financial theory.

The 'hard' approach to risk

The argument denying the need for managers to control risk privileges the owners as the most important stakeholder group for any enterprise, in some senses the only stakeholder whose interests matter. The single goal of any enterprise is to maximise the price of the shares held. The shareholders are seen as in a much better position to control risk either, where risk is unsystematic, by diversifying the portfolio of assets held, or where risk is systematic, by adjusting that portfolio of shares to take account of the risk attached to any particular enterprise, risk which is, therefore, reflected in its price. The context in which risk is considered is, therefore, that of its marginal effect on a well-diversified shareholder.

In such analysis, there is an assumption of strong or semi-strong market efficiency, that all relevant information is reflected in prices. The analysis assumes that systematic risk is reflected first in the risk premium attaching to a particular asset and secondly in the level of 'betas' which indicate the level of co-variance of the returns of a particular enterprise with the overall market return. It assumes the existence of stable betas and risk levels knowable from past data. It asserts that the shareholders are uninterested in any risk control by managers; any attempt by managers to change the betas, i.e. to manage risk, will be offset by a movement in the price of the relevant shares. A corollary of these arguments is the separation principle (Modigliani and Miller 1958), the notion that the investment decision and the finance decision are separate, the former made by managers and the latter by the shareholders as financial investors.

The capital asset pricing model provides a template for the inclusion of risk in the appraisal of any investment (see Dumas 1993 on the global asset pricing model – GAPM). Any asset (or project), or in a world of co-variation any portfolio containing such an asset, must yield an expected return greater than the risk-free return, plus a premium which compensates for systematic risk, plus a term which allows for idiosyncratic or non-systematic risk.

The conventional formula is:

$$r(j) = r(f) + b\{r(w) - r(f)\} + e$$

where $r(j)$ is the target rate of return for the particular enterprise, and under certain conditions a particular project, $r(f)$ is the risk-free rate of return, and $r(w)$ is the (world- or country-)market expected return. e is an error term which captures any non-systematic risk.

A key constant is beta, which is defined in the following way.

$$b = cov\{r(j), r(w)\}/var\{r(w)\}$$

The beta reflects the divergence of the return on this asset from the market return or more precisely and more formally the co-variance of a particular asset's return with respect to the market return, divided by the variance of the market return.

There are three distinctive risk premiums commonly separated and relevant to investment appraisal –

- a systematic market risk attached to the particular class of assets, reflecting its riskiness over and above a minimum risk-free level (usually taken as the rate for a New York treasury bill), say equities in a particular country or in the world market. The risk-free return is sometimes defined differently for separate countries (Moosa 2002: 207–210).
- a systematic asset- or enterprise-specific component, which can either increase the systematic market risk premium or reduce it. The asset or portfolio beta is most commonly measured on the basis of past data, but also with reference to real characteristics which impart a persistent and systematic divergence from the market level – at the enterprise level, by the size of the enterprise, its degree of debt leverage or variability of earnings; at the country level by elements included in the country risk assessment which have the same impact on variability of return by country.

The usefulness of such an analysis rests on the stability of such betas, including the elements which determine the betas. If betas are not stable, they do not identify elements of behaviour useful in determining the relevant risk premiums. One significant aspect of risk is proneness to a change in the level of risk itself.

In the absence of a world market it is interesting to ask whether stable country betas exist, indicating a persistent tendency for riskiness to differ from country to country. In a sense, the assertion of the importance of country risk is an assertion of a systematic beta-like tendency for market movements in particular countries.

- any non-systematic asset-specific risk independent of the behaviour of the market.

It is assumed that this element can be managed away by diversification of assets, provided that there are enough different assets in the relevant portfolio. There should therefore be no risk premium for private risk. If for some reason shareholders cannot diversify in the way desired, an enterprise should deliberately acquire a portfolio of unrelated assets in different sectors of the economy, since any non-systematic risk will be diversified away by a careful choice of enough assets. Whether country risk can be diversified away depends on whether it is regarded as un-

systematic risk and, even if the latter, whether there are enough countries to build a large enough portfolio to do this. There are both controllable and uncontrollable elements in this component (Aaker and
Jacobson 1990).

On this argument market frictions establish the need for risk control
(Doherty 2000: chapter 7), because they impede efficient market operation, give rise to positive transaction costs through agency and bankruptcy problems, and interfere with optimum investment decisions.
There are inefficiencies in the markets for strategic resources, notably
the intangible resources specific to all enterprises, and even for real
options (Miller 1998: 511). An enterprise may also deliberately compensate undiversified stakeholders, such as the managers of the enterprise, for the risk bearing arising from the operation of the enterprise
(Miller 1998; 511; further developed in chapter 6).

How risk is measured

In any financial investment there are assumed to be many assets, with
varying combinations of return and risk, which could make up a portfolio. Any which yield a given return at a higher risk or a given risk
with lower return should be ejected from the portfolio. Those left constitute the market security line, an efficiency frontier. The choice of
preferred outcome from an efficient set of projects reflects a trade-off
between risk and return, underpinned by a clear stance towards risk,
which is usually expressed as a set of indifference curves each representing combinations of risk and return yielding an equal level of
utility.

Risk is defined in a way that allows it to be measured as the variability of possible returns. In most of the financial literature risk is usually
taken as the variance of returns, which are normally distributed (that
is, the square of the standard deviation, which measures the average
deviation from the mean). If we know the first two moments, the
mean and the standard deviation, we can easily infer the probabilities
of different outcomes occurring (Culp discusses this issue at some
length). This approach ignores the possibility that the distribution is
non-normal. Risk control must confront the danger of 'lower-tail outcomes', extreme events. The object of risk management is seen as the
minimisation of variance, or a variant such as the reciprocal of the
coefficient of variation. Adopting as target the maximisation of a
return adjusted in a particular way for risk, for example the return
divided by the standard deviation (the Sharpe ratio) prejudges the

appropriate attitude to risk, by subjecting the analysis to a formulaic approach (Hirschleifer and Riley 1992).

Sometimes the use of variance is indirect. For example, the World Investment Reports in both 1998 and 1999 use the coefficients of variation of investment flows into particular countries as a measure of the risk facing potential investors in those countries. This is to put the cart before the horse. Any such measure should be treated as an independent variable in a study of the determining influence of country risk on FDI. This is an example of the illegitimate practice of taking a consequence of risk as part of the defining characteristic of that same risk.

The main weakness of the variance approach, particularly when it is estimated ex post, is that it misrepresents the situation on risk. Only if the distribution is normal (symmetrical) is it possible to say that variance exhausts the meaning of risk and provides an accurate measure of that risk. Such a focus on variance assumes no skewness or kurtosis. What is relevant is downsize risk (Aaker and Jacobson 1990), the negative behaviour of returns as represented by the lower half of the distribution. The approach produces obvious anomalies, if applied mechanically, such as the classification of businesses with predictable but rapidly growing returns as highly risky and those with stable or slowly declining returns as not risky. There is much evidence that the world is not 'normal', not conforming to a normal distribution: there is considerable skewness or kurtosis. Extreme events matter. Even financial markets have been on occasion subject to extreme swings, becoming hopelessly illiquid as the result of mood changes sparked off sometimes by an apparently minor event. A normal distribution predicts that a 10% decline in the capital market is a very rare event, whereas such declines occur much more frequently than predicted (Stulz 1996: 21), happening, for example, on the American stock market on 100 days in the twentieth century. Such instability makes most hedging impossible and risk control breaks down at the very time that it is most needed. In the event of a dramatic meltdown, even the most sophisticated of risk management ceases to be effective.

Large unprecedented, unexpected events cannot be accommodated with normal portfolio management techniques. It is difficult to know how far these meltdowns can be predicted, but comprehension of the relevant chains of causation is highly relevant. There are disasters or catastrophes which can cause major financial distress, even the bankruptcy of a company, and threaten the position of particular stake-holder groups, notably managers or owner-managers who have considerable enterprise-specific capital. These risk-generating events might include natural disasters such as earthquakes in California or Kobe or hurricanes in Florida, as well as terrorist attacks such as those of September 11 2001. Such events are rare, but their impact can be devastating. At other times, there is the build up of small changes, which at some stage grow to constitute a threshold beyond which there is a run-away effect. Identification of such events is vital to survival. A precondition for successful risk control is a realistic awareness of future probabilities.[2] Worst case scenario generation focuses directly on the threat of such extreme events. In certain circumstances rather than aiming at reduction of the 'average' risk associated with a given project risk control should be about the identification of the possibility of 'lower-tail outcomes' and their elimination. The more recently developed 'value at risk' approach recognises this by focusing, as a measure of risk, on the maximum possible loss at various confidence levels, the latter chosen according to the degree of risk aversion of the investor (Dowd 1998). For example, it might consider the maximum loss which occurs with a 95% or a 99% confidence level. Any greater loss is only likely to occur on average once in 20 or 100 years.

Problems with the conventional approach

The starting world for financial theory is the following:

- a developed set of efficient markets in which risk is traded, both along with and in financial instruments separate from the products and services exchanged in those markets,
- a range of derivatives, or contingent claims, which cover every contingency confronting decision makers, including those making investments, and derive their value from some underlying asset.

In the words of Moss (2002; 35), 'Standard economic models actually envision a world of complete contingent markets, where any risk – no matter how small or unusual – can be bought or sold in the marketplace.' In such a market system, all prices fully reflect risk and there is no need to account for risk or uncertainty separately. The premiums attached to prices reflect the level of risk as revealed by the probabilities in the various markets. An investment decision maker would then be operating in the equilibrium world of an Arrow or Hirschleifer. The market for risk may not be as developed as this suggests for a number of very good reasons (see Moss: chapter 2). The concern is not so much the faults of the underlying Capital Asset Pricing Model (Roll 1977), about which there is considerable debate (Fama and French 1992), as its usefulness to the appraisal of foreign direct investment. There are four good reasons why the CAPM approach cannot be used without significant adaptation. The space devoted to the first reason shows its paramount importance.

- The argument is based on a series of highly restrictive assumptions inapplicable to the real world. It is possible to relax some of the assumptions and retain the theory, but not all. There is a point at which relaxing the assumptions creates a different world.

There are four crucial assumptions (Culp 2001: 63). The first is the existence of strongly efficient markets, notably capital markets. Although assets in the financial market are unspecific, homogeneous in key attributes, designed to be easily exchanged, and usually divisible, and there are many buyers and many sellers, there is overwhelming evidence that at best the weak market efficiency assumption holds.

One problem is asymmetric investment in a transaction. The influence of different stakeholders on decision making is important because they have different risk exposures, that is different investments, and different abilities to diversify. Shareholders are unusual. Other stakeholders often have assets which are heavily committed to activities linked to the relevant enterprise. Workers and managers have most of their assets locked up in human capital which over time becomes more and more specific to the enterprise for which they work. Many such stakeholders may be unable to diversify their assets. This is particularly significant for managers. Human-capital risk cannot be diversified away in a private market because claims on human capital cannot be bought or sold; this would constitute a form of slavery. This gives managers a particular interest in the risk to which the enterprise is exposed. There is little doubt that the old have no choice but to hold too much, and the young too little, human capital in their portfolios of assets. There are comparable issues for the community living around an enterprise, which may not only have human capital tied up in employment in a certain enterprise but housing whose value is linked to the prosperity of the relevant enterprise. Even the provision of schools and hospitals may be so linked. It can also apply to governments who generate a large proportion of their revenue from a limited number of projects, or suppliers linked to one or a few customers.

Another problem emerges with respect to the credibility of the commitment to any business relationship. The role of one important group of stakeholders is usually ignored, the next generation. It is impossible to commit future unborn generations to current risk sharing arrangements through private contracts. There is a danger future generations may reject such contracts, sometimes through the political process, sometimes not. Complete intergenerational risk sharing is ruled out. Nor can any private entity ever credibly commit *not* to default on its future obligations; there is always some default risk. An individual may default deliberately as a matter of strategy or be forced to default by circumstances beyond his/her control. Sometimes the default has a significant negative impact on the conduct of business.

Another difficulty is that some benefits and costs, including particular types of risk, are not fully reflected in the price of a product, but are externalised. Externalities exist at every level of an economy. They may simply be external to a project but still internal to an enterprise or external to the enterprise but internal to an industry.

There may also be dangerous feedback loops such as financial panics resulting from contagion effects. Depositors will withdraw money from an otherwise sound institution simply because there is danger that others will do so. In a race to get access to liquid assets many depositors may lose out and the institution may go bankrupt regardless of its initial state. The same might apply at the country level with a run on a country, resulting in a rapid and large outflow of financial assets. All market economies operate on the basis of perceptions and therefore of confidence.

Network effects are a positive manifestation of an externality, where the value received by a consumer in his/her consumption reflects the number already consuming. For example, the greater the number of consumers operating a third generation mobile phone, the greater the potential benefit to be derived by a new consumer. It does matter how many other consumers you can link up with. This is similar to the old bootstraps argument which was once advanced on the basis of pecuniary external economies, that is, that the simultaneous implementation of a number of linked projects favours them all, if only in the increased demand generated.

A second assumption is that all players have similar knowledge, that is, they are exposed to the same new information, perceive it and are capable of processing it in the same way. In the literature on both risk and FDI there has been an increasing focus on imperfections in access to information. Much uncertainty or risk arises because of ignorance, a lack of adequate information on possible risk-generating events. The frequency of occurrence of some risk-generating shocks cannot be predicted because there is simply not enough information to make such a prediction. The causal chains may be unknown, and perhaps unknowable with the current state of knowledge or in any feasible future state, whatever the resources devoted to an information strategy. In some cases neither of the potential parties to a transaction involving risk can obtain adequate information about the risk in question, because the information either does not exist or is prohibitively expensive to acquire.

The problem is also the unevenness of the spread of information. The main example of asymmetry is that between insiders and outsiders, those who are privy to particular decisions and those who are not. There is nearly always a difference in the accessibility of information by two partners in any economic transaction. The reality of business is that some enterprises have knowledge that others do not. Much of the current analysis of risk management is increasingly premised on such asymmetries of information, notably that between owners and managers. Investors, particularly large market-leaders, deliberately seek to segment the market, creating asymmetries of information in order to generate profit-generating situations. Insiders actively seek to create a perception of bimodal or skewed distributions. There is a motivation to conceal relevant information.

Asymmetric information of this kind creates incentive problems which can increase overall risk. Principal/agent relations are universal, arising wherever one partner to a transaction(s), the principal, hires the other, the agent to perform a particular task. The principal cannot know what the agent knows about the detailed circumstances of the performance of that task. If the two have differing interests in the outcome of the transaction, there is a risk for the principal that the agent will pursue his/her own interests rather than those of the principal.

Moral hazard arises when the partner to a risk-management transaction providing the hedge or insurance knows less about possible risk contingencies and their impact than the hedged or insured partner. Any gain from mitigation will be captured by the insurer or institution providing the hedge and not by the insured or hedged. There is, therefore, a diminished incentive to engage in such mitigation behaviour. Risk management in this situation may increase the level of risk to which an economy is exposed.

Adverse selection arises when the seller of a product or service knows more about the quality of the sales item than the prospective purchaser. An individual knows more about his/her medical condition or the seller of second-hand motor car knows more about the quality of the car relative to the average being insured or sold. More relevantly, it also occurs when the insured knows more about their level of risk than their insurers, or the receiver of a loan more about their creditworthiness than the bank making the loan. Those who are most at risk have an incentive not only to conceal their risk but to take the relevant insurance or sell the car, and those who are least at risk have an incentive to refrain from incurring the costs of the same insurance or to withdraw the car from the market and sell it privately. There is a process of self-selection which could subvert the effective operation of the market.

Even if the same information is available it may be perceived differently (Tversky and Kahneman 1979). Perception problems may result from the way a problem is 'framed', which often depends on the context in which the problem first makes its appearance. The shear quantity of information available makes this likely. There is an abundant literature showing that individuals do not behave according to the standard view of what is rational. Market participants do not make decisions as rational economic men/women, maximising income, utility or some easily understood maximand. They have neither enough information nor the capacity to process that information. They may lack the inclination, in many situations trusting their own gut feeling or intuition (for an argument in favour of the use of intuition see Mandron 2000: 1012). They may adopt a range of simplifying tricks or heuristic devices which allow them to impose order on a rather uncertain world and to frame the relevant problem in a way which makes it easier to deal with (Moss 2002: 43–34). This framing may be done in terms of the status quo, or rather aspirations relative to the status quo; information may be used which is readily available or striking and ambiguous information rejected or downplayed; or there may be an optimistic bias, a preference to use good news rather than bad news, for example the tendency to ignore the possibility of extreme events. There are many such simple rules used to put the information available into some kind of working order.

The third assumption is that investment strategies are already given, that is, the investment decisions of enterprises are determined independently of financing decisions. All the possible values of a given project are 'spanned' by assets already sold on the capital market (Dixit and Pindyck 1994: chapter 5). This means that it is possible to find an asset or to construct a dynamic portfolio of assets, whose price is perfectly correlated with that of any project because its risk/return profile can be replicated by those assets. In the simplest case of no risk, it is a risk-free bond. Any decision currently being made is assumed to be within the span of existing projects – it has no effect on the prospective range of returns and risks. This is equivalent to saying that the decisions of the relevant enterprise do not affect the opportunity set available to investors. This is untrue of many projects such as those involving research and development or the introduction of a new product. Any additional investment project extends the span of existing projects.

Finally, it is assumed that everyone has equal access to the capital market and on the same terms, whether to lend or borrow in that market. The interest spread of similar financial instruments shows that this is not the case. It may be impossible for some players to borrow at all. This ability may also vary over time. This assumption is a fundamental departure from reality.

These problems are the principal reasons why the market cannot fully handle the existence of risk and why existing theory fails to take full account of the complexity of relevant decision making (Moss 2002). The world is not at all as the theory of the text books describes. The divergences of the real world from such an ideal world has significant implications for investment appraisal, as we shall see later.

• The second reason for having reservations about CAPM theory is that most treatments of risk deal only with the redistribution of existing risk, the level of which is taken as a given.

The analysis is usually couched in terms of a fixed and known amount of risk. Insuring or hedging does not mean that overall risk is reduced. Structural change does mean that the potential impact of risk, or risk exposure, is reduced, although the level of risk itself is not. In the 'hard' risk literature genuine risk mitigation is usually not dealt with at all or in a trifling way.

• The third is that, despite the main argument of financial theorists, even they find in the multiple failings of the market so many justifications for managing risk that they might just as well assume from the beginning the need for managers, in addition to financial investors, to manage risk of various kinds.
• A final problem relates to the large contradiction between theory and practice, in particular the assertion by decision makers that they follow the CAPM method in investment appraisal and the inconsistently high 'hurdle' rates used in such appraisal (Jagannathan and Meier 2002). The true market risk premium might have been as low

as half the historical US equity premium during the last two decades. Surveys of decision makers in enterprises (Poterba and Summers 1995) have indicated the application of much higher hurdle rates of return than would be suggested by the CAPM approach (Fama and French 2001). These rates also unexpectedly vary greatly from project to project within the same industry, and even the same enterprise. Such discrepancies require an explanation.

The peculiarities of foreign direct investment (FDI)

There are serious reservations concerning the extension of the 'hard' risk management, or portfolio, approach to foreign direct investment[3] (Elton and Gruber 1975).

- Portfolio analysis looks backwards rather than forwards: it rests on the availability of detailed information about past behaviour, notably that concerning the level of the risk-free return, the market returns on different assets, and return co-variances. The analysis also assumes stable past behaviour so that there is an unambiguous risk-free return, risk premiums for different markets and betas for different enterprises. Otherwise each will change according to the time period selected for the estimate.
- The relevant time horizon, reflecting a commitment over a protracted period, although not necessarily the lifetime of the assets, is much longer than for portfolio choice. The commitment of resources for such a long period guarantees a higher level of uncertainty.

The first two reservations, indicating very different time perspectives for financial and physical investment, makes it doubtful whether the approach is appropriate for FDI (Calverley 1985 is one of the few to directly address this question). FDI has a much longer time perspective and requires anticipation of future events which are not simply a re-run of the past. Estimating variance, or any other measure of risk, from past data assumes a stability of the environment which is illegitimate. In normal times, i.e. periods of stable behaviour, the past can be used to anticipate the future. In abnormal times, i.e. periods of instability, this does not work. The latter are frequent enough to cause enormous problems for investors if they are ignored.

- There is a commitment of a wider range of assets to such investments, including entrepreneurial and technical inputs as well as financial resources, creating very different risk exposures.

- FDI involves investment in highly specific assets, usually in large indivisible units. There is a lumpiness about the investment which creates what economists call discontinuities.[4]
- The segmentation of many markets for physical assets by asymmetric information is ignored. This is linked to the fact that for many assets there is a liquidity risk which reflects the lack of a market for such assets which can be accessed at any time without serious loss.

Together these three reservations have significant implications. It is extremely rare that an enterprise holds facilities which are completely independent of each other, assets which yield no economies of scale and scope.[5] At the very least for international projects there may be a sharing of promotion costs or of research and development. For a given enterprise, because of the existence of significant world-wide value-adding networks, the returns and risks attached to different assets may be highly correlated; there are serious interdependencies and very considerable co-variance. For a 'global' portfolio of physical assets held by a multinational enterprise there is, therefore, no risk which is completely non-systematic. This makes it very difficult to diversify away risk by simply having a large portfolio of different assets. Inclusion of a new asset may change the whole pattern of returns and risk for existing assets. If different country markets fluctuate independently of each other, entry into a large number of such markets might create such a portfolio, but this involves exporting as the entry mode rather than FDI.

- The range of events which threaten the value of foreign direct investment is much greater than for normal portfolio investment. The kind of threat is different from that which affects portfolio choice.

As a result of these reservations, the portfolio approach is only marginally relevant to an international investment project. The risk premiums advocated in the capital asset pricing approach are unlikely to be appropriate to such a project.

3
Risk and Risk-generating Events

There are never likely to be enough major capital investment decisions facing a company within a reasonable period of time for it to be proved statistically that decisions taken on the basis of an analysis of the risks are better than those taken without any such analysis.

It should be recognised that the use of risk evaluation in business is in essence an 'act of faith'.

(Hull 1980: 135)

This chapter starts by indicating how necessary it is to bring together the disparate approaches to risk in a genuinely integrated manner which assimilates all risk factors and the different disciplinary approaches to risk. It defines what risk is and shows the universality of that risk with careful distinctions made between incidence, impact and response. The analysis shows how such risk-generating events might be classified. One method of classification is by the different levels at which risk arises and has to be controlled. The analysis then turns to the response to risk by considering the appetite for risk, or degree of risk aversion, of those confronting risk. Part of such an analysis is consideration of the nature of risk exposure for organisations and individuals, notably different stakeholder groups. In conclusion, the chapter analyses the connection between risk and return which is considered a positive one by financial theorists but paradoxically has appeared in the empirical data to be negative; successful organisations are able to increase returns and reduce risk simultaneously.

There are six sections in the chapter:

• The first section argues the need to take an integrated approach in dealing with the various risk factors.

- The second confronts the need to define risk in a preliminary way.
- In the third the focus is on the interaction between incidence, impact and response and on the universality of risk.
- The fourth section makes an introduction to the different types and levels of risk relevant to FDI and to the risk exposure of particular assets.
- The fifth section considers the risk appetite, that is, the degree of risk seeking or risk aversion, which characterises individuals or organisations.
- The final section discusses the relationship between risk and return in a dynamic context, particularly whether there is a trade-off between the two.

Integrating the treatment of risk

Risk is not a purely negative element since inherent in any opportunity is some risk. Risk is everywhere, the ever-present associate of progress in general or of any specific entrepreneurial challenge in particular. It inevitably accompanies the attainment of a good pecuniary return. It is both impossible and undesirable to avoid all risk since the opportunity cost in lost income is too large. Controlling risk is part of the challenge of taking full advantage of any opportunity. Risk is therefore central to any decision and strategy made.

The literature dealing with risk is unhappily fragmented and often apparently inconsistent in its approach. It deals with disparate aspects of risk, often with variable definitions and large omissions of relevant risk types. For example in a well-known and generally sensible treatment of risk Olsson (*Risk Management in Emerging Markets* 2002: 35) defines country risk as the risk that a foreign currency will not be available to allow payments due to be paid because of a general lack of foreign currency, or a relevant government rationing what is available. For most commentators this is a small part of country risk. The adoption of such a 'particularist' viewpoint with a concentration on one area is unfortunately common. This has led Moosa to rightly comment, 'Considerable conceptual confusion surrounds the idea of country risk' (Moosa 2002: 131).

There have been a number of attempts to standardise the general terminology used. The significant example is ISO/IEC Guide 73: 2002 Risk Management. Vocabulary. Guidelines for use in standards. This terminology has been taken up by a number of organisations and theorists, although usually modified to suit the purposes and views of the relevant users (see for example Aven 2003: Appendix 2, or at the more practical level, A Risk Management Standard drawn up by AIRMIC, ALARM and IRM, 2002). The present book seeks to keep within this terminology, only adjusting it to take account of the FDI orientation of the analysis.

In an excellent paper published in 1992, Kent Miller emphasised the fragmented state of the treatment of risk, which he described as reflecting a tendency to take a particularist approach, analysing specific uncertainties in isolation rather than taking an integrated risk management perspective (for a comment on Miller's article see Werner and Brouthers 1996). The criticism continues to be valid. Miller pointed out the stress in the existing literature on particular uncertainties, whereas in his view there should be a 'multidimensional treatment of uncertainty' (Miller 1992: 312). The present book seeks such a multidimensional perspective.

There are an increasing number of papers which have explained the proliferation of different results by weaknesses which could be dealt with by a genuinely integrated approach. The weaknesses include:

- ambiguities of definition, in particular what should and should not be included in any definition of risk,
- illegitimate assumptions of a direct and universal relationship between particular kinds of risk-generating events and variability in a key performance indicator,
- a failure to accord proper respect to the uniqueness of specific circumstances and of event sequences which create a significant path dependency, thereby marking out risk as highly specific (Fatehi-Sedeh and Safizadeh 1989).

In a later paper Miller describes his attempt to analyse risk in an integrated manner as 'a perceived environmental uncertainty measurement instrument' (Miller 1993: 694).

According to Miller an integrated approach involves two necessary reorientations: firstly, taking a general management, or strategic, view of risk, that is bringing together the separate treatments of risk by international business theorists and analysts of strategy, and secondly, giving explicit consideration to numerous kinds of uncertainty. The former means, for example, removing the apparent gap in the treatment of country and industry risk (Miller 1993: 694), the latter analysed by strategists and the former by international business theorists. From another perspective, it also means bringing together the hard approach to risk management, which is espoused by financial theorists, and the soft approach which is applied in the area of foreign direct investment, with the aim of linking market risk with country and other types of risk in a coherent conceptual framework.

Since the publication of Miller's original article, nobody has taken up his challenge in a systematic way, despite the fact that Miller has provided a good foundation on which to build an integrated framework with a coherent set of categories. There have been few published empirical applications of Miller's conception of integrated risk management in international business, and even fewer theoretical explorations (Shrader, Oviatt and McDougall 2000).

There is plenty of scope for an integrated approach satisfying a number of aims:

- a comprehensive classification of the different types of risk with a consistent use of terminology, one which can be tailored to the particular problem under analysis (Miller 1992),
- the pursuit of enterprise-wide risk management (EWRM) (Culp 2001: chapter 11), which comprises every kind of risk to which the enterprise is exposed,
- consideration of risk control in a general strategic context in which opportunity and risk are two sides of the same coin (White 2004: chapter 5),
- a fusion of the approaches of different disciplinary orientations, whether economic, financial, managerial or any other one relevant,
- an integration of the various areas in which decision making needs to be made compatible – valuation, planning or strategy, performance measurement and compensation schemes with their incentive implications (Mandron 2000).

One way of integrating risk control is to make it part of the general strategy of the enterprise, which includes, for example, simultaneous decisions on the capital structure and financing of the enterprise and on the investment projects to be implemented.

A definition of risk

Miller starts by stating, 'The strategic management field lacks a generally accepted definition of risk.' (Miller 1992: 311). The first requirement in any analysis of risk is an appropriate definition.

Perhaps a reasonable starting point is Culp (2001: 14): 'Risk can be defined as any source of randomness that may have an adverse impact on a persona or corporation.' The first half of the statement picks up the fact that the events, or relevant interactions, engendering risk are somehow unexpected. Risk is not simply a matter of ignorance, since it is possible that even expected events can have unexpected negative consequences because the enterprise does not turn out to have the capabilities its strategy makers think it has (Miller 1998: 508). The second half stresses the negative impact of such events – it is the downside that matters.

This rather general definition begs a number of critical questions. It is appropriate, and not unusual, to start such analysis with the distinction between risk and uncertainty. Since there is still considerable confusion in the use of the two terms, risk and uncertainty, the ambiguity needs to be clarified. The distinction which is common in the literature goes back to Knight (1921). Knight argued that uncertainty lay within the province of the entrepreneur, not the insurer or hedger who dealt with risk. This is the source of the distinction between finance and business risk already discussed in the introduction. In the literature, the distinction between risk and uncertainty is usually made in a simple way.

- Risk is the set of calculable possible future outcomes for a relevant performance indicator, a known set of probabilities.
- By contrast, uncertainty relates to what cannot be known because it is in some sense unpredictable and therefore non-quantifiable.

Graaff has aptly commented, 'Uncertainty is not to be thought of as a quantitative thing like the chance or numerical probability of a coin showing heads when tossed a large number of times. It refers to something qualitative. It is a description of a degree of knowledge, of lack of knowledge. It arises whenever one has incomplete information on which to act' (Graaff 1963: 116). The distinction is further developed by Meldrum. He points to a *continuum* between pure risk and pure uncertainty, emphasising the distinction between an event whose occurrence is frequent enough to yield a statistical function amenable to probability analysis and one lacking these requirements. 'For example, the probability of death from an auto accident qualifies as a risk; the probability of death from a nuclear meltdown falls into uncertainty, given a lack of nuclear meltdown observations. Many of the individual events investigated by country risk analysis fall closer to uncertainties than well-defined statistical risks. This forces analysts to construct risk measures from theoretical or judgmental, rather than probabilistic, foundations' (Meldrum 2000: 33–34). There is a natural desire on the part of both theorists and practitioners to translate uncertainty into risk in order to make quantification possible.[1]

Miller notes a more subtle confusion between two uses of the term risk – to refer on the one hand to a general lack of predictability in firm performance outcomes, and on the other to the unpredictability of organisational and environmental variables which have an impact on performance predictability, or simply a lack of information concerning these variables (Miller 1992: 312). Miller prefers to call the first risk, although he makes no presumption that it is quantifiable, and the second uncertainty. In this sense, risk arises because of the existence of uncertainty. This is the rationale for Olsson's definition of risk, 'risk is the uncertainty of future outcome(s)' (Olsson 2002: 5).

In rejecting the Knightian distinction on the grounds that 'it violates the intuitive interpretation of risk which is closely related to situations of unpredictability and uncertainty' (Aven 2003: 39), Aven is taking the same approach. He argues that all probabilities are subjective assessments of uncertainty. Therefore 'for the uncertainty situation we interpret the probabilities as measures of uncertainty, as subjective probabilities expressing degrees of belief. Alternatively, the probabilities can be interpreted as subjective estimates of true, underlying, objective probabilities.' (Aven 2003: 28) According to Aven there are two categories of uncertainty to go with these two interpretations – 'stochastic or aleatory (= variations of quantities in a population) and knowledge-based (epistemic) uncertainty'. (Aven 2003: 17) The former is the uncertainty which can be expressed in exact probabilities, such as a toss of a dice (the alea). The latter reflects lack of knowledge about the world (i.e. system performance) in general and of observable quantities in particular. This lack can never be completely removed. In the words of Aven, 'risk is uncertainty about the world' (Aven 2003: 50).

Since the world is characterised by uncertainty, it is unsurprising that the problem of dealing with risk is rather more difficult than often assumed. The enterprise exists as a separate and well-defined organisational system within a single integrated environment but one which has many aspects – political, economic, legal, technological, and socio-cultural. It is critical to distinguish that environment from the enterprise itself. Instability is a property of that environment and risk a property of the enterprise. There are certain relevant

events, of differing provenance, which occur within that environment and constitute a significant part of that instability; in so far as
they also have an impact on the operation of the enterprise they
create risk.[2]

The level of uncertainty is never binary, there is never a simple
either/or situation. Such a binary position grossly oversimplifies the
world. In reality, there is neither zero uncertainty (complete certainty),
nor on the other hand complete uncertainty (complete ignorance)
(Courtney, Kirkland and Viguerie 1997). The world has regularities
which are the basis of the possibility of meaningful strategy. Complete
uncertainty is a situation which entails what Shackle calls 'powerless
decision' and can be disregarded.

In terms of the managerial perception of these events and their
outcomes there are four possible states of affairs (Kobrin 1979):

- a nearly definite future,
- a number of discrete alternative possible futures (scenarios),
- a broad but continuous range of possible futures with clear boundaries which demarcate what is impossible,
- an ambiguous future fraught with unknowns, that is a nearly
  complete uncertainty.

Incidence, impact and response: the universality of risk

The diagram below articulates what has been the source of much of the
confusion concerning risk, a failure to identify the difference between
the defining characteristics of the concept and the causes and consequences of different levels, or changes in the level, of risk. It is possible
to link causes, characteristics and consequences with incidence, impact
and response in a simple way.

Defining risk.

Causes	A set of risk-generating events or changes in behaviour, sometimes called shocks usually interacting closely with the relevant contexts	Incidence
Characteristics	Significant unpredictability of a key performance indicator(s) which indicates	Impact

the achievement of an important strategic objective(s). (Variance in the performance indicator)

| Consequences | Long-term consequences – structural or organisational change e.g. the choice of organisational form such as the introduction of limited liability | Response |

Medium-term consequences – the adoption and implementation of generic risk control strategies by key players (= country risk function)
- information strategy
- assessment strategy
- avoidance strategy
- mitigation strategy
- management strategy
e.g. the adaptation of the capital structure

Short-term consequences – at the micro level, specific investment decisions and their financing; at the macro level, specific inflows of FDI into particular countries

The three – incidence, impact and response, while in theory are independent of each other, interact in an inevitable way, particularly where government is successful at controlling risk levels. There is no objective measure of the incidence of risk-generating events, let alone an estimate of their probability of occurrence. It is impossible to measure objectively the frequency of events which are the source of the kinds of risk described above (White 1987 and 1992). Clearly, the response influences the impact and the incidence. It is common to take some measure of impact as a measure of the incidence or of the riskiness of an environment, as in the treatment of 'hard' risk. This makes analysis dangerously circular.

It is appropriate to return to a provisional definition of risk:

- Risk is the possibility of an unanticipated event, or change of behaviour, which has a negative impact on a key performance indicator or on the achievement of some strategic objective, one sufficiently significant to justify a response by relevant decision makers.

There are the same three elements – the unanticipated events, the indicator or objective affected in a negative way and the response by decision makers. Any risk involves the unpredicted, which must be placed at the centre of a definition. Often the indicator negatively affected is taken as profit or the value of an enterprise. The impact should be seen in a broader perspective: risk has an impact on the achievement of all strategic aims. It is possible to extend the definition of risk to include, not just a negative effect on a quantitative performance indicator, but also any impediment to the achievement of strategic business objectives (Rugman and Hodgetts 1995: 356). In strategic analysis the balanced scorecard approach shows the range of different indicators which ought to be considered (Kaplan and Norton 1996). The actual outcome, however superficially good, must also be related to a desired outcome. This further increases the difficulty of quantification.

Types and levels of risk

It is necessary to be systematic about the classification of risk. The classification must fit the specific problem under analysis, which in this case is the determination of FDI. There are numerous ways of classifying risk, each reflecting the particular focus of interest. For example, an economic historian interested in the influence of risk on the process of economic development might define a risk-generating event as inherently capital-destructive or labour-destructive. Such an historian might argue that the environments of different parts of the world differ in the bias of their factor destructability (Jones 1987). Or a classification might be made which distinguishes natural, social, market or power (political) risk according to their different sources. The course of economic development is marked by phases during which the different risk types predominate (White 1987). Moss (2002) has produced a model which considers phases in the USA which differ according to the nature of government intervention to control risk. On the other hand, concentration on financial markets has yielded a very different classification of risk (Saunders 2000). The main emphasis is on the distinction between systematic and non-systematic risk but a much more ad hoc classification is made regarding the sources of risk. The classification lacks coherence, largely because the source of the risk is considered irrelevant to an analysis which concentrates on the impact. All financial textbooks contain such a classification, usually differing in detail but covering the same ground. This classification focuses on the impact of risk on the value of the enterprise, its cash flows or returns, mostly on market or credit risk, taking into account risk elements such as price, notably interest, risk, differing maturities risk, even credit risk and off-balance sheet risk. It includes as separate elements, liquidity and insolvency risks. Often there is some reference to operational risk or technical risk, that is, the difficulty of mastering a new technology, and to political and transfer risks.

From the perspective of this book it is necessary to develop a different classification, one appropriate to FDI, a process begun by Miller (1992). The second section of the book completes this process, whereas this section explores the principles by which such a classification should be made. We can start with the question, what sort of events are relevant to direct investment in general and to FDI in particular? Such events range from those occurring at the macro level, natural events such as storms or earthquakes, or human-initiated shocks such as economic recessions or terrorist attacks, to those occurring at the micro level, the bankruptcy of a creditor or the failure of a vital piece of machinery. The frequency of incidence and both breadth and depth of impact differ from shock to shock; in particular cases the impact is strongly mediated through strategic and structural responses by decision makers acting within the relevant organisations.

It is also necessary to refer to the risk which arises from the competition between strategy makers, which might be called strategic risk, at the international level, a combination of competition risk and country risk. The term strategic risk is used since it describes the risk which arises from ignorance of the strategies of others and of the pattern of action, response, and reaction which ensues from the implementation of any particular decision (Smit and Trigeorgis 2004). The indeterminateness of unfolding scenarios is shown both by the different solutions to problems set up as games and by the path dependency of actual outcomes, which often reflect the potency of apparently small events to influence a historical path (David 1985; Arthur 1989). Any investment decision must be viewed in the context of the strategies of all other significant players.

Risk exists at different levels of the system – global, national, industrial, enterprise, project and individual. The relevant level can be defined by the source of the risk-generating event, by its area of impact or by the location of risk responses. At all levels the relevant risk-generating events have a powerful potential impact on business, but only after a filtering process makes specific the impact. From an economic perspective the significant impact might be defined by some performance indicator, anything from the GDP growth of affected countries to the profit of a particular enterprise experiencing the impact or the return on a particular project.

Risk is systematic to the level to which it refers, particularly above the level of the enterprise. It affects those on whom the risk has an impact in a similar, although not identical, way. The most relevant type of risk, country risk, affects to a varying degree all those investing in a particular country. On the other hand, industry risk affects all those investing in a particular industry. Global risk has the potential to affect everyone. The key levels are dealt with in separate chapters in part three of the book.

The risk facing an enterprise arises at all levels. It is possible to combine in a simple way the generic industry and country risks relevant to a project, with one type of risk on each axis of the matrix. This investment risk diagram can be constructed with the help of quantitative measures of risk (see Moosa for the use of such a diagram for another purpose).

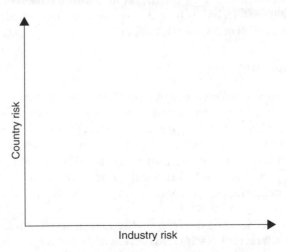

Figure 3.1   The matrix of country and industry risk

The slope of the boundaries reflects a trade-off between the two kinds of risk. In some cases, the significance of industry risk may be much greater than of country risk, in other cases the ranking may be reversed. One enterprise may be relatively intolerant of the risk in a particular country although it has expertise in the relevant industry. Another may be happy with the country location, but be operating in an industry which is a fast changing one.

The critical risk levels for the purpose of this book are not those at which generic risk arises, but the enterprise and project levels. Since an enterprise is unique in its various identifying features – resources, structure, strategy, personnel and history, and has a set of capabilities or competencies which include the control of risk specific to the enterprise, the higher level risk is filtered to the enterprise in a unique way through relevant control responses. There is therefore what might be called vertical overlapping between the risk levels. There is also horizontal overlapping in that different shocks may bunch because of some causative connection. Natural catastrophes are often linked with war. Economic risk is a source of political risk. The nature of risk at these different levels is discussed in chapters 4, 5, 6 and 7.

The potential impact of particular events is described as the risk exposure. This is the extent to which external contingencies threaten the value of the enterprise (Miller 1998: 497, 499). Such an impact reflects the nature and value of the assets affected. In order to specify exactly what value is at risk, it is necessary to specify both the probability distribution of relevant events, including any skewness or kurtosis of the distribution, and the assets or income streams at risk. The confidence level selected to help determine the value at risk reflects an important third element, the risk appetite.

The risk appetite

There is no objective measure of risk; there is an inevitable subjectivity to any assessment of risk, since there are different perceptions of the same environment, any particular perception reflecting the risk appetite of the person perceiving. The same possibility of project outcome in terms of risk and return can be differently regarded. The attitude to risk is referred to through general terms such as appetite, sensitivity or tolerance. Decision makers can be risk averse or inclined to risk taking.

Two issues arise – the degree to which an individual has stable dispositional characteristics towards risk which ensure a within-person across-situation consistency, and the degree to which there are group norms, for example how far investors from one country share a common risk appetite. Groups of decision makers in different countries can see the same environment in a different way Hofstede 1991. Uncertainty acceptance and uncertainty avoidance are one of the five scales by which Hofstede identified cultural differences between societies, indicating the significant degree to which risk tolerance differs from country to country.

All decision makers are often assumed to be risk or loss averse, having a limited appetite for risk. The proposition of diminishing marginal utility of income provides the underpinning for the general existence of such a risk aversion. The rate of diminution may differ from individual to individual, and for decision makers from enterprise to enterprise. There may also be stretches of income where marginal utility does not decline, in particular there may be very different attitudes to a loss and to a gain.

It is common to conceptualise this risk aversion as one reason for the existence of a risk premium, to be added to the target return which is expected of a particular project. The more risk averse the enterprise, the greater the risk premium demanded. Such a sensitivity to risk can vary over time and therefore imply a changing risk premium. For example, there is evidence that decision makers became more risk averse after the terror attacks of September 2001 (Fan 2004; White and Fan 2004). Another source of a risk premium is the riskiness of the risk environment, tempered by the degree of exposure of the relevant enterprise. It is usually assumed that the more risky the environment, the greater the risk premium demanded of a relevant project. The riskiness of the environment and risk tolerance are implicitly linked. It is not always possible to distinguish the influence of the two. Effective risk management requires the taking of an explicit attitude to risk and the careful consideration of the actual riskiness of possible outcomes.

The risk appetite reflects six main elements which differentiate the attitude of key decision makers to risk.

- the personality and motivation of the strategists interacting in the decision-making process. Some individuals are more risk averse than others. By definition entrepreneurs have a greater appetite for risk than the average. In reality, few decision makers can afford to be deliberate risk takers. Even the most adventurous seek to control risk. Some are stimulated by the challenge of overcoming risk but always seek to control the level of risk to which they are exposed.

The perception of possible performance outcomes is coloured by the position of the observer and reflects the confidence with which expectations of the future are held by that observer. A single dominant personality, the leader or dominant entrepreneur, can be the critical input in the willing acceptance of risky projects. Without a champion with a belief in a successful outcome the project is never undertaken. It is often the role of the leader or entrepreneur to provide such confidence. Risk aversion often reflects the past history of such an individual. Recent catastrophic events can have two opposed outcomes: they tend to reduce the appetite for risk and increase risk aversion, or they induce a mood of desperation in which dramatic risks are acceptable.

• ignorance of or unfamiliarity with the relevant area of risk.

The degree of risk aversion might vary according to lack of relevant experience or knowledge, for example, of a particular country. Some commentators believe that decision makers equate risk with difference and that previous experience dictates how far it is possible to live with and control the level of relevant risk. For example Brouthers writes, '....as the differences between countries becomes greater on the items being measured, the perception of risk increases' (Brouthers 1995: 22). Familiarity may reduce the degree of risk aversion. Certain decision makers may be more sensitive to particular types or components of risk than others, particularly those to which they have not been previously exposed.

• the economic health of the enterprise.

The more vulnerable the enterprise in which the decisions are made, the greater the reluctance to accept risk. Vulnerability may be a matter of:

• chronically low profits,
• persistent loss making,
• high leverage or gearing (how much debt there is relative to equity),
• an illiquid position: low financial reserves and poor borrowing ability.

An enterprise which has few reserves to tide it over during unexpectedly bad times is bound to be more sensitive to risk than an enterprise which has ample reserves which can tide it over anything but the most extreme of events. There are various such reserves, from cash held to assets which can be easily realised on the market or used as collateral for a loan.

- the culture of the enterprise.

Corporate culture almost invariably involves an easily identifiable atti-tude to risk and risk taking. A corporate, just as a national culture, can encourage or discourage risk taking. Whatever the views of a single powerful CEO, such a person needs support; an appropriate corporate culture helps. The culture of an enterprise is partly the result of past behaviour and its outcomes – what succeeded in the past and what failed, and partly the result of the attitude and influence of leaders, both past and present.

- the 'political' interaction between key decision makers.

Risky projects usually require for success a careful alignment of all the relevant stakeholder groups and an integration of all functional areas. Conflict can either be channelled into positive attitudes to risk or prevent decisive action and encourage risk-averse behaviour. Fear of a mistake can increase in a context of conflict. Different interest groups clash and prevent decisive action. As a result the whole process of decision making may become much slower. It also becomes a matter of unstable compromises. Sometimes these tendencies are built into organisational structures. The matrix organisation has been particularly vulnerable to paralysis of such a kind (White 2004).

- the 'framing' of decisions.

A critical issue is how decisions are presented to the decision makers. The same problem or decision can be presented in different ways and elicit responses which appear to reveal very different degrees of risk aversion. One well known theory is prospect theory developed by Tversky and Kahneman (1974, 1981) which argues that decision makers evaluate risky options through a subjective value system char-acterised by a reference point such as the status quo or the aspirations that individuals have relative to that status quo. An individual's esti-mate of the psychological value of an option differs systematically from the actual value of that option according to the reference point used for evaluation. Individuals frame the situation in terms of gains or losses relative to that situation, but can shift their reference points, that is have adaptive aspirations.

Individuals are also loss averse, that is relative to the reference point they weigh a unit of loss more highly than a unit of gain, i.e. they are faced with a S-shaped value function, which is concave for gains and convex for losses. This is the opposite of the function shape assumed by Friedman and Savage (1948) in order to explain why the same individuals simultaneously insure and gamble. According to prospect theory, if the outcome is framed in positive terms, the individual is much more likely to be risk averse; if it is framed in negative terms he/she is likely to be risk seeking. Empirical studies support this, suggesting the view that losses are weighted about twice as much as gains.

The problem is to identify the relevant frame for the important decision makers. There is evidence that managers tend to take less risks when their companies are performing well. Troubled firms take more risks. Such behaviour can lead to virtuous and vicious circles and is reinforced by high debt leverage when managers acting for themselves and/or for owners may take more risks, because they enjoy all the possible gains from the upside but pass much of the downside losses on to creditors.

In the context of the investment decision, the general relationship may hold but there is also a specific one. Where opportunity dominates threat – the gain domain, a risk-averse approach may be adopted by individual decision makers. Where threat dominates opportunity – a loss domain, a risk-seeking approach may be adopted. However quantitative is the approach to decision making there is often considerable uncertainty about future revenue and cost streams and considerable discretion in the choice of the numbers to be put into the investment appraisal. The positive or negative framing of decision scenarios is important because the same situation can be described as either a gain or a loss position and can give rise to different estimates.

It has also been argued that individuals adopt little tricks (heuristic devices) which produce systematic biases into decision making. They overweight available information, are ambiguity averse and have an optimistic bias. They do not know how to deal with events with a very low probability and therefore also have a central bias.

Reactions to a particular situation are therefore based on an interaction between the attitude to risk and the actual riskiness of a particular project. The risk matrix diagram described earlier is without usefulness if it only records some measure of the riskiness of the relevant environments. It needs also to display risk aversion. This can be done by dividing the matrix into three different zones – a zone of acceptable risk levels, one of unacceptable levels and one which is uncertain. The location of the boundaries between these zones indicates the degree of risk aversion. The closer is the situation to the zero corner, the greater is the degree of risk aversion. The breadth of the zone of uncertainty may reflect a lack of familiarity with either country or industry risk rather than aversion as such. It is better, if possible, to separate the riskiness of an environment from the perception of that environment which reflects the degree of risk tolerance.

The risk/return trade-off

It is an often-quoted tenet of financial theory that there is a strongly positive relationship between return and risk, measured by the mean and the variance of the distribution of a performance indicator such as profit. It is common to draw a risk/return frontier which encapsulates the trade-off between the two. The rationale is simple. If decision makers are risk averse, any higher risk must be compensated by a higher return. By contrast, those exposed to a lower risk are willing to take a lower return.

For efficient markets, this trade-off is true by definition since the movement of prices guarantees it. Risk aversion is expressed in a preference for securities with lower risk, which would have their prices pushed up by increased demand to the point at which the return is low enough to compensate for the lower risk. On the other hand, high risk securities would be in less demand, with their price falling so that the higher return compensates for the higher risk. The link rests on the assumption of a single object for the enterprise, that of maximising the market value of shares, at a given moment of time. In such a world, any enterprise engaging in unnecessary expenditures or making non-optimal decisions is taken over and has its decisions changed.

This association is true of the market for financial assets, but it is not necessarily true of the world of investment decision making. As Bowman (1980: 25) has written, 'It may be argued that equilibrium conditions will tend to eliminate this discrepancy, but clearly equilibrium *within* the capital marketplace comes much more rapidly than equilibrium *between* the capital marketplace and the firm, if it comes at all.' Studies of the empirical data for enterprise performance, usually longitudinal, have shown a negative rather than a positive relationship between risk and return, measured in the conventional way (see the classical paper by Bowman 1980 which gave birth to a considerable debate). Higher returns are associated with lower risk and lower returns with higher risk, not for all industries but for most.

There are several possible explanations, which introduce real time rather than the imaginary time of equilibrium analysis:

• There is every motive for both artificial and real income smoothing of profits or revenue streams, in particular in the latter case by judicious timing of expenditures and investments. This kind of behaviour is very common.

• Some theorists have recognised that controlling business risk lies at the heart of good strategy, especially where oligopolistic or monopolistic elements prevail in an industry. In this world, non-systematic risk is more important than systematic risk and risk mitigation more important than risk management. The enterprise seeks to reduce total risk and to mitigate it. Good management, including effective strategy making, can bring about both higher returns and lower variance within an industry as enterprises seek to control the environments relevant to decision making and its outcomes. By doing this they will enhance operational efficiency, stimulating not just an even but an increased cash flow. This is true only in dynamic ones.

• Prospect theory also indicates that in a loss situation, i.e. a situation of low return, enterprises may be deliberately risk seeking (Tversky and Kahneman 1979). There is now considerable support for this kind of behaviour. In other words, troubled enterprises take more risks (Bowman 1982).

In a dynamic context, a successful enterprise can aspire to both lower risk and higher returns. The enterprise which innovates successfully simultaneously secures both. This is a natural result of good strategy. The book rejects the assumption of a normal distribution of future returns which allows a reduction of the risk control problem to a simple return/risk (mean/variance) trade-off (Culp 2001: chapter 2). Scenario building usually implies a non-normal distribution of returns which can be described as bi- or tri-modal.

4
Home Country Bias in Foreign Direct Investment

> In the home-trade his {the wholesale merchant's} capital is never so long out of his sight as it frequently is in the foreign trade of consumption. He can know better the character and situation of the persons whom he trusts and if he should happen to be deceived, he knows better the laws of the country from which he must seek redress.
>
> Adam Smith (Vol. 1, 1976: 454, quoted by Gordon and Bovenberg: 1057).

This chapter analyses in what sense and why the aggregate level of foreign direct investment is lower than might be anticipated. It begins by pointing out the ambiguities of definition and the limitations of the estimates made of FDI. It goes on to explore the degree to which all economic actors, whether they are individuals, governments or companies, prefer their own. This applies to where a person works, where he/she places savings, or to the origin of the goods and services consumed by that person. It also applies to where a company invests in productive facilities, who it employs and where it purchases. It explores three arguments advanced to establish such a bias, analysing in turn the arguments based on deficiencies in market integration, the tendency for equality between national savings and national investment, and a pronounced domestic orientation in the composition of portfolios of financial assets. The chapter defines home country bias, indicates how it might be measured and seeks to explain it. It concludes by making a link between country risk and home country bias in FDI.

There are six sections in this chapter:

- The first section focuses on the nature of FDI, distinguishing it from international portfolio investment.
- In the second section the main implications of a home country bias in investment decisions are set out.
- The third concentrates on the definition and measurement of home country bias.
- Section four examines the arguments for home country bias and the relative immobility of capital.
- The fifth section reviews possible causes of a home country bias.
- The last section briefly explores a relationship between risk, notably country risk, and home country bias.

The nature of FDI

Imad Moosa (2002: 265) asserts: 'FDI is the process whereby residents of one country acquire ownership of assets for the purpose of controlling the activities of a firm in another country.' Foreign direct investment is, unfortunately, an ambiguous concept for three principal reasons.

Firstly, such investment embraces three related but distinct activities – funding, ownership and operation, all critical aspects of foreign direct investment but capable of separate implementation by specialised agents. Confusion arises because it is unclear which of these functions is being talked about. The usual definition of FDI distinguishes it from portfolio investment through the level of ownership and the control of operation, not the source of funds.

Funding starts with the savings decisions which free the resources required to allow an investment to occur. Savings are commonly channelled into financial intermediaries which move the funds to those who finance investment. Individual savers and financial institutions hold the savings in the form of a portfolio of financial assets, hence it is called portfolio investment. Some part of foreign direct investment is matched by financial flows created by the issue of shares or bonds to finance a project initiated by the productive investor, and therefore shares certain aspects with portfolio investment. Sometimes the savings decision involves the reinvestment of retained profits by enterprises, in which case the saver and the investor are one and the same. Because of the importance of intermediation, there may be no particular link between the savings decision and the investment decision, but no Investment is possible without a matching savings decision, made by someone somewhere, not necessarily in the same country. Foreign investment often involves savings and investment decisions made in different countries.

Ownership is a matter of who directly owns the productive assets created by the investment, often a large multinational corporation which can own directly, through subsidiaries or even joint enterprises. The ownership chain might be long. A corporate legal entity holds the assets on behalf of the ultimate owners, the shareholders, who may be many, various and highly dispersed, even globally.

Operation involves the appropriate organisation and integration of the relevant resources in the process of creating something of value to a market. It is also the control part of ownership and control. Any productive assets can stand alone, being managed separately, be linked to a network of suppliers and purchasers in the host economy, or be part of a genuinely international value chain of linked producing units.

The second source of ambiguity is that each of the terms in the expression, foreign direct investment, lacks a precise meaning.

For which function does foreignness apply – saving, ownership, control, or all three? The term international production is often used carelessly. In theory, a subsidiary of a multinational corporation might raise capital on the market of the host country or borrow from a local bank; all the funding, and therefore the saving, is domestic, coming from the host country.[1] This might imply a dilution of foreign ownership of the relevant organisation. Such a flow of capital is usually excluded from an estimate of foreign direct investment and the use of the term foreign is taken as requiring the actual import of funds from abroad, except where the subsidiary of a foreign enterprise is using retained profits. If the corporation is taken to be the foreign investor – which is commonly the case, how is it possible to determine the nationality of a multinational corporation which raises capital from a multitude of different sources and has to a varying degree severed its links with the home country? Is the nationality simply defined by the location of its headquarters? Next, what does direct mean? Usually, it is taken as indicating both a long-term commitment to the project and control of the relevant production facility. Ownership and control do not necessarily go together. A corporation can hire all the necessary resources, thereby controlling but not owning, or it can rent out resources it owns, thereby owning but not controlling. Finally, in what does the investment consist? Is it the financial flow generated by the investment, as is often assumed, or is it a 'real' movement of resources? If the latter, does the term comprise just production goods, or include associated entrepreneurial expertise and technical knowledge, a package of related resources transferred with the production goods?

Thirdly ambiguity arises because the analysis of foreign direct investment requires a multidisciplinary approach, involving:

- the financial theory relating to capital markets, a sophisticated body of theory, which includes a burgeoning literature on risk management and capital budgeting, and various attempts to apply the theory relating to financial options to real options,[2]
- the management theory relating to strategy, particularly that which has developed to explain competitive advantage through the resources possessed by an enterprise (Wernerfelt 1984), and also the mode of entry into international business transactions,
- the theory of the firm, including the recent literature on capitalist organisation in general, sometimes referred to as institutional economics.[3] Related is the growing body of economic theory relating to informational economics,
- political theory which explains the causes, characteristics and consequences of political change.
- neoclassical economics relating to production and to trade (Krugman and Obstfeld 2003),
- game theory, applied to strategic problems.

There should be a clear distinction between foreign direct investment and portfolio investment. The two distinguishing criteria are control and a link to a specific increase in productive capacity, not just a change of ownership. The intent to control is the key defining feature of direct investment, but actual control can reflect different levels of ownership. The US Department of Commerce defined foreign direct investment as: 'the movement of long-term capital to finance business activities abroad, whereby investors control at least 10% of the enterprise' (see Meyer, S. and Qu, T. 1995: 1). After careful consideration, the OECD concurred with this view. The World Investment Report adopts the same position, as have most relevant international organisations. An investment of anything less than 10% is deemed a portfolio investment. While 10% might give control, if another organisation holds 51%, even 49% is not necessarily a controlling interest.

Any addition to productive capacity can be achieved by the movement of production goods but it does not have to. On the one hand, an increase in productive capacity may reflect the reorganisation of an enterprise acquired (Lee and Caves 1998). It is possible for foreign debenture holding to support an extension of productive capacity through the transfer of consumption goods. The sale of debentures involves abstention from consumption in the home country, followed by the export of consumer goods to the host country and their consumption by workers constructing the enlarged productive capacity. Portfolio investment can indirectly support an increase in productive capacity, provided an effective transfer of the relevant goods can be made. The economic circuit is indirect. The distinction between portfolio and direct investment is a difficult one to fully sustain and in the main literature is deliberately not sustained.

Following usual statistical practice, the present book recognises the simplifying assumptions made to avoid these ambiguities. FDI includes three main elements: the transfer of equity funds, any lending by headquarters to subsidiaries abroad and the investment of retained profits by those subsidiaries. The first is critical since FDI only occurs if there has been a transfer of ownership abroad of at least 10% of the capital of an enterprise.

What is the problem?

In the past, government policies have been deliberately protective of domestic economic activity, but at the same time deliberately promotive of foreign investment. Traditionally, tariffs on the import of goods have been used to encourage an inflow of FDI. Recently, attention focused on the need for government to remove all the barriers to the free movement of goods, factors of production or knowledge. In a global world without such barriers, the existence of national borders would allegedly place no obstacle in the way of the free movement of goods and services and the flow of the mobile factors of product, labour and capital. An emphasis on globalisation suggests that the level of international transactions reflects a willingness of key players to cross international frontiers without any reluctance, or an indifference as to whether the players engage in domestic or international transactions; place is irrelevant. This indifference to international boundaries is in practice uncommon. Much more common is a simple preference for the domestic over the international.

The conventional wisdom is firstly, that the degree of capital mobility is high, notably for industrial countries, and has been rising at an accelerating rate in recent decades; and, secondly, that this is related to increasing market integration, that is the two go together. It is often assumed that market integration and capital mobility are one and the same; this is not the case.[4] With perfect integration of markets and perfect mobility of goods and factors of production, decisions on location might be made without any consideration of the existence of national borders. In such a world arbitrage – the riskless exploitation of price differences for profit – would cause all relevant prices to be equalised. The realisation of the law of one price would be evidence for such an integration. Production is located and factors flow according to the dictates of relative returns, tending to equalise those returns at the margin. However markets might be fully integrated, but with a weak resulting flow of goods or factors of production, if there is little profit to be derived from such flows.

A main proposition of this book is that there is still a significant home country bias, especially for the use of capital, caused by the existence of country risk. Financial markets in the world are the closest to the perfect competitive ideal of the economists and the most fully integrated of all markets; they should display the least home country bias.[5] If existing evidence shows a significant home country bias for capital markets, it is highly likely that the bias will exist for other markets. In practice, the FDI inflows are much lower than might be anticipated. In some cases, the level of country risk completely closes off the relevant economies, in other cases, where the risk level is low, investment in that economy may approach more closely the expected level.

It is impossible to consider the investment decision in isolation from other decisions. There are two principal reasons. The first relates to the fact that FDI consists of a package of inputs, comprising not just financial assets but technical knowledge as well as entrepreneurial and broader labour inputs. Secondly, the movement of goods and of capital are linked, any obstacles in one area restricting movement in the other. The problem is the interaction in the balance of payments between the current and the capital accounts. If the level of international reserves are assumed constant a deficit in one must be matched by a surplus in the other and vice versa – it is an accounting identity. This accounting identity reflects a more important relationship. Any movement on the capital account is meaningless without a matching movement of goods and/or services on the current account. In a world of floating exchange rates, an increase in the flow of savings into an economy from abroad, which causes a surplus on capital account to emerge, will also cause the value of a currency to rise above what it would otherwise have been. With the usual demand conditions, the price of exports relative to that of imports will rise, influencing relevant expenditure decisions on exports and imports, and causing a matching current account deficit to appear. With fixed exchange rates, the mechanism would still be through price movements, but the time delays would be much longer as an inflow or outflow of domestic currency might trigger the relevant monetary and price movements.

If there is an international differentiation of goods so that such goods are not regarded as fully substitutable at the international level, the mechanism described above will not operate freely and without friction. If the matching goods flows do not appear, there is what has been described as a transfer problem. This would make an inflow of savings difficult to validate. Capital mobility is therefore difficult without product mobility.

The definition and measurement of home country bias

In a world where there was no home country bias of any kind, the ratios of international as against domestic transactions in the different markets would reflect exactly the overall size of the relevant markets, for example the level of GDP, or the overall level of the labour force, of world savings or consumption, or the aggregate of total gross fixed capital formation. If the country under analysis represented 10% of the world economy, however defined, unbiased behaviour would result in 90% of managers and workers working abroad, 90% of savings being invested abroad and 90% of commodities consumed being imported.

The world is not like this. Non-US investments represent substantially more than half of the world equity portfolio, yet between 1980 and 1993 the share of US investments in foreign equities only grew from approximately 2% to 8% (Levi 1996: 451). At the end of 1996, Australians who presumably can invest where they choose owned only 2% of the world's corporate shares. Following the logic of the argument non-Australian citizens should have owned 98% of the shares in companies listed in Australia, but owned just 31% (Bryan and Rafferty 1999: 13). Returns from investment are not randomly distributed throughout the world since it is more profitable to invest in some countries than others. Rather, a bias should be defined as a preference which appears irrational from an economic point of view, a preference which cannot be explained solely through relative returns.

Another approach is to compare what happens within countries and what happens between countries. The levels of movement within a country can act as a way of defining and measuring bias. Home country bias exists, where taking out the influence of the size of an economy and of distance still leaves, in Helliwell's words, strong border effects, differences in the level of intra-national movement compared with international movement. After adjustment for size and distance, inter-provincial trade flows within Canada were more than twenty times those between Canadian provinces and American states (Helliwell 1998: chapter 1). This is surprising for two reasons. Firstly, Helliwell (1998: 3) quotes survey evidence showing that trade experts, students of economics, and others without special training in economics thought that trade linkages were at least as tight between provinces in Canada and states in the USA as among provinces. This seems the conventional wisdom. Secondly, similarities of culture and language, combined with the impact of the North American Free Trade Area, apparently justify such a belief and identify the USA/Canada link as more likely than any other to reveal a mobility of goods unimpeded by national frontiers.

The degree of home bias, although it differs markedly from country to country, is very high. Despite globalisation few workers work abroad, most savings are retained within the domestic economy and most commodities consumed are of domestic origin. There are some interesting patterns. There is more bias in labour markets than in capital markets, more bias in physical than financial investment. The inhabitants of small countries have less bias in all markets than those of large countries. It is interesting to ask why the bias exists and what factors cause differences in the level of bias.

One explanation is that the movement across international frontiers is not free; even today it is regulated, sometimes in ways not immediately obvious. There are barriers to such movement, usually imposed by governments – restrictions on immigration, tariffs and non-tariff barriers of various kinds on commodity imports, exchange controls and restriction on foreign investment. While there has been a considerable freeing up of such restrictions, there is a long way to go before the movement is as easy internationally as domestically. Often the regulations impeding movement are hidden and indirect. For example, the operation of anti-dumping or inspection laws limit international trade.

For an economist, a significant cause of bias is relative costs, here the higher cost of engaging in international transactions. It is expensive for a manager or worker to relocate to another country, in some cases very expensive if the time devoted to the relocation is considered. There are transactional costs involved in importing over and above the costs related to goods consumed domestically. Distance is a problem. Switching funds into another currency may involve further costs.

However, the economic restrictions on the movement of goods or capital are growing less important over time. The costs are relatively small, although not trivial. Neither physical restriction nor costs seem barriers large enough to explain a significant degree of bias.

There is a qualitative difference between the movement of people and of commodities or capital. People become immobile because the factors which influence them are as much social or psychological as economic. Labour does not like to move because people have an attachment to a place where family and friends live. The further they have to move to take a job, the greater is the reluctance to move. They grow to like a particular style of living. They may be daunted by the need to use a different language and to learn to live within a different cultural milieu. The extent of the bias suggests that the individual decision makers are not solely motivated by economic factors. Even irrational preferences are often translated, however imperfectly, into cost differences, for example higher rewards for expatriates and therefore higher costs for a foreign investment project. Capital and commodities are not as subject to the same impediments on movement as people.

Home country bias and the immobility of capital

The argument for immobility is indirect and rests on three main elements:

- The existence of real interest-rate differentials across countries, which indicates a failure of the law of one price and by implication a lack of mobility of capital.
- The close relationship between national savings and national investment and their tendency to move together, with the implications that savings tend to stay at home to finance domestic investment
- The heavy specialisation of individual portfolios on domestic securities, in spite of a strong theoretical case for large potential gains from international diversification

Price equalisation

The first requirement in any analysis relating to markets is to consider price (Frankel 1992). The law of one price says that in a fully integrated frictionless market one price will prevail (see Appendix 1 for what this means in a formal sense). The existence of such an equality of price is used as evidence of full mobility and indirectly that FDI is at an expected level.

In the market for financial capital, the law of one price is initially represented as the equality of nominal interest rates (uncovered interest parity). Such an equality does not take account of changing exchange rates. Nominal interest rate parity would hold only if there were a zero exchange risk premium. A more rigorous condition would be covered interest rate parity, with any non-zero exchange risk covered. The condition for financial market integration is that the covered interest differential is zero, i.e. there is covered interest parity between countries. Real interest parity makes a further requirement, that exchange rates change only to accommodate different expected price movements. This is referred to as purchasing power parity.

Purchasing power parity describes a relationship between weighted average price levels of a typical basket of goods in different countries. The evidence shows that purchasing power parity is departed from significantly and for lengthy periods of time. The work of Taylor has shown that a strong purchasing power parity argument does not hold but a weak one does (see in particular figure 3 in Taylor 1996). Although current exchange rates differ from PPP exchange rates, as both the World Bank and the Economist's Big Mac exchange rates so graphically show, there are relatively small deviations in exchange rates from the PPP rates in the periods before 1914 and after 1960. The interwar period was an era of large deviations from PPP. Although the existence of PPP rates is a test of goods-market arbitrage, it is identified by Taylor as a necessary condition for the most stringent of capital market integration tests, the international equalisation of real interest rates. Free international capital flows, it is argued, should achieve PPP. In practice, there is no purchasing power parity and no real interest parity. Generally, the evidence is that the law of one price does not hold (Buckley 1996). One implication is that the forward exchange rate is noticeably worse than the current spot exchange rate as a predictor of the future spot exchange rate (Helliwell 1998: 69).[6]

Savings-investment equality

There are two groups of decision makers relevant to any home country bias in capital markets – savers and investors. The savings of enterprises and households are converted into financial assets by the financial system. The financial system has the links, both international and domestic, which allow it to distribute those savings in a way which provides the risk/return combination most appropriate for savers. Both individual savers and intermediating financial institutions build up a portfolio of assets, including both foreign and domestic assets. On the other side are those who invest the savings in productive assets, finding the resources for that investment either from their own internal funds or from the financial market in equity raised or debt incurred. The balance of sources is structured to suit the needs of the enterprise. Some part of the investment in a particular country is undertaken by foreign enterprises.

There are four possible situations – first, domestic investors use domestic savings to undertake an investment; second, domestic investors use foreign savings to undertake the investment; third, foreign investors use domestic savings to undertake the investment; and fourth, foreign investors use foreign savings to undertake the investment. The latter three situations all involve international transactions. The first does not, and therefore is the vehicle for the expression of home country bias. The two groups may display differing degrees of home country bias. Suppose that savers have a high degree of bias but investors do not, the first and the third will be the predominant situations. If investors have a high bias and savers little, the first and the second would be predominant. The fourth holds only if both groups have little home country bias. In this last case, the savers and the investors might be different people but it is unlikely.

A long indirect intermediation chain makes it difficult to track particular savings streams. A more indirect approach has to be taken. Each country has a total savings pool and a total investment effort. In a closed economy, the two are equal since the savings go to finance the investment. Economics teaches us that ex post they must be equal, provided a country's exports and imports are in balance, in other words provided there is no capital flow into or out of the country. Equality between the savings and investment does not mean that both are entirely internally generated.

There can be offsetting flows in both directions. In a world of specialisation, the more developed is an economy, the more likely this is true. In an extreme case, all the investment in a country could be financed from abroad and all the savings could go abroad to finance investment in the rest of the world, indicating little bias. Some countries, such as Australia, are persistent importers of capital, tapping the savings of the rest of the world. Others, such as Japan, may be persistent exporters of capital, sending out their savings to other countries. Most developed countries are sometimes in surplus and sometimes in deficit. If there is a surplus or deficit on the current account, there must be an offsetting deficit or surplus on capital account.

A path-breaking paper by Feldstein and Horioka in 1980 highlighted the issue of home country bias since it undermined the assumption of a unified global capital market. In a world of perfect mobility of capital, one in which the savings and investment decisions are independent, it is possible for savings, attracted by better returns, to move to finance investment wherever it occurs in the world. For any country there is no reason why savings and investment acts are correlated – the correlation should be zero. Even if national savings were high, national investment might be low, and vice versa. Feldstein and Horioka discovered the opposite, that for OECD countries in the 1960s and early 1970s the correlation between national savings and investment rates was high. Furthermore, a movement in one rate was closely, but not perfectly, associated with a movement in the other. This contradicted what might be expected in a world of capital mobility, where a fall in savings in one country could be made up by borrowing from abroad at the current world interest rate and need not drive up the domestic real interest rate or 'crowd out' domestic investment. In a world of imperfect mobility, domestic interest rates would rise and domestic investment be crowded out.

The form of the underlying equation is simple:

$$I/Y = a + b(S/Y) + u$$

where I is the level of capital formation, Y national income, S national savings and u other factors that help determine investment. b is interpreted as the national retention ratio for savings, zero in a world of perfect capital mobility. The estimates of b turned out to be closer to one. Savings were retained in order to finance local investment. Such estimates can be made from either cross-sectional or time-series estimates. In the former case, the savings retention ratio, if estimated over a sufficiently long period, say 5 to 10 years, a period typically covering the whole business cycle, can be given a 'natural' interpretation as a reflection of long-run stability. In the latter case, b can be interpreted as a measure of short-run stability.

Critics of the argument have tried to show that with an assumption of full mobility of capital, it is still possible to have a close relationship between savings and investment. The first argument is to claim that the equality is an identity. Savings and investment are by definition equal, if they are measured properly in the national income accounts (Coakley, Kulasi and Smith 1996, Sinn 1992). In a closed economy b = 1. This is asserted to be true in an open economy. Estimated over a long enough period, savings and investment are equivalent to their permanent or life-time values and permanent investment must equal permanent saving, plus some constant reflecting the initial level of wealth. If a solvency constraint is introduced into the analysis – that is an assumption that the bigger the current deficit and the larger debt, the greater is the risk premium demanded of those who invest in that country, provided the time period of analysis is long enough, savings and investment will always tend to be equal, again with an allowance for initial wealth holdings.

The second argument relates to the catch-all term u. An implicit assumption of the analysis is that savings are exogenously determined. Savings rates may be endogenous in that the same factors might influence both savings and investments rates, causing the identification of a spurious relationship. In the equation above, u is related to S/Y. Such factors might include the influence of the business cycle, of demographic structure and population growth rates, of relative prices, taxes, growth or productivity shocks, or of government behaviour, including policy reactions to current account imbalances. With suitable assumptions about the patterns of such shocks and the nature of the business cycle it is possible to show a positive correlation between national savings and investment.

A third argument reflects the size of the economies under study. If the country studied is large by world standards, e.g. the USA, it can influence the level of world interest rates because the savings and investment flows between this country and the rest of the world are significant. A fall in national savings in this country might push up world interest rates and prevent the inflow of savings from outside which might offset the initial fall.

These objections have been aired and rebutted. In a rather fitful way there has appeared a significant literature which, despite the vigorous attempts to disprove the argument, has tended to confirm the main contention. Taylor has referred to the general view that this is now 'a robust result – stylised fact' (Taylor 1996: 7). Further studies by Feldstein and others have supported his original contention. Even those attempting to rebut the argument accept the robustness of the results. Under numerous alternative specifications, the data show a consistently significant correlation between savings and investment.

What does the value of b say about the level of capital mobility? What is a high level? Taylor (1996) has argued that the strength of the argument is greatly increased in a comparative context, either inter-temporal or inter-spatial. There is a growing number of long-term comparisons.

Taylor has taken the analysis back to the 1860s. Before 1914, the level of b was very much lower than today. It is true that rises in b tend to co-incide with recessions. The interwar period was economically a poor one. Since then the savings retention coefficient has been tending to fall, decade by decade, which might be expected in a world of increasingly integrated capital markets. Work by Taylor suggests that the fall in the second half of the twentieth century is only a recovery of the capital mobility lost in the first half.

A second comparison can be made with movements within countries. Sinn (1992: 1168) argues that the evidence on intra-national capital mobility may serve as a benchmark against which to assess the international evidence. He shows that the value of b for investment and savings within American states is not significantly different from zero, well below the highly variable international levels which range from 0.4 to 0.9. Provincial or state boundaries do not appear to act in the same way as national boundaries in segmenting economic activity. In the words of Helliwell and McKitrick (1999: 1171), 'National borders continue to mark sharp divisions between markets for capital as well as for goods and services. Provincial borders apparently do not.' The evidence certainly suggests that domestic markets are integrated in a way untrue at the international level.

Portfolio composition

Studies of the composition of the international portfolios of financial institutions produce the same conclusions as the previous two arguments. They show that the inclination of savers is to hold their savings in domestic assets.

A powerful theoretical argument is put in all finance textbooks, that it pays to hold a portfolio of financial assets which includes international as well as domestic stocks because of the implied reduction in risk (Levi 1996: chapter 18). An integrated world capital market would have prices of stocks move together, through arbitrage; all risk would be systematic. In practice, prices move independently. Returns yielded by different international assets are seen as more independent of each other than those from domestic assets, because of the pursuit of differing policies in different countries. There is more non-systematic risk at the global level (Levi 1996: 435, 450). There is a strong body of evidence to show that prices differ substantially and markets are segmented. The degree of correlation between the returns in different markets is low and this is not due to the different compositions of the market by industry, rather to idiosyncratic economic circumstances. This is true, for example, of pension portfo-lios in both the USA and UK (Helliwell 1998: 70). For Nordal (2001: 18), country risk is all unsystematic risk. There is even disagreement as to whether systematic risk, perhaps in normal times insignificant, becomes much more important in abnormal times when a high level of instability occurs (Goodman 1986) or whether, as Shapiro (1999: 661) asserts, 'only bear markets seem to be contagious, not bull markets'.

In this environment a significant proportion of risk can be diversified away by individual financial investors holding a wide spread of inter-national assets. The gains from diversification are potentially very large. For Buckley (1996: 27), 70% of a typical enterprise's shares' vari-ance is accounted for by unsystematic risk, a proportion which comes down as the portfolio is expanded until with 20–30 assets it is close to zero. Such a portfolio can help an investor reduce risk for a given return or increase the return for a given level of risk. According to Lessard (1985: 18), international diversification lowers risk to 33% of that of a typical stock, compared with domestic diversification's 50%. According to Levi (1996: 441), an internationally diversified portfolio typically has less than half the risk of a domestically diversified portfo-lio. The risk of US portfolios of over 20 stocks, measured by the stan-dard deviation, is approximately 25% of the risk of a typical security, whereas the risk of a well-diversified international portfolio is only about 12% (Solnik 1974: 51, quoted in Levi 1996: 440). The benefits for a German or Swiss investor were shown to be even larger.

It is possible from the range of returns and risk on different assets to forecast the ideal composition of a portfolio, including the share of international assets, and to compare the actual with the predicted holdings. The share of international assets in most portfolios falls well below the predicted levels. It may be that the relevant models are mis-specified – they are very much models based on the usual economic assumptions for perfect markets, or it might be that the inputs into such models are wrongly estimated. Such input errors might include transaction costs differing between countries, or the omission of assets, such as human capital, from the investor's opportunity set. It is possi-ble to contradict each argument. The transaction costs argument is undermined by the fact that there is considerable evidence showing more 'churn' for international than for domestic assets (Tesar and Werner 1994, quoted by Helliwell 1998: 71). No single adjustment will explain the home asset bias, although a combination of assets might (Glassman and Riddick 2001). Unfortunately they come up with the phantom asset or assets, whose characteristics are known but which is not identified. It cannot be human capital since a high correlation with returns on domestic assets would mean that the holding of foreign assets should be even larger than usually forecast in order to compensate for the domestic bias of human capital (Baxter and Jermann 1997).

Levi (1996: 451) refers to both direct barriers such as legal restrictions on the holding of foreign stocks and discriminatory tax treatment, or indirect barriers such as 'the difficulty of finding and interpreting information about foreign securities and reluctance to deal with foreigners' (Levy 1996: 451). Helliwell (1998: 71) turns to the 'perceived advantages of dealing within familiar and trusted networks, institutions, and markets', which are seen as greater than the potential gains from further international diversification. He goes on to suggest that the border effects 'involve a subtle combination of information networks, national systems of accounting and regulation, and assessments of foreign risks that are often poorly grounded.' He continues, 'The weak basis of information for the assessment of the riskiness of foreign markets and institutions makes those assessments likely to change rapidly whenever the credibility or prospects of foreign markets are called into question' (Helliwell 1998: 72).

The causes of home country bias

Adler and Dumas (1983: 925) write: 'To distinguish between the domestic and international settings, one needs an economic concept of nationhood.' They might have added political and cultural concepts. Nationhood involves the existence of many such boundaries, for various reasons difficult to cross, particularly where they have existed for a long time. The boundaries have obvious political aspects, such crossing implying the entry into another jurisdiction or sovereignty, but they also involve economic and cultural differences, some obvious such as the use of different currency or language systems. Adler and Dumas (1983) point out that the economic concept of nationhood differs according to the relevant branch of economics. There are two conceptions in conventional trade theory. Ricardian theory sees nationhood as reflecting different technologies and tastes. The Hekscher-Ohlin theory selects endowment with factors of production as the defining characteristic. Monetary economics identifies the existence of separate currencies as the key element. From the perspective of foreign investment theory there are more ramifications. For portfolio theory two alternative conceptions are discussed – nations as zones of common purchasing power (purchasing power parity) and nations as manifestations of sovereignty exercised notably through taxes and border controls of various kinds.

There are other relevant features which are referred to by Helliwell in considering the size of border effects. National borders divide outsiders from insiders. The differences comprise attitudes, values, behavioural patterns and institutions, the whole paraphernalia of culture. There is inevitably much greater familiarity of insiders with what is inside. Perception is critical. There is a tendency for outsiders unfamiliar with a particular country to exaggerate difference. A survey of Australian enterprises on risk control conducted by one of the authors showed that those not engaged in FDI in developing countries tend to have a view of the level of risk in those countries which is higher than those actually engaged in investing there (Fan 2004: 175–176)!

In the past, there was a tendency to explain home country bias through a particular area of government policy – the establishment of barriers which either prevented the relevant flows or changed the price system to favour one's own. For investment, this might mean exchange controls or inconvertibility of the currency and restrictions on the purchase of enterprises by foreign companies. Both have been largely dismantled over the period since the 1970s. This dismantling has had a positive effect in encouraging international mobility and has reduced the size of border effects, including a reduction of the value of b in the equation on savings and investment. However, government policy still changes in unpredictable ways which deters international exchange. It is much more difficult to anticipate the actions of foreign than domestic governments. The emphasis in this argument is on the nature of the polity and political institutions, notably government. The relevant national boundaries may coincide with both cultural and economic boundaries, imparting particular potency to so-called border effects.

There are important cultural issues which are relevant. There is a growing literature putting the argument that no market can operate without an appropriate infrastructure of attitudes and institutions supporting it. All economic behaviour is embedded in particular social structures and the social networks which characterise those structures. The social and cultural structures of all societies reflect particular historical experiences. They differ markedly one from another, although there may be links which make one structure closer to another and amenable to easier interpretation by outsiders who have a similar background. The degree to which social networks extend beyond political boundaries helps determine patterns of FDI (Collier and Gunning 1999: 87). Norms of behaviour which stress trust are critical to all economic activity. The problem is how to achieve, in a large rather than a small group, a level of trust which reduces transaction costs – search, negotiation and enforcement costs, to levels which allow those transactions to occur.

A significant factor which reduces the uncertainty and mistrust obstructing economic exchange is identity and the reputation associated with it. This identity is relevant both to internal transactions within the relevant group and to external transactions between the group and others. Identity acts as a signal of the quality of a product or service provided. Trust becomes an important element in establishing that any information given is accurate and not deliberately deceiving. It reduces relevant transaction costs and is particularly important for risk control. Some economic transactions take place only between clearly identified parties. Such identity applies best to smaller institutions, families, groups of friends and firms (Ben-Porath 1980) but also to communities and nation-states (Helliwell 1998: 120–121), creating expectations about rights and responsibilities, highly specific for the smaller institutions but more general for the larger. The identity may emerge as a consequence of actions which have nothing to do with economics, and may be deliberately constructed. The establishment of that identity requires the investment of resources, both as fixed costs in setting-up identity and as variable costs in maintaining the identity. Ben-Porath talks in terms of 'specialisation by identity' (Ben-Porath 1980: 1), that is, individuals deal only with the same person or with specific small groups (Ben-Porath 1980: 9). This is the origin of various networks which act to promote exchange of various kinds. Nations do the same thing. There is often an obvious asymmetry of information between those within a network and those outside. Insiders are more familiar with the way in which things are done and the networks which are relevant. Outsiders do not have this information but may wish to link up with the relevant networks. The clusters of nations receiving FDI from a common source illustrate well these arguments.

Home country bias and country risk

One persuasive explanation of a home country bias rests on the existence of risk, particularly country risk. The placement of savings reflects the need for an acceptable combination of return and risk. In a perfect market returns would be equalised everywhere with a risk premium added to take account of the different risk environments. By a simple measure such as the returns on government paper, the spread of notional risk premiums is clearly large.

Country risk is partly associated with ignorance about future conditions in other countries which are the destinations for FDI. Decision makers may not be aware of investment opportunities. The concept of asymmetrical information captures the divergence in knowledge between insiders and outsiders. It is of the nature of competitive advantage that some enterprises have in relevant areas more information and knowledge than others. They have a better ability to read risk in those areas. Those within a country have more knowledge about that country than those outside the country. This applies to those who have developed a familiarity with a particular country environment compared with those who lack that familiarity. With each additional investment in a particular country, there is a learning process which reinforces existing patterns of familiarity. The pattern of foreign investment for any country clearly reflects this familiarity (see the concentration of Australian outward FDI on the USA, the UK and New Zealand, English-speaking countries with strong cultural ties: Fan 2004: 208–209). Ignorance can be reduced to a cost, by assuming that the ignorance might be dissipated by the commitment of the necessary resources to appropriate information gathering. This is not as easy as it sounds since there is a need to know where to look. Selection may be biased by existing patterns of knowledge and investment. It is impossible to gain all the necessary information.

Helliwell has summarised the implications of his confirmation of a strong home country bias in all relevant areas, including trade, prices, investment, technological knowledge and migration. 'The striking size and pervasiveness of border effects reveal that the global economy of the 1990s is really a patchwork of national economies, stitched together by threads of trade and investment that are much weaker than the economic fabric of nations.' (Helliwell 1998: 118) This book seeks to explain the existence of such a significant home country bias through the existence of a high level of relevant risk.

Part II

Different Perspectives on Investment Appraisal

> It is gradually becoming clear that human decision making cannot be understood by simply studying final decisions. The perceptual, emotional and cognitive processes which ultimately lead to the choice of a decision alternative must also be studied if we want to gain an adequate understanding of human decision making.
>
> (Quoted from Sandberg, Schweiger and Hofer 1988 in Fried and Hisrich 1994: 13)

It is necessary to begin by analysing the nature of the decision-making process at the micro, or project, level. The apparent simplicity of an investment decision, as presented in many textbooks, belies its complexity. This book is concerned with unravelling that complexity. There is a need for a better understanding of the nature of an investment project, achieved by considering such projects from different perspectives – the financial, strategic and organisational.[1] The different perspectives prompt the asking of three groups of questions.

- How might an international investment project be appraised? What are the decision rules and measurement systems appropriate to such an appraisal? How does such an appraisal take into account uncertainty?

The financial perspective treats the project as a set of financial flows.

- How does the project fit in with the strategy of the enterprise or business unit? What is the nature of any relevant interdependencies? How far is the success of future projects linked to that of existing projects? How is it possible to take account of the overall strategic situation in the appraisal of a project?

Any investment has linkages with other projects, both contemporary and future, and will elicit strategic responses from other enterprises.

* How is decision making organised? What risk exposures exist for different stakeholder groups involved in the investment project? What kind of assets are at risk? How far can the different stakeholders diversify against risk?

The organisational perspective recognises the enterprise as a coalition of many stakeholders with an interest in any decision, more for an international project than for a domestic one.

Each of these perspectives is the focus of a chapter in this section.

5

The Investment Process and Decision Making: the Financial Perspective

> There is little doubt that the single most difficult part of risk evaluation is the generation of good input data.
>
> (Hull 1980: 140)

This chapter emphasises the importance of avoiding two types of mistakes, making a poor investment and ignoring a good one. It continues with the articulation of the formula for estimating the net present value of a single project, initially in which there is no uncertainty. The next section explores the significant measurement problems for inputs into such a formula, including the problems following from its international nature. The assumptions of the analysis are made explicit. Later sections show how such formula over-simplifies the appraisal of an investment project, by ignoring the key issue of uncertainty. The chapter goes on to analyse the impact of uncertainty on decisions making, assuming that all the relevant risk is epistemic risk, risk arising from a lack of the relevant information. This uncertainty relates both to the identification of the project and to the reading of the environment in which the project will operate and its influence on the project. The real options approach which allows for a reduction of uncertainty is discussed.

There are five sections:

- In the first section there is a review of mistakes which might be made in investment appraisal and their likely cost.
- The second section introduces the net present value formula.
- In the third section there is an analysis of the difficulties in estimating the different inputs into the present value formula.
- The fourth section attempts an incorporation of uncertainty into investment appraisal.

- The final section introduces the real options approach as a way of coping with uncertainty.

The possibility and cost of mistakes

It is helpful to consider the investment decision in terms of making a mistake and its consequences. Making the right decision can be interpreted as avoiding making a wrong decision. This does not mean that projects are accepted only if there is certainty of an excellent return. An excess of caution has its own cost, a neglect of potentially rewarding projects. The following diagram indicates one way of classifying the nature of any mistake.

A type 1 error is one in which a potentially good project is rejected, whereas a type II error is one in which a bad project is accepted. Usually more attention is focused on the latter. Accepting a project which is a failure has more obvious negative consequences for the decision makers than passing by a potentially good project. A failed project can have a number of consequences – it can generate an identifiable loss, varying in size with the project size; it can even threaten the existence of the enterprise, if other projects are in difficulty. Profits decline or become losses; growth rates of revenue decelerate; cash flows cease; share prices fall. By contrast, there is no obvious manifestation of failure in the case of neglect of a potentially beneficial project. Consequently, there might be a greater fear by most decision makers of making a type 11 error, particularly when they are closely associated with such a project. This might lead to a bias in which a project is only accepted if it has a decisively positive present value.

	Project	
	Good one	Poor one
Accepted	Correct	Type II error
Rejected	Type I error	Correct

Figure 5.1 The error matrix

This interpretation is only part of the story. In the longer term, the consequences of a type I error can be as bad as those of a type II error, for both the enterprise and its key decision makers. Innovative investments are usually associated with a high level of risk, but are critical to the retention by any enterprise of a continuing competitive advantage. In a situation of strategic drift an enterprise finds its strategy increasingly out of line with a changing external environment because of the rejection of projects which could maintain its competitive advantage. If the gap becomes large enough the enterprise may enter a 'turnaround' situation when all performance indicators begin to show a marked deterioration. Mistakes of type 1 can accumulate unrecognised for a significant period of time and are more difficult to identify since they include projects which the relevant enterprise never seriously considered.

On the other hand, financial theory suggests that ambitious managers, sometimes encouraged by owners, may have a bias in favour of risky projects, particularly if the enterprise has high debt leverage. They reap most, if not all, the upside but only a small part of the downside (chapter 7): the burden of any failure, and of ultimate bankruptcy, falls largely on the creditors because of the existence of limited liability. There are other reasons why managers prefer projects which generate growth rather than profits (Marris 1964). Such considerations increase risk for those providing finance, supporting the inclusion of higher premiums in any interest charge. However, for most enterprises it is unlikely that this tendency will fully offset that described above.

One reason why Type 1 error might be a common occurrence is a general anti-failure bias in decision making, which is referred to as 'an obsessive bias' (McGrath 1999: 27). The reasons for such a bias are threefold: a tendency to extrapolate the perceived circumstances of past success into the future, the existence of cognitive biases of various kinds, and errors introduced through actions to avoid the appearance of failure (McGrath 1999: 17–19).

The first follows from the tendency to over-sample success; from a routinisation of established procedures and their application in inappropriate contexts; and from a tendency to hold to already tried methods whatever the change in environment. The second includes the confirmation bias, the tendency to reject information which is negative for existing views and to accept the general consensus; the tendency to attribute success to one's own efforts and failure to bad luck; and the general rejection of anything that has failure associated with it. The third consists in straight forward manipulation of the numbers that go into the appraisal; the inclination, and to some degree, the interest of all stakeholders in banding together to hide a failure; but finally the inclination of all to concentrate the costs of a failure on a scapegoat.

The implications of this bias for the values fed into any appraisal are clear. Incremental investments (sustaining innovations) have values put in which are often optimistic whereas new strategic investments (disruptive innovations) have pessimistic values inserted and require very positive values to be seriously considered (Christensen 1997; Christensen and Bower 1996; and Christensen, Johnson and Rigby 2002). To offset the anti-failure bias and its influence on the numbers fed into the appraisal a strong championing of disruptive innovations is required (Burgelman 1983, 1985, 2000; and Burgelman and Grove 1996).

A type-II error can be detected through the impact on key performance indicators, whereas type-I can be detected only through a strategic audit. Even in retrospect, with all outturns known, it is difficult to know whether a right decision has been made. The acceptance of any project is followed by unanticipated changes, some arising because of changes in relevant environmental circumstances, such as the level of market demand, others because of changes to the parameters of a project, its technology and organisation. It cannot be known whether an alternative would have yielded more beneficial cash streams, sufficient to have tipped the balance in its favour (Liebowitz and Margolis 1995). This is sometimes the source of path dependence (David 1985; Arthur 1989).

Investment appraisal

Capital budgeting is 'the process of analysing capital investment opportunities and deciding which, if any, to undertake' (Moosa 2002: 102). It comprises developing an appropriate decision rule and estimating procedures for the relevant input variables. A decision rule indicates whether an individual investment project should be implemented. The simplest rule says, adopt any investment project which has a positive net present value. This sets a threshold which is easy to understand. For the moment, any decision is a now or never decision since a competitor enterprise can take up a project with a positive value if the relevant enterprise delays a decision. There is one scenario with fully known constant net cash streams, denoted X. The investment costs are initially zero.

The next step is to derive a present value from the future cash streams. Since any investment involves cash streams at different times, an appraisal takes the form of an estimation using discounting to translate future values into present ones. The future cash streams are discounted at a relevant risk-free discount rate r, also a constant. In a world of certainty, the economics of such a decision are simple (Hull 1980: chapter 1): the net present value is X/r. A thousand dollar net cash stream would be valued at twenty thousand dollars if the interest rate were 5%.

Usually there are investment costs, denoted as K, for the moment all incurred at the beginning of the project. If the project is irreversible, with no exit from the project possible at any time, the capital costs cannot be recouped. The net present value is then: $- K + X/r$.

It is always beneficial to bring forward revenues or to delay costs where this is possible, with the result annual streams sustained over a finite project life of n years, $X_1, X_2, X_3 .... X_n.$. The net present value is then defined as: $NPV = - K_0 + \Sigma X/(1 + r)^n_{t=1}$. If there is some reversibility, there is at any time a known salvage value, including at the end of the project's life a notional value, S_n. This can be added to the stream of net positive cash flows and discounted in the same way. $NPV = - K_0 + X + S_n$.

Any appraisal is only as good as the accuracy and appropriateness of the figures used to represent the cash streams, the life time of the project, and the rate of time discount.[1]

The inputs into the estimation of present value

There are difficulties in estimating the values of the inputs inserted into the present value formula, which are discussed in turn.[2] The analysis notes particular complications introduced by the international orientation of an investment project. There are three preliminary issues.

The first relates to the degree of disaggregation. The more specific the information required, the easier it is to acquire and the more accurate it is likely to be, which argues in favour of as much disaggregation as possible. However, the longer the lines of communication, the greater is the likelihood of distortion, both deliberate and inadvertent. When these lines of communication cross international borders, the problems multiply. Any inputs used should come from independent sources of information.

This raises a second issue – the existence of correlations between the different variables. Such dependencies can cause complications in estimation, since the value attached to one variable is conditional on the value of another. The greater the level of disaggregation, the greater the probability of the existence of such dependencies. For example, the investment costs incurred may influence the nature of the ongoing inputs required. For international projects, these interdependencies are particularly important (Buckley 1996: 159).

A third issue relates to whether attention is focused on the cash flows generated by the project in the host country or on the remittable cash flows available to the shareholders in the home country (Buckley 1996: 162–164).[3] There might be a significant disparity in such cash streams because of linkages with other parts of the multinational's empire, which have an impact on the net cash position of the parent. For example, there must be a deduction from net cash streams for any export sales by the parent or other subsidiaries which are replaced by the new sales sourced in the host country. It is also necessary to take account of such issues as relative tax rates, exchange controls, remittance policy, fluctuations in exchange rates, even differences in the relevant discount rate (Moosa 2002: 106). Where there are exchange controls, the relevant cash flows to the parent may consist of a mixture of management fees (net of any costs), royalties, interest on loans, dividend remittances allowed, and repayments for loans extended by the home country enterprise. Another relevant issue is the exchange rate used to convert into the home currency. Often this is an exchange rate which fails to reflect purchasing power parity, i.e. involves relative inflation rates out of line with expected movements in the exchange rate.

The perspective adopted is partly an issue of who owns and who controls the enterprise (Moosa 2002: 104). If the project is controlled by the subsidiary but the subsidiary is fully owned by the parent, a focus on the subsidiary is probably appropriate. It seems appropriate to make the basis for any appraisal of the project itself, and then to consider the project from the perspective of the parent company, if there are notable differences in the relevant cash streams. The account below is written on the assumption that the local managers have full autonomy and remit all profits to the parent. If this is not the case, issues such as the possible blocking of transfers of profits, forced retention of profits or the imposition of withholding taxation, become relevant, as does the movement of the relevant exchange rates. It is necessary to distinguish actual differences in such policies from the threat of action which might create such differences.

Cash flows

The Xs are the revenues minus the costs for relevant years during the lifetime of the project, which vary from year to year, even turning negative in some years. The net cash streams are estimated as earnings before tax, then as earnings after allowance for tax payments. Tax rates are a problem where there are differences in the rates between home and host countries and where credits granted may be variable. There may be some discretion as to where the cash flows appear, which raises the whole question of transfer pricing (Vonnegut 2000).

The main uncertainty arises from the primary variables which underpin the revenue and cost streams.

- Revenues are the number of sales times relevant prices, both of which need to be forecast. The further into the future the appraisal is aimed, the more uncertain are the values of both variables. Some methods of forecasting, such as univariate or multivariate analysis, are sophisticated, others take full account of the uncertainty concerning both unknowns. Sales reflect the overall growth of the market for any relevant product or service and the market share attained by the relevant enterprise.

Decision makers can consider prices in real, not nominal, terms. Futures markets provide information on the movement of prices over the lifetime of a project, but often not the whole lifetime. Future changes are to some degree under the control of the decision makers concerned with the relevant project. The managers of the enterprise may consider that their information is better than that held by the market.

- Costs are both variable and fixed. Variable costs such as wages, raw material, component and energy input costs, fluctuate with the level of output or sales. The process of learning by doing and the movement down the experience curve will affect future cost levels. It is necessary to anticipate different cost scenarios. Fixed costs are incurred irrespective of output levels and should be included in K. The initial capital costs, K, generate streams of costs, including depreciation allowances and interest charges. The former may be matched by maintenance and upgrading expenditures. There is much difference in the way in which depreciation is estimated in different countries and different industries. There is some difficulty in moving from cash streams to earnings streams because of the arbitrary nature of costs such as taxes, interest payments and depreciation allowances.

The movement of prices and cash streams may reflect the anticipated strategy of other players and the level of competition in the relevant sector of the economy. The degree of competition in any market and the interaction between the strategies of competitors creates a risk for the enterprise making an investment decision since what the competitors do has a direct influence on prices, output sold and even on the level of costs.

Discount rate

There are two elements to any discount rate, time and risk elements. The latter disappears in an environment of certainty, when the discount rate is a risk-free rate, perhaps LIBOR (London Interbank Offered Rate) or the rate on a treasury bill issued in New York. Even a rate of time discount may differ from period to period, from person to person or from organisation to organisation. The discount rate can be nominal or real, that is, it can ignore or take account of the rate of inflation, provided all cash streams are consistently measured.

Choice of an appropriate discount rate is central to any attempt to consider uncertainty. This means selecting an appropriate risk premium to be added to the rate of time preference. Once uncertainty is introduced there are many complicating issues:

- Individuals attach different utility to income
- Risk may differ from period to period
- Risk may differ from one kind of project to another.

There may be different rates for cost reducing investments, capacity expanding investments or investments introducing new products, or for different business units at different points in their life cycle (Hull 1980: 13–14).

- Risk may differ from country to country
- Risk may differ from one cash stream to another

Since the discount rate is intended to correct for the specific risk in each period, there should be multiple rates. Using a single rate reflects implicit assumptions (Mandron 2000: 998–1001):

- that uncertainty dissipates at a constant rate with time (the shape of the probability distribution of cash flows expected in adjacent periods is unchanging).
- all cash flows have identical per-period-risk.

Clearly, these are illegitimate assumptions. In the words of Mandron, The traditional DCF model is ill-suited for projects characterised by varying degrees of risk resolution across time (Mandron 2000: 999).

The discount rate can be interpreted as the target rate of return for the project or as the cost of capital, often the weighted average cost of capital. It should be a marginal rather than an average rate. It is often assumed that the debt/equity ratio remains constant, which removes the problem of average versus marginal cost. In simplified cases, a 100% equity financing is assumed in order to avoid the uncertainty created by debt leverage (Mandron 2000: 1004–5). The cost of capital on any project depends on the use to which the capital is put since the latter determines the level of risk. The separation principle between investment decisions and finance decisions falls down in practice (Mandron 2000: 1003).

Initial investment cost

Capital costs are those incurred independently of the level of output but necessary to the operation of the relevant project, in the simplest situation all incurred today (year 0). The capital costs include the working capital required to start operations and any promotional or distributional costs associated with the sale of a new product. The capital costs are usually incurred over a number of years and are flexible in their timing. Any such instalments need to be discounted to give a present value.

The cost of the investment may not be fully known, particularly for international projects. Sometimes the parent company contributes existing equipment. There may be some ambiguity about the valuation of equipment provided by an enterprise to a subsidiary abroad rather than that bought on the market or constructed by the relevant enterprise. The valuation can be the current purchase price of equipment in a similar state of wear and tear, the net realisable value of the equipment, or the present value of future earnings generated by the equipment. These values may differ. This issue of the relevant valuation is discussed at some length by Buckley (1996: 164–167).

Project lifetime

The choice is initially arbitrary. Depreciation is likely to assume a given life, particularly if it is based on the straight-line method which simply divides the capital cost by the number of years of life.

Salvage value

This term is the most difficult one to estimate. The further into the future a project is likely to conclude, the less is its influence on present value. This value can reflect net revenue streams beyond the termination date.

In practice the estimation of the values to go into the formula occurs after a long assessment process in which the key decision makers deal with many uncertainties. The same appraisal framework can be adopted, even if the future cash streams are not fully known. There are two possibilities:

- The uncertainty yields either discrete possibilities or the limits of a feasible range of values. It is common to assume a normal distribution of returns with the extremes clearly specified, and common to attach probabilities to all future outcomes. Often, a weighting by probability and the averaging of possible outcomes is the approach adopted in finance texts. The Xs are, in that case, the mean expected values of these distributions. Averaging different scenario outcomes is a dangerous procedure if there are a limited number of possibilities. The nature of the distribution is important, particularly if there is a skewness or kurtosis implying the possibility of nasty outcomes.
- Alternatively the uncertain streams could be reduced to certainty equivalents, that is, the managers could state cash flows which, if obtained for certain, are equally as desirable as the projected uncertain cash flows. This may be difficult to achieve.

In both cases the estimation is done as if all the values were known with certainty. This has prompted Vonnegut to comment, 'The ENPV rule [expected net present value] is flexible in that a wide range of uncertainties and probabilities can be incorporated into the state space for each time period.' (Vonnegut 2000: 84).

Implicatluiis of the analysis

There are three initial questions

Firstly, why use net present value, when there are alternative decision rules (Hull 1980: chapter 1; Trigeorgis 1996: chapters 1 and 2; for the methods used by American enterprises see Buckley 1996: table 6.5, p. 171)? Discounted cash flow methods include the internal rate of return or profitability index. The internal rate of return estimates the return on the declining balance of funds tied up in a project which reduces any positive net streams to a zero present value. The decision rule for the investment project is that the investment yields an IRR greater than a cost of capital, or if there is a choice between a number of variants, selecting that which yields the highest IRR. The measure has disadvantages over the net present value measure. It does not take account of the size of the investment and of the value created. In some circumstances there is more than one rate, which reduces the net returns to a present value of zero. Further, it can give a recommendation which differs from the net present value measure, particularly if much of the positive net returns are concentrated in the earliest years of a project – this is because the IRR is not the rate of return on all the initial funds invested in a project. There are good reasons for believing that the net present value approach is preferable (Buckley 1996).

Much more commonly used by managers is the target payback period. Before the 1960s when discounted cash flow methods became popular, the payback period was widely used and is still used more commonly than thought (Buckley 1996: 172; Jagannathan and Meier 2002: 8–10). The payback period is the number of years it takes to recoup the cost of an initial investment by additional positive net cash flows. The decision rule is, invest if the actual period is less than the target period. This has a number of serious weaknesses. The choice of target payback period is arbitrary. Like the IRR, it docs not take into account the size of the investment or return. It ignores any positive net income streams which come after the payback period and the timing of such streams within the payback period itself.

Secondly, what kind of investment decision is relevant?

- whether to invest in the development of a new product or process
- what variant of an investment project to choose
- whether to continue existing projects
- whether to acquire or merge with another enterprise

The application of the decision rule in all these appraisals should be consistent. Any project emerges as a set of variants, with variations relating to the timing of implementation and completion, to the scale of operation, to the mix of outputs or inputs, and even to the timing of implementation and abandonment. A relevant formula should be capable of dealing with the options made possible by different staging or pacing decisions, with the flexibility inherent in the nature of any investment project.

A neglected consideration is whether there are limitless funds available for investment or a fixed sum to be allocated between projects. If there is a limited pool of investment funds, the ranking of projects in terms of value will determine where the cut-off falls. Models based on the weighted average cost of capital take account of the different costs of capital, notably as between internal cash, debt and equity. Existing cash flows may be significant in determining the level of investment since they provide the internal funds available for such investment, and therefore indirectly determine the cost of capital. Moreover, the same argument can be applied to the resource position of the enterprise more generally, in particular a finite availability of managerial or organisational inputs, which may limit how many projects can be considered and/or adopted at any given time (Jagannathan and Meier 2002: 3 and 19).

Thirdly, how do we know whether the use of the simple net present formula yields the right decision? Theorists usually consider from an equilibrium point of view whether the decisions resulting from the method are optimal and whether the incentive structure encourages an appropriate choice. Often, the procedure adopted is to define an equilibrium set of conditions which determine all relevant prices and then to estimate whether a project adds value to an enterprise and its shares. There are a notional set of optimum investment decisions which result in positive net present values. Such an approach is acceptable in a theoretical treatment. An individual enterprise cannot repeat the exercise of estimating equilibrium prices each time it makes a decision, even if it were possible; the cost would be prohibitive and any time delay excessive. Nor is it possible to estimate shadow prices which might be used to yield an optimum. Even if possible, this represents a social optimum, which might bankrupt any enterprise which tried to use them.

An enterprise has no option but to accept the existing structure of prices as given, despite some serious reservations. The use of existing prices is based on the assumption that they result from the operation of efficient markets, in which inputs are priced competitively at their opportunity costs. Decision makers are seen as price takers rather than price makers. However, price policy is a strategic issue and the history of particular prices reflects the history of the implementation and interaction of relevant strategies. The present analysis simply takes prices in existing markets as a given without making any assumptions about the degree to which enterprises make those prices. These issues point to the centrality of strategy as the context in which any specific investment project must be appraised – an issue dealt with in chapter 5.

Another assumption privileges the shareholders in that an enterprise is seen as running in their interests. In practice, the decision making unit is a complex organisation with many decision makers participating in that decision and many stakeholders influencing and influenced by the relevant decision. Some stakeholder groups may be located in the home country, others in the host country. The enterprise is a network of different stakeholders threatened in different ways by risk. The interests and aims of stakeholders differ. Negotiation and bargaining between stakeholders over the sharing of costs, benefits and risk is important to the success of any project. Once the assumption that everyone is a price taker in a perfect market is relaxed, the issue of price becomes a strategic one relevant to the treatment of all stakeholder groups. This is the world of price makers, whatever market is considered. Prices result from negotiations and bargains struck which take into consideration both the competitive positions and the strategies of the different stakeholder groups and help to distribute the value created by investment projects. A project may have hidden in its cost streams values generated and distributed to a variety of stakeholders. For the moment, the focus is on adding value without specifying for whom – an issue dealt with in chapter 6.

Incorporating uncertainty

'Any long term major allocation of funds will be considered to be a capital investment' (Hull 1980: 1). Examples are a five-year training programme, a major advertising campaign, an investment in R and D, as well as the classic investments in plant and equipment. Most literature on capital budgeting is written as if all investments are independent, irreversible investments, the classic once-and-for-all, accept or reject, decisions based upon static expectations of cash flows and on a passive acquiescence by relevant managers in the implications of the decision. The usual starting point is a single project with, at least implicitly, a single decision maker and a single decision. A simple objective of profit or share price maximisation is commonly assumed.

Such a profile means an over-simplification of the relevant problems. Dixit and Pindyck (1994: 3, 23–25) emphasise three characteristics shared by many investment projects:

- irreversibility – there is some element of sunk costs about any investment which involves assets specific to the enterprise or industry,
- uncertainty – mostly about future net revenue streams,
- timing – there is flexibility about the timing of all investments.

The following offers a classification of relevant investments with these three factors in mind (Trigeorgis 1996: 2–3):

- Independent investments for which there is an option to defer, including staged investments, or investment by instalments, at each stage of which there is an option to delay (or to exit). Any single project involves discrete decisions spread out over time. The deliberate staging and pacing of decisions is an important matter (White 2004: 631–33). Sometimes there are natural stages in an investment project, e.g. in the exploration and development of an oil field, in the development and testing of a pharmaceutical drug or in the development of real estate. Part of such investment is the preliminary identification of a relevant project through research and development.
- Reversible investments where there is a realistic option to abandon, i.e. the relevant plant can be sold at close to its original cost. This might apply in a capital intensive industry, such as airlines, where there is a good market for the relevant capital equipment. The reversibility is limited where the investments are highly specific or where all enterprises within a sector experience the same cyclical fluctuations.
- Investments made to increase flexibility, allowing at low switching costs a change in either inputs or outputs, in some cases being based on modular development, or an expansion or contraction of scale, including a temporary closure. The first applies to any industry in which there is a significant energy input or in which product customisation has become important, e.g. automobiles. The second might include the fashion industry. The group includes investments made as an insurance, for example deliberately built-in

overcapacity, where there is strongly seasonal demand, such as electricity generation.

- Growth investments, including any type of research and development expenditure. Such investments make possible other investments, e.g. buying licenses in telecommunications, in mining exploration or development and testing in the pharmaceutical industry. They include deliberately interdependent investments, serving other investment projects, sometimes generating temporarily negative net cash streams. One option may be to acquire another option, creating a compoundedness of options.

The existing resources of the enterprise predispose decision makers to certain kinds of projects, already implicit in the knowledge developed in the implementation of operating projects. New projects are the result of a long process of development and learning but the trajectory of development of a new technology is not known in advance. The future learning process must be allowed for. It is illegitimate to think of the financial blueprint of an investment project as complete.

While all the factors important for domestic investment are important for international investment, there are other complicating factors (Moosa 2002):

- the different perspectives of home and host countries which may mean that the values of key variables are modified, e.g. the rate of time discount,
- greater complexity, e.g. more interactions between projects in a value adding chain,
- usually a much larger commitment of resources, raising the initial level of investment,
- greater risk, notably country risk.

The investment decision is the result of many determinants operating within the highly specific circumstances relevant to a given project. It is difficult to come up with all the information needed for an investment appraisal, particularly the exact value of relevant inputs. Uncertainty may result from an inadequate information strategy, an inability to forecast accurately, or a recognition of the unavoidable uncertainty about day-to-day returns and the likely occurrence of risk-generating events. This section considers how a company allows for the existence of such uncertainty in the valuation of an investment project.

A simple and well-tried method of taking account of the uncertainty is to vary the length of the target payback period. The greater the risk, the shorter the target period. In extreme cases the decision maker may require payback in a period as short as one to two years. This technique requires little information and little sophistication in its calculation, which explains its popularity and its weakness.

Uncertainty can be taken into account by a significant adaptation of the decision rule. There are two basic methods. They are both based on the assumption that an investment project can be delayed until uncertainty is reduced. The first method requires for immediate implementation of the investment that its value covers the opportunity cost of losing the option of waiting. The second method includes in the estimation of net present value a term which allows for the value of waiting or of any other options specifically created by the investment project. The value of the option of waiting may convert a negative net present value into a positive value.

Alternatively uncertainty can be built into measurement of the inputs into net present value. Moosa refers to three – adjusting the discount rate, adjusting the cash flows and estimating the sensitivity of values to variations in relevant variables.

- The discount rate can include a risk premium. The problem is to determine the level of the risk premium. One rate can be applied to all cash streams or the discount rate can be varied according to the riskiness of the particular streams, with a higher premium for streams further into the future.
- Cash flows can be adjusted by 'certainty equivalents' which differ for different time periods. Discounting is then applied at the risk-free rate. This approach has the virtue of separating the time element from the risk element for discounting.
- Sensitivity analysis assumes an investment project with provisional values for all inputs and analyses the ability of the project to sustain positive net present values after changes in key variables. It is widely used to identify which variables have a significant effect on value. One approach is to extract from managers optimistic and pessimistic values for all key input variables, defining these in a consistent manner, for example as those for which there is a 95% confidence that the variable will be less than the optimistic level or greater than the pessimistic level. It is not easy to extract such information from relevant managers. Doing this for all variables and estimating net present value can show whether it is worth con-

sidering the project, clearly not in the case of a negative overall outcome using optimistic inputs, or whether there needs to be time devoted to risk analysis at all, clearly not if there is a positive outcome using pessimistic inputs. It is possible to weigh the importance of individual inputs and make as accurate as possible the most important variables. This is done by varying their value by a small amount, holding all others at their expected level, and estimating the impact on the net present value. If the results are trivial, the expected value can be used, ignoring the distribution of probabilities. Otherwise, the probabilities are important.

Such subjective probability distributions are constructed from the judgement and experience of one person or a group of people, often insider managers, but where appropriate, using the Delphi method, a panel of experts who have the 'alleged' virtue of objectivity. The result is a set of probability distributions for all key variables and for the key performance indicator, in this case net present value. Such distributions can be constructed with the help of historical data, but the past is not often directly relevant to the future.

The procedure for extracting relevant information is critical. There are biases which can affect any information elicited from the relevant managers or stakeholders, some motivational and some cognitive (Hull 1980: 50–53). These result from the interests of the relevant managers or stakeholders and the spin they are likely to put on the estimates. Probably the most common bias is the central bias, the tendency of managers to see too narrow a distribution for any performance indicator. Managers have most difficulty with extremes, particularly if the distribution is of its nature skewed.

An alternative technique is to use the Monte Carlo method to select random values for the variables in order to produce from such simulations a probability distribution of net present value. Ambitious simulations can be carried out with different values of key variables yielding a probability distribution of net present values. The level of any significant variable which produces a break-even net present value could be carefully analysed to see whether it represents a likely outcome.

A focus on the mean and variance is justified if the distributions are expected to be normal, not so under differing but likely conditions:

- if the investment has a number of associated and potentially valuable options (expansion, contraction, abandonment),

- if the relevant variables are non-linear in their impact,
- if there are dependencies between non-linear variables,
- if the number of uncertain variables is small, even just one.

All techniques share a common weakness in including uncertainty as a negative factor. They assume that in order to take account of uncertainty a larger risk premium should be included in the discount rate used to yield a present value, or lower cash flow values should be selected. In both cases the impact of higher risk is to reduce present value, in some cases converting a positive into a negative present value. Such techniques encourage decision makers to think of uncertainty as a factor always negative for any project. The greater the uncertainty, the lower the value of an investment project and the less likely that it will be implemented.

There is a sense in which the opposite it true – the greater the risk, the potentially more beneficial the project. There is usually an upside and a downside to any variation in a measure of risk. With a normal distribution, the outcomes are symmetrical. For most distributions, a larger variance offers the prospect of both more advantageous and more disadvantageous outcomes. If the downside could be avoided but the upside exploited, the project will be more advantageous, not less. The potential value of a riskier project is higher, provided that the increased upside is not matched by an increased downside. If there is flexibility in the timing of an investment the option to delay can deliver value, particular by revealing more information on the likely outcome. If the worse outcome occurs, the possibility of exit, at least at a low cost, can limit the downside. If the better outcome eventuates, the project can go ahead. The so-called cone of uncertainty widens the longer we look into the future, so that the longer we wait the greater the possibility of an upside (Amram and Kulatikala 1999: 14), other things being equal such as the absence of pre-emption of an opportunity by a competitor.

Sometimes, it is useful not just to wait in a passive manner for information, but to make opportunities for acquiring relevant information, particularly, if it involves a possible upside. This may involve deliberate strategies – implementing a relevant information strategy, developing a pilot project, or staging an investment in such a way that the immediate commitment is limited. It may be possible to modify the project in the process of learning more about the risk confronting the enterprise: for example, threatening risk factors can be mitigated.

The real options approach

The real options approach can be regarded as a measurement tool which assists in accommodating criticisms of the net present value approach. There is a parallel between a financial option, notably a call option, that is, an option to buy, and an option to invest. As a matter of symmetry it is possible to view abandonment of an investment project as a put option. Whether a financial option is exercised or not depends on the relationship between the underlying price of the asset and the exercise price, which determines whether it is in or out of the money. With a call option, where the former exceeds the latter the option should be exercised and where the latter exceeds the former it should not. There is a non-linearity in the payoff which means the option holder can reap most of the upside but avoid the downside. For an investment there is the same relationship between the value of the underlying asset and its cost. An option to abandon an investment project can be compared with a put option, an option to sell if the underlying value of an asset falls below the exercise price.

The main weakness of the real options approach is ownership since the underlying asset of a real option is not owned in the same way as the underlying asset in a financial option. Lack of ownership means that others may pre-empt your action by making a similar investment or similar abandonment.

It is possible to take account of the positive value of uncertainty by retaining the same decision rule – invest if the present value is positive, but adding a term for the value of the option to wait in order to see if circumstances improve. The formula for the value of a project then becomes:

Strategic net present value = conventional net present value + the value of the option

Even if the conventional net present value is negative, if the option value is greater, the project should not be rejected.

Immediate investment has an opportunity cost which is the loss of the value of flexibility on commitment to an investment. This perspective might persuade us to change the decision rule so the net present value must exceed the total of the investment cost and the opportunity cost of losing the option to wait. In the event of the decision being a mistake there is a loss of value. If the decision is to drop the project, the loss is the possibility that the net present value, which is currently negative, becomes positive in the future. If the decision is to go ahead, the loss is the possibility that the net present value which is currently positive becomes negative.

Such a view assumes there are variants of the project which differ by their timing. By distinguishing the different variants, the real option approach puts a value on the ability to consider different options. It is necessary to determine the differing threshold levels of net present value which would justify outright rejection and immediate investment. It is necessary to value any option in order to estimate an expanded net current value. Otherwise if there is a desire to retain the positive net current value rule, the opportunity cost approach should be adopted which requires an addition to the conventional investment cost.

The real options approach requires identifying the information relevant to a investment decision and necessary to value the advantage of flexibility in the timing of an investment. The two methods which are commonly discussed in the literature, the Black-Scholes formula[4] and the binomial method (see chapter 11), identify five main factors which influence the value of a real option, analogues of those used in valuing a financial option.

Table 5.1   **Mapping an investment opportunity onto a call option**

Call options	Variable	Investment opportunity	Effect on value
Stock price	S	Present value of a project's net cash flow	+
Exercise price	X	Expenditure required to acquire project assets (the investment cost)	−
Time to maturity	t	Length of time the decision may be deferred	+
Riskiness of project	σ^2	Variance of returns assets	+
Risk-free rate	R_f	Risk-free rate (time value of money)	+

The general approach can usually handle two types of uncertainty, three at most, the Black-Scholes formula less.

The first task is to identify the underlying asset. The approach seeks to link the estimation of relevant values to market valuations, where possible. It is often difficult to find an asset sold on the market which exactly reflects the project. The problem is avoided by creating a synthetic portfolio with the same characteristics as the project. The underlying assets for a real option are portfolios of securities traded in the financial market with an equivalent risk, whose fluctuations are used to determine the value of the option. For example, if it were an investment in expanding a semi-conducting manufacturing facility, the option value reflects the future price of chips as the underlying assets. Or the underlying asset for oil exploration is the appropriate oil futures contract or an index of such contracts.

Traded contracts price in a convenience yield while spot prices do not. There are non-contingent cash flows which attach to the underlying asset, some positive and explicit, such as rents, dividends, interest, royalties or license payments, or implicit, benefits such as convenience yields, some negative and explicit (reflecting inventory held for what Keynes called the precautionary motive), losses such as storage costs, taxes, licensing or royalty fees, insurance cost loss from perishable damage. These are significant for certain kinds of investment. Spot prices reflect supply and demand, whereas the value of assets, such as futures contracts or other options, reflects information about relevant cash flows. Despite the effort to link real options to financial markets, the usual method of valuing the underlying asset is to use the discounted value of free cash flows generated by the sales of the chips or of the oil.

The further into the future that the investment project is implemented, the more difficult it is to estimate its cost. The time to maturity is a variable; it is the time that the enterprise retains some monopoly control over the source of competitive advantage, the time allowed by the expiry of a contract or a patent or simply the period during which a competitive advantage exists since it takes time for competitors to imitate the competitive advantage. It is not easy to know how long such an advantage might last. The reduction in the time to maturity is a fresh source of uncertainty. Generally, the longer the time to maturity, the greater the uncertainty faced by the decision makers.

Risk is the volatility of the cash streams generated by the project. It can be either the variance of a probability distribution, usually assumed to be normal, or the full range of possible returns, the gap between the most optimistic and the most pessimistic forecasts. The basis for estimating such a volatility may be existing historical data or even, and preferably for some, the volatility of a traded option relevant to the underlying asset. Volatility is related to a relevant time unit. It is common for the pricing of contingency claims or options to take account of a further source of uncertainty – unpredicted extreme events, specifically their frequency of occurrence and severity of impact. How this is done is discussed later.[5] The risk-free interest rate is that which reflects the value of time. There are various ways of valuing real options and of incorporating the real options approach into the net present value formula, discussed in chapter 10.

6
The Investment Process and Decision Making: the Strategic Perspective

> Strategic analysis provides a framework where the value lies not so much in providing answers, but rather in the guidance of decision making, the comparison and evaluation of alternatives, and studying the source of business successes and failures.
>
> (Rogers 2002: 35)

This chapter turns from the project level to the enterprise level, mainly because an appraisal which considers an investment project in isolation is inadequate. An enterprise perspective is necessary. The chapter, therefore, adopts a strategic perspective on investment decision making, one which places the appraisal of a single investment project in the context of the overall enterprise strategy, including its relationship with other projects – past, present and future. Such a perspective stresses the role of the enterprise as a maker of strategy. It is consistent with a view which interprets most strategy as emerging from a learning process. It also discusses the strategic risk arising from the strategy of other players before presenting an expanded version of net present value and a decision rule which takes full account of uncertainty. It follows up with a review of the requirements of a relevant information strategy. The chapter concludes with an analysis of a critical aspect of strategy, the appropriate mode of entry to be adopted into international business transactions.

There are six sections in this chapter:

- The first section explores the different ways of interpreting the nature of the enterprise.
- The second section shows the importance of strategy in the interaction of investment projects.

- The third section considers strategic risk, that is, the negative impact which competitors' decision can have on an enterprise.
- In the fourth section there is a discussion of how an individual investment project can be properly appraised only within the context of the overall strategy of the enterprise.
- The fifth section concentrates on the role of a risk control strategy, particularly an information strategy, in the overall strategy of an enterprise.
- The sixth section illustrates how the choice of direct investment as a mode of entry into international business transactions is influenced by risk.

Strategy and the nature of the enterprise

The nature of the enterprise in which an investment project is located has become a focus of considerable interest. Much economic theory assumes that the enterprise is a black box into which inputs pass and outputs emerge (the production function approach). The nature of what happens in the black box is of no consequence, largely because in perfect competition there is no room for strategy making. Since in imperfect competition there is scope for the pursuit of distinctive strategies, what goes on in the box does matter. Because the enterprise is a complex entity there are various ways of viewing it. It is possible to distinguish two main approaches, called here the structural and the strategic approaches.

In the new institutional theories of economics there is assumed to be competition between, and to some degree a deliberate choice, among different organisational structures (Williamson 1985) for the economy as a whole. The focus of interest is the transaction, which might involve a labour input, the making of a loan or the sale of a commodity. The raison d'etre of any organisational structure, including that in which the enterprise is prominent, is to minimise the costs associated with all transactions. This way of viewing the enterprise stresses the relative efficiency of different organisational forms, such as markets and business enterprises, in the allocation of resources. Often the level of costs for transactions internalised within enterprises is significantly lower than that which would characterise a system based entirely on market relations.

First the enterprise is viewed as a structure or configuration of interacting parts, that is, an organisational or administrative unit with a bureaucratic structure based on vertical hierarchy and clear boundaries both between it and the outside world and internally between its horizontal divisions. It is an organisation continuously seeking to reconcile the need for specialisation (horizontal division) with that for integration (vertical division). Any structure has both formal and informal aspects. The formal configurations exist independently of who occupies particular positions in the hierarchy. There are also informal networks of interaction between the members who at any given time occupy those positions.

A supplementary approach interprets the enterprise as a network of contracts, some explicit, some implicit, which together determine the nature of economic relationships. There is a tendency by some to see the enterprise as simply a network of such contractual relationships without the need for any permanent hierarchy of any kind. Contracting is seen as a means of reconciling conflicting incentives through negotiation and bargaining with minimum damage to the enterprise. The persistence of contractual links may vary from enterprise to enterprise. A second variant stresses the nature of the enterprise as a coalition of different stakeholder groups with different interests in the performance of the enterprise. Such an approach, as with the contractual approach, reduces the importance of the boundaries between the enterprise and the outside world. A third variant is the behavioural theory of the firm which sees the enterprise as a system of standard operating procedures, or routines (Cyert and March 2001), such as control systems or incentive structures. There are patterns of behaviour within the enterprise which persist over time and define its nature.

In the second view, the enterprise is seen as a strategy making unit (Rumelt 1984), a vehicle for the articulation and implementation of strategy – not the only one, since other types of organisation, notably governments, also have strategies. The interaction of the strategies of different organisations is important in establishing the competitive environment of the enterprise and influencing all key decisions, including those on investment projects. The enterprise justifies its existence by creating and retaining competitive advantage, largely through value innovation (Kim and Mauborgne 2005), and by controlling risk.

The enterprise has a competitive advantage in certain core areas and an ability to control risk which is denied to other enterprise with different core activities. The strategic view of the enterprise sees the enterprise as consisting mainly in a set of resources, capabilities or competencies (Wernerfelt 1984). This includes intangible as well as tangible resources, the former fast rising in importance relative to the latter. This approach focuses particular attention on the role of knowledge. All the relevant resources or competencies are closely linked with the core activities of the enterprise and with the ability to realise relevant investment projects. In its more sophisticated version this approach seeks to dynamise the picture, emphasising the process of learning, the development of dynamic capabilities and the movement of dynamic transaction costs (Teece, Pisano and Shuen 1997). In one incarnation, the enterprise is seen as a learning organisation (Quinn 1992).

Each of these two definitions has implications for the investment decision-making process and for the risk control function. This chapter explores the strategic dimension of investment decisions and the next chapter the organisational dimension.

The full range of investment options

The principles underlying the present value formula are the same for an enterprise as for an individual project: the managers of an enterprise are interested in the difference between the position the enterprise will be in if it goes ahead with a project and the position it will be in if it does not (Hull 1980: 3). They are interested in any future incremental cash flows generated by a project. An appraisal involves comparing the cash flows which will occur if the project is undertaken but will not occur otherwise, and the cash flows which will occur if the project is not undertaken but which will not occur if it is undertaken. The relationship between different projects influences these net flows.

The capital budgeting and strategic approaches to investment decision making were developed separately (Myers 1984, Trigeorgis 1996: 7–9) and widely regarded as incompatible approaches. There, therefore, emerged two streams of thinking about resource allocation within the enterprise, including the nature of investment decisions (Trigeorgis 1996: 7–8)). One is the capital budgeting approach which decentralised decision making to the project level and concentrated on the discounting of particular cash streams to a present value. The other is the strategy making approach which focused on the creation and maintenance of overall competitive advantage in the longer term. The previous chapter has illustrated one way of reconciling the two approaches, through the real options approach, which makes possible a valuation of the benefits which the opening of strategic options can bring to a particular project. The real options approach is partly a tool which assists in the appraisal of individual investment projects, but also an expression of a strategic approach which affects all business decisions.

The emphasis on flexibility not only focuses attention on identification of the full range of choices open to those making a strategy but also emphasises the particular interpretation of strategy as emergent strategy, which has at its centre a learning process in which ignorance and uncertainty are dissipated over time, sometimes by deliberate action and sometimes by a simple unfolding of events. Learning can be directed to developing particular options and not others.

Any strategy has as a starting point a set of options for the use of the investment funds available to the enterprise. At the core of any strategy are investment projects, some already up and running and some at an early stage in their development. The return from any investment project reflects in part the context created by other investment projects already accepted. There are significant interdependencies between existing investment projects and between present projects and future projects. The typical portfolio of projects of a healthy enterprise comprises both, projects at various stages in the life time of a product, process or even industry. The strategy is the mechanism for selecting appropriate investment projects and for allocating the resources required to implement them.

There are two main kinds of projects, operational and strategic. The former, characterised by good profits but limited growth potential, generate most of the existing profits and the latter, characterised by poor profits, if not losses, but great growth potential, create the potential for maintaining performance in the future. Classical strategy describes a strategy in which most projects are of the former kind. Since strategy looks to the future it is about projects which open up the possibility of future profits. Much of the market value of an enterprise, particularly in such fast-changing industries as electronics, communications, biotechnology or pharmaceuticals is accounted for by growth potential rather than current cash streams (Myers 1984, Smit and Trigeorgis, 2004: 6–8). The strategic projects spawn both operational and further strategic projects, whereas the operational projects only spawn to a slight degree (Kasanen 1993).

Embedded in alternative investment projects are options (Kemna 1993). At any time a strategy consists of various options, only some of which will be exercised. In the words of (Foss 1998: 10): 'Optimal flexibility corresponds to the plan of action that enables the firm to acquire the set of options that maximise the net present value of the firm.' Strategy needs to be flexible enough to take account of uncertainty and is emergent, reflecting learning done at all levels of the enterprise. The interdependence of investments must be recognised in a strategy consisting of linked options. Strategy stresses their compound nature, the fact that future successful projects depend upon the realisation of previous options. For example, a successful pharmaceutical enterprise has projects at various stages of development, from the initial concept, through various clinical trials, to the process of regulatory approval for a new drug or process and its marketing. Since early project stages have a negative net present value, all the value is generated in the final instalments.

The previous chapter sidestepped the issue of interdependency, the possibility that a project influences the cash flows of other projects. A project might add value to other projects undertaken by the relevant enterprise, or create potential for adding value in the future. There are two kinds of interdependency. The first involves synergies of revenue and cost between existing projects. It is possible to refer to such synergies as realised interdependencies. Various economies of scope fall under this heading. Any shared facility has the effect of reducing costs for other projects. A branding exercise has a 'rub-off' effect on any products or services sold. This term can be denoted RI, and included in an expanded formula.

On the other hand, there are unrealised interdependencies which are common. The existence of unrealised interdependencies generate value as real options, which can be grouped into three main kinds as shown in the table below.

The existence of such options has a significant value for a strategy. Any research and development project is analogous to an option, since it can create a valuable opportunity without committing the enterprise to investing in the commercialisation of that opportunity. Some of the options are more tactical than strategic, notably those described as insurance options. Because of the existence of switching costs for the insurance options, there is a significant degree of path dependence for the cash streams in any relevant strategy.

Table 6.1 A classification of options

Learning options	Option to wait
(before investing)	Option to 'stage' an investment – to make it in instalments
Growth options	Option to innovate
(while and after investing)	Option to expand
Insurance option	Option to contract
(while and after investing)	Option to switch inputs or outputs
	Option to abandon or shut down temporarily

The full option value can only be estimated within the context of a specific strategy which has identified all the possibilities. In the words of Copeland and Antikarov (2001: 5): 'we would go as far as to say that NPV systemically undervalues each project'. It does this because that technique 'fails to capture the value of flexibility' (ibidem: 13). A further term should be added to the expanded net present value formula, one denoted UI (unrealised interdependencies). It is the value of all the options which attach to a given investment project, not a simple sum of those values since some options are mutually exclusive. For the sake of completeness the existence of both positive and negative externalities should be recognised. The existence of interdependencies provides a good reason for adopting some projects with a negative net present value or rejecting other projects with a positive value.

Strategic risk

It is impossible to appraise the investment project by focusing only on the strategy of the relevant enterprise. The strategies of actual and potential competitors, as well as complementors, must be taken into account since they influence the value of an investment project. There are alternative scenarios reflecting the behaviour of both competitors and complementors, streams of action, response and further reaction, constituting scenarios which offer different pictures of how the future will unfold. It is unclear which scenario will prevail, but each scenario is associated with a different valuation of the relevant investment. The future is only partly under the control of those who make strategy.

One aspect of market risk is therefore strategic risk. Strategic risk is the negative consequences on a key performance indicator of the relevant enterprise of an unanticipated action of an outside strategy maker. There is inherent in any strategic context a significant degree of uncertainty. So far uncertainty has been dealt with through the real options approach which assumes a known maturity period, that is a period during which there is no cost attached to delaying an investment. As Smit and Ankum have pointed out, 'A project in a monopoly situation is more analogous to a call option, since it involves an exclusive right to invest. A project under perfect competition, on the other hand, is like a "public good" of the whole industry. In this case, there is a loss in value from postponement caused by the early entry of competition' (Smit and Ankum 1993: 243). There is no exclusive right to invest. In the extreme case, a failure to implement a project means that a competitor immediately takes up the opportunity The time to maturity of an investment prospect may be very uncertain. There may be rapidly increasing costs in waiting to implement an investment. In the event of immediate pre-emption by a competitor there is no extra value attaching to the option to delay.

How the strategies of other players influence an enterprise's strategy depends on market structure. The assumption so far is that the relevant enterprise is a monopolist. Under perfect competition, strategy can have no influence on the key market parameters, notably price. Above normal profits and the associated competitive advantage are quickly competed away. Both extremes are unusual. A multinational will be reluctant to invest abroad unless the monopoly rents associated with oligopoly or monopolistic competition are present. The norm, particularly at the international level, is therefore monopolistic competition or oligopoly (Buckley 1996: 115). Any such market imperfection will create space for strategy to have an influence.

In order to simplify the situation, a situation of duopoly is often assumed, described with the aid of simple game theory. Games can be zero-sum games or games that favour all players. There exists a mixture of such games which are conducted simultaneously. Enterprises both compete and cooperate. It is not difficult to set up in a game a prisoner's dilemma situation for any specific investment (White 2004: chapter 13), in which both players rush to invest in a new international market to avoid being pre-empted by the other, rather than cooperate in a strategy of waiting, which increases the value of the investment for both. Both lose by rushing into the investment.

Commitment and signalling become relevant strategic issues. Reputation is another key issue in repeated games. The possible responses of competitors affect both the overall quantity supplied to any market and the level of prices in that market. By denying an enterprise potential economies of scale and the benefits of experience, they may indirectly raise cost levels. This may greatly raise the level of risk since it is uncertain how the market situation will evolve. It will affect the value of the net cash streams which go into the appraisal. There is a new term to be incorporated into the net present value formula which could be called the strategic effect, which depending on market circumstances and the strategies adopted can have an effect of varying sign and size. If negative, it may be negatively correlated with the term for the value of waiting.

Strategy and the individual investment project

It is impossible to ignore the strategic context in which an investment decision is made. Strategy is concerned with identifying specific opportunities and risks, and is expressed in the strategic evaluation and appraisal of different investment projects. In many cases the evaluation is cursory. Already before any specific appraisal a selection of projects has taken place, sometimes unconsciously. Certain projects are more interesting, meriting consideration within the specific strategic context of the relevant enterprise, or are championed by influential stakeholders. Investment projects are dismissed with little attention if they do not fit the general strategic orientation of the enterprise and may be neglected if they have no champion. This is inevitable given the limited ability of decision makers to process all the data available to them.

At its inception an investment is simply an idea, identified in the course of strategic thinking and championed by a particular individual or stakeholder group, a process sometimes referred to as intrapreneurship. It becomes a set of evolving constituent elements taking shape as relevant decision makers interpret the environments in which the project is to operate. Just as a strategy is said to emerge, so its constituent parts, the various investment projects making up the enterprise strategy, can also be said to emerge. No investment can be regarded as an off-the-shelf proposal, although for simplicity this is usually taken as the starting point for the process of investment appraisal. In the process of evolution of a project, those developing the project mould the proposal to suit the various environments of opportunity and risk to which the enterprise is exposed. Projects build on existing resources, capabilities and competencies and often add to these new but related assets. Existing competitive advantages act as filtering mechanisms largely determining which projects survive to a point at which appraisal becomes appropriate.

Investments eventually chrystalise as significant commitments of funds, with the prospect of a stream of significant future net returns. In order to properly appraise an investment project the value of the various options and interdependencies should be added to the conventional net present value of the project. This gives an expanded form of the net present value formula.

Strategic, or expanded, net present value = Conventional NPV (the intrinsic value) + the value of waiting + RI + UI +/– any allowance for strategic risk

The formula appeared to define a clear decision rule: go ahead if the value of SNPV is positive (remember that whereas NPV, RI and the allowance for strategic risk can be either positive or negative, VW and UI can only be positive, since they can never fall below zero).

The valuation depends on the five variables already indicated: the underlying value of the relevant assets (S); the investment cost (X); the risk-free interest rate; the cone of uncertainty, often the standard deviation (σ) or variance; and the time to expiry (t). In two articles Luehrman (1998a and 1998b) has shown how it is possible to reduce the number of variables to two option metrics – the value-to-cost metric (S divided by the present value of X) and the volatility metric ($\sigma\sqrt{t}$). If the former is greater than one, it means that the project has a positive conventional net present value. The higher the volatility metric, the more likely it is that a project not currently having a positive net present value will have a positive one in the future. It is possible to map the location of any project on a two dimensional diagram according to the value of the two metrics.

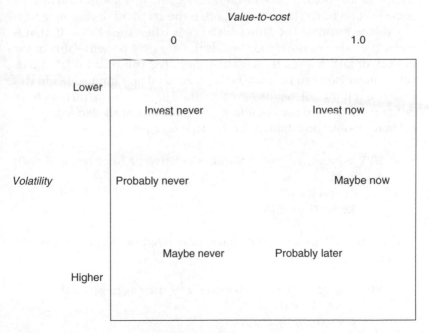

Figure 6.1   Mapping an investment strategy

The definition of the boundaries of these regions is arbitrary. Few projects are likely to have a return which justifies immediate investment. Many are never considered or rejected after a cursory examination. Those which offer a present value which lies between the two thresholds of outright rejection or acceptance, are of greatest interest. Over time, as the years to expiration pass, a project moves in the direction of both a lower value-to-cost metric and a lower volatility metric. The present value of the investment cost rises and the cumulative volatility, or chance of an upside in returns, declines. If it is a project that has never been a project with an 'invest now' location the project will tend to finish as an 'invest never'. This can be countered by two factors, luck – conditions change in favour of the project – or by active management, that is deliberate action to increase revenues and reduce costs. The latter is much more important for strategy making, although an ability to ride one's luck is an important attribute of good strategy making.

Others have collapsed all five variables to one metric, described by Alleman, Suto and Rappoport as the uncertainty-adjusted or risk-normalised NPV and referred to in their work as d, a ratio similar to the Sharpe ratio – the net present value, $S - X$ (the first metric), divided by some version of the latter metric, often the standard deviation, σ. It is possible to estimate the ratio which holds when the SNPV = 0, that is when the value of the option equals the negative present value of the project, or rather when it ceases to be negative: this is called D*. A relevant comparison can be made between actual d and implied D*. In this case the number of regions on the strategic map is defined as four, rather than six, and the boundaries are unambiguously defined.

There are four possibilities for the decision rule.

> NPV is negative and VW either positive or negative, and their aggregate < 0
> > or $d < - D^*$
> > Reject the project

This is an obvious case; not much time need be committed to the appraisal.

> NPV is negative but VW positive, and their aggregate > 0
> > or $- D^* < d < 0$
> > Keep the project alive

The closer to zero the average expected NPV and the greater is its possible variance or standard deviation, the more likely it is that this situation will arise. Much of strategy making is concerned with such projects.

> NPV and VW are both positive but NPV < VW
> or 0 < d < D*

Wait until the value of the option falls below the present value and then invest.

In this case, it will be appropriate to delay the investment. The same arguments apply in this case as in the previous one.

> NPV and VW are both positive, but NPV > VW
> or D* < d
> Invest now

This is an obvious case where the project should be undertaken immediately. This represents the core area of any strategy, a core which has to be supplemented by marginal projects.

This same picture can be depicted in terms of a difference between what might be called an upper hurdle rate of return beyond which immediate investment is called for and a lower hurdle rate at which complete rejection occurs (Jagannathan and Meier 2002). The size of the difference between the two rates, coined by Jagannathan and Meier – the hurdle premium, indicates the value of waiting. The greater the gap, the more valuable it is to wait. In practice, decision makers use such hurdle rates, well above the discount rate suggested by the CAPM approach. The exact level of the hurdle rate reflects the constraints of managerial and organisational capacity within an enterprise and the nature of the project under consideration.

The main problems for strategists are created by the middle two regions in which the conventional net present value is close to zero and there is considerable uncertainty. The third region is particularly problematic and more unusual than the second since, in most conditions, investing now in a project with a positive net present value seems an obvious thing to do: it is not. Investment now commits the enterprise to a project which has a real chance of failing, whatever the expected value and distribution of possible cash flows, or which precludes the exploitation of significant benefits in the next period:

- if there occurs between now and the next period technical changes which must be embodied in new plant and equipment. These benefits would be lost if the investment occurred now, using an old vintage technology. The maturity period must be long to make this a likely event. On the other hand, learning by doing makes no difference to the timing of an investment since it occurs as soon as the investment is made,
- if the total possible output is fixed – there is a limited reserve of some natural resource such as oil or timber involved or some well-located but limited supply of land, and if the price of the relevant output is likely to rise following an increase in demand, it might be beneficial to wait in order to take advantage of the increased price,
- if the period of exploitation of a competitive advantage is fixed by license or patent and delay reduces the period of advantage,
- if the level of risk declines over time and the value of a project rises with a lower rate of discount applied.

Control of risk and an appropriate information strategy

Any successful enterprise has particular knowledge which enables it to control risk in a way which others cannot. The adoption of appropriate risk control, by reducing the impact of the relevant risk-generating events, brings risk down to levels not achieved by other enterprises. By exposing the enterprise to such risk in a controlled manner the managers make possible the earning of an above normal return. To achieve this requires a carefully worked-out risk control strategy. There are three main areas in which a risk control strategy is important – an information strategy relating to risk, risk assessment, and a risk response strategy. The later two are treated in detail later in the book, but some preliminary remarks are made about risk assessment relevant to an information strategy.

The assessment of risk involves the identification, measurement and monitoring of relevant risk. How each of these is done depends on the industry in which the enterprise is positioned, the country of location and the nature of the investment project itself. Much work on classification has as an aim a facilitation of identification. The check list approach (Nagy 1979) requires such a comprehensive typology but depends for its effectiveness on an appropriate classification.

Measurement means a quantitative evaluation of the riskiness of the environment, the ideal being a risk measure which is unique and comprehensive. To produce a single index requires a specification of all the relevant components and sub-components of the different risk types, a use of quantitative proxies for such components where direct measurement is not possible and a weighting of the individual components. The measurement can be done within the enterprise or an external agency can implement it. Assessment is a major task and requires a considerable commitment of resources. It cannot be repeated frequently because of the cost involved. Moreover, the risk situation needs to be monitored between assessments. Monitoring means finding a signal(s) which indicates an increase or decrease in the relevant risk level and hopefully when a major revision of the assessment system is needed.

The previous chapter explored the kind of information which is needed in order to make an investment decision. Resources must be committed to gaining such information. A successful information strategy would identify all the relevant data needed to estimate the variables in the expanded version of the net present value formula. An effective information strategy also analyses the implications of the inclusion of a project in the overall strategy. Acquiring the relevant information is critical to accurate risk assessment. There are issues which any information strategy must address:

- what maximum level of uncertainty to aim for,
- what resources to commit to removing uncertainty,
- selecting the relevant 'readers' of the external environment and institutionalising the process of reading that environment,
- how to identify relevant information from the general environment,
- what resources to get access to, and mechanisms to develop, for processing available information,
- how to link information gathering and processing to strategy making.

Decision makers rarely know probabilities concerning the future outcomes of their decisions. It is important for them to put together scenarios relevant to a particular investment project. There may be bi-modal or tri-modal probability distributions which reflect the more likely realisation of certain scenarios and indicate which scenarios should be investigated. An important aim of any information strategy is not so much to move decision makers from a higher to a

Table 6.2   **The different time perspectives**

	Degree of stability	State of uncertainty	Information strategy
Short term	Predetermined elements predominate	Almost complete certainty	Exact prediction
Medium term	Mixed strength	Discrete options, or continuous but limited range.	Scenario building
Long term	Critical uncertainties predominate	Total ambiguity	'Make the future'

Source: White (2004: 128).

lower state of uncertainty, as to remove downside risk or exclude negative scenarios, and to discover ways of increasing, by deliberate action, any possible upside.

The level of uncertainty reflects the degree to which it is necessary to look into the future (for a relevant discussion see White 2004: chap. 4, Reading an uncertain future). The above table indicates the nature of the problem confronting decision makers in doing this.

The duration of the long and short term differ from industry to industry and from enterprise to enterprise, partly according to the length of life of an investment project.

The aim of reading the environment is to recognise opportunities and threats, whether preliminary to an early recognition of an opportunity or building on existing opportunities to articulate a new project. It is the activity of identifying relevant information in the changing environment of the enterprise. It is also necessary to identify who are the relevant readers, with the obligation, or rather opportunity, of making the necessary reading. There are both inside and outside sources of information. Private consultancies and rating agencies have an important role to play. Reading involves four separate steps – scanning, monitoring, forecasting and assessing (White 2004). The information gathered is incorporated into strategy thinking about emerging investment opportunities in order to articulate them as specific projects. It is also incorporated into the ensuing investment appraisal process. Reading is not a neutral process; it is of its nature a 'political' process intended to serve conflicting interests, involving the following steps:

• selection or the identification of relevant information,

- transmission by designated conduits of the relevant information to decision makers or strategy makers. These may be long and indirect,
- incorporation of relevant information into a strategy or, more specifically, into an investment appraisal process.

Different ways are discovered of reducing risk. This involves a number of processes – recognition of a threat, prioritisation of threats discovered and mobilisation of the resources to deal with the relevant threat. The 'political' problems to be confronted include deliberate suppression of the existence of a threat, reinforcement of an existing view which excludes the possibility of such a threat, and poor response to a threat, reflecting the weak bargaining strength of readers and fragmentation of decision making within the relevant enterprise. This means that any relevant information is likely to be distorted.

It is also necessary to identify opportunities. This requires identifying what are called 'shadow options' (Bowman and Hurry 1993: 763). Any information strategy must start by identifying all the available relevant options. The real options approach clearly identifies the nature of the information relevant to a desirable strategy. This is a matter of reading the environment for the relevant opportunities, since options come into existence when existing resources and capabilities allow preferred access to future opportunities (Bowman and Hurry 1993: 762). In the words of Bowman and Hurry, 'Options ..... form the choice mechanism that underlies strategy' (Bowman and Hurry 1993: 764).

It is only possible to value the options on the basis of relevant information. The specific information required might not be available to make the relevant valuations with any exactness. An option value initially arises because of the uncertainty created by the passage of time and the ability, even the need, to delay investment expenditures. Time provides two particular advantages – the advantage of earning a return on the resources freed by deferred expenditures (the present value of the investment cost reduces with the length of the delay) and the possibility that the world may change in a way that increases the value of the project. This assumes that future states are already given, whereas a significant difference between a financial option and a real option is that decision makers can strategically change the boundaries of both costs and revenues, deliberately increasing the upside and reducing the downside. The decision makers can also avoid the downside by *not* making an investment if unfolding events suggest that the outcome is a negative one.

This method allows the full value of an investment to be considered. By plugging into financial valuations yielded by the market, it seeks to impose a discipline on any investment appraisal, for example using the future prices of key products such as oil or gold. However, it does this in a way which avoids taking an attitude to risk tolerances. It also allows total risk to be considered, not just systematic risk, but also non-systematic risk, which cannot be diversified away with direct investments.

There are some difficulties in the use of the real options approach as an instrument for organising information in decision making:

- a lack of simplicity of the method. There are many attempts to show how the method can be explained to managers in a lucid manner,
- dealing with more than two kinds of uncertainty. If uncertainty is too great, the real options approach cannot be employed.

There is clearly a sequence of steps to move the approach beyond its role as a more systematic way of strategic thinking, in order to make it also a superior investment evaluation technique:

Qualitative result = identification of real options
↓
Approximate valuation = identification + elementary model parameters
↓
Exact valuation = identification + elementary model parameters + all the model assumptions met

A paper by Dimpfel, Habann and Algesheimer (2002) proposes a gradual applicability with differentiated prerequisites and results.

Some of the model assumptions which may not hold and therefore may prevent the movement to the third stage include:

- the existence of imperfect markets for real option rights and their valuation,
- the fictitious nature of the underlying assets and the nature of basis risk which reflects the failure of the asset chosen for the replicating portfolio to track accurately the value of the relevant project,
- the sharing of ownership of options among different market players (or stakeholders) – there is no clear maturity date since there is no control over others who might exercise the option,

- the interdependence of most real options attached to a particular project and, therefore, of their values.

It may be possible to define upper and lower limits to the values of the relevant options. Since it is impossible to include all possible variants and all possible scenarios – the computational requirements would be too great, the technique is based in most cases on a degree of qualitative judgement concerning the strength and significance of the relevant information. A strategic assessment should exclude from the appraisal most possible variants and concentrate attention only on certain scenarios.

Direct investment as the preferred mode of entry

There are alternative strategies for participating in international markets. For a specific project, there is a choice, not simply of whether to implement a particular investment project or not. It is also a choice of where to implement, in home or host country, and of who should implement, the main enterprise or a licensed partner. The choice could be made on the net present value of the different options. Although the choice may appear to be simply one of location or of who makes the investment, whether a foreign partner is to be involved, the implications are strategic. They require some modification of the decision rule and the net present value formula.

Associated with each mode on entry are different risk/return combinations. With this in mind, the choice could be regarded as an expression of the risk appetite of the enterprise. Given the relatively high level of risk involved in foreign investment, it is difficult to understand why an enterprise would prefer investment as a mode of entry over exporting or licensing (Buckley 1996 and Whittington 2001). It is possible to regard the move to foreign investment in a more dynamic context, as part of strategy making. Rather than simply a choice at a given moment of time the move is the result of a learning process in which the level of risk associated with the investment decision is reduced. There is a sequence of decisions involving an increasing level of foreign involvement which follows either an increase in potential return or a decrease in anticipated risk (White 2004: 532; Buckley 1996: 111).

If all markets were fully competitive, there would be no international transactions since of their nature they have higher costs than domestic transactions. Foreign investment is never the preferred mode unless

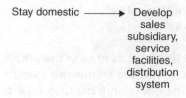

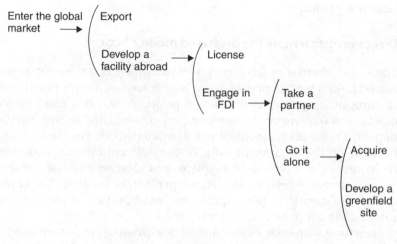

Figure 6.2 The mode of entry decision tree

there are significant market imperfections which allow monopoly rents to be earned either because of advantages of locality or, much more likely by the internalisation of existing significant competitive advantages which are enterprise-created and mobile. Unless there is some sustainable competitive advantage which offsets the range of difficulties associated with operating abroad (Buckley 1996: 118), there is no point in investing abroad. The aim of international investment is to exploit these competitive advantages more fully and to maintain them as long as possible.

One illuminating way of considering the problem of choice is in the context of real options (Buckley 1996: 147–153). Different participation strategies open up differing future options. Foreign direct investment provides a much better opportunity for the enterprise to identify and exploit valuable options than other modes. It also provides a much better opportunity to gain the information required to make an accurate appraisal of the full potential of operating within a foreign economy (Buckley 1996: 151). Entry into a new foreign market might be initiated by a pilot project on a minor scale in order to achieve this learning.

It is possible to express the problem in terms of net present value analysis. For each mode there is a base net present value. Choice may be characterised initially by the following situation:

NPV(Ex) > NPV(Lic) > NPV(FDI with partner) > NPV(FDI after acquisition) > NPV(FDI after greenfield development) > 0

However, the addition of an allowance for options values changes this order dramatically, so that for example:

NPV(FDI – greenf.) + Opt(FDI – greenf.) > NPV(Ex.) + Opt(Ex.)

It is likely that, given the importance of particular competitive advantages, the value of the relevant options may be high (Buckley 1996: 150).

7

The Investment Process and Decision Making: the Organisational Perspective

...the goals of a business firm are a series of more or less independent constraints imposed on the organization through a process of bargaining among potential coalition members and elaborated over time in response to short-run pressures. Goals arise in such a form because a firm is, in fact, a coalition of participants with disparate demands, changing foci of attention, and limited ability to attend to all organizational problems simultaneously.

(Cyert and March 2001)

The present chapter takes an organisational perspective, focusing on the structure of an enterprise. The analysis concentrates on the nature of the enterprise as a network of stakeholder groups who are affected by, and have an influence on, the investment decision. This chapter explores the way in which the joint stock limited liability company privileges the one stakeholder group, the shareholders, and how various risk environments have influenced the development of the organisational framework and the relevant law, notably in the areas of limited liability and bankruptcy. It goes on to show how the way in which key decisions are made reflects relations between different stakeholder groups. These relations determine the distribution of both value and risk. Further sections consider key stakeholder relations, notably those between owners and managers, and between creditors and owners. The organisation of the enterprise and its capital structure provides the context in which investment decisions are made. The capital structure of an enterprise can influence the way in which risk affects the investment decision. The chapter concludes by considering the general nature of the decision-making process.

There are six sections in this chapter:

- In the first section there is an outline of the network of stakeholder groups relevant to any investment decision.
- The second section considers the structure of the modern enterprise and how it accommodates risk.
- In the third section the mechanisms for distribution of risk and of the value created by investment projects among relevant stakeholder groups are analysed.
- Section four considers the implications for investment appraisal of the divorce of ownership and control in the context of the risk situation of the two stakeholder groups, owners and managers.
- The fifth section turns to the relationship between creditors and owners in the context of the capital structure of an enterprise.
- Section six reviews the nature of the decision-making process.

A coalition of stakeholders

While financial theory privileges the shareholders as the most important stakeholder group by assuming that the sole aim of the enterprise is to maximise its value, the enterprise is a coalition of different stakeholder groups. While the classical approach to strategy sees only one decision maker in the enterprise, the CEO with the sanction of the Board, there are always many who influence the relevant decisions and many ways in which this influence manifests itself. The classic definition of a stakeholder (Freeman, R. E. 1984: 46) is: 'A stakeholder in an organization is any group or individual who can affect or is affected by the achievement of the organization's objectives.' This relates the stakeholder interest to the strategic intent of the organisation and applies also to the investment decision.

The direction of influence is twofold – the influence of a project on the stakeholder and the influence of the stakeholder on a project.

- The stakeholder has an interest, sometimes, contractual, in the performance of the enterprise, one of potential benefit or harm. The interest might be as a supplier of equipment, a potential worker on the project, a member of the local community in which the relevant facilities are located, or a government concerned with the impact of a project on tax revenues or employment opportunities.
- The stakeholder has an influence on the decision making of the enterprise and the successful outcome of relevant projects. That

influence may be institutionalised with clear lines of communication, or informal; indirect, through the process of strategy making, or direct on the particular investment decision.

The nature of stakeholder interests and the source and level of any stakeholder risk differs from investment project to project. With asymmetric information each stakeholder group holds specific information relating to its role, which others do not have.

There are various ways of classifying stakeholder groups who have an interest in a particular investment project. The number of such groups depends on the degree of disaggregation adopted in the classification.

Each of these groups could be subdivided, notably the strongly differentiated managers and suppliers of finance. The financial group for a multinational enterprise could be divided according to degree and length of commitment: shareholders into local strategic investors, international strategic investors, local portfolio investors, international portfolio investors, international policy lender, investors with a controlling strategic interest, and local government if it participates; creditors into local banks, international banks, and other significant suppliers of credit. As the enterprise gets larger, there is a growing specialisation of organisational units and an increasing proliferation of stakeholder groups with differing interests in the performance of the company. The need for more capital than the original owners can provide is usually the cause of a company going public. That action further expands the range of stakeholder groups as the suppliers of capital multiply. Internationalisation of the enterprise's business activ-

Table 7.1 Stakeholders in an investment project

Outsiders	Insiders	Outsiders
Contractual		Non-contractual
	Board of directors	
Finance		Local community
Shareholders	Managers	Government
Creditors	Workers	Trade associations
(debt holders)		Trade unions
		Environmental groups
Market		Media
Suppliers		Social and political
Customers		action groups
Strategic allies		
(complementors)		

ities increases dramatically the number and variety of the relevant stakeholder groups.

For an international project it is necessary to consider a wider range of stakeholder groups. With any international investment project it is possible to divide stakeholders into two groups, those who are located in the home country and those in the host country, including relevant government organisations and the various insider groups of the relevant subsidiaries. There may be a conflict of interests between the two sets of stakeholders. The geographical split is capable of producing different interests and different roles, even for similar stakeholder groups. The influence of different stakeholder groups on decision making is relevant, whether they are managers of the multinational, managers of the subsidiary or other owners of the subsidiary apart from the multinational. The group of relevant managers is split according to where they are based and their role in the decision-making process. The local managers may be either from the home country or the host country, or they may be genuinely cosmopolitan. This will partly reflect how far the subsidiary is integrated into the broader organisation. Usually it is impossible for the local subsidiary to ignore local culture, including institutional and behavioural arrangements.

There may also be stakeholder groups in third countries. The subsidiary may supply other subsidiaries within the broader enterprise or be supplied by other subsidiaries.

Table 7.2   International stakeholder groups

Home country stakeholders	Host country stakeholders
Senior managers and strategists responsible for foreign activities	Local managers responsible for implementation and control of the project
Home owners	
Suppliers of equipment or components	Local workers and unions representing them
	Government at various levels
	Local owners (if there are such)
	Local suppliers of credit (if there are such)
	Local suppliers of equipment and components
	The local community and its representatives
	The suppliers of complementary goods and services
	Local customers

It is necessary to note key characteristics of stakeholders which have an influence on the investment decision:

- the degree of organisation of stakeholder groups
- the nature of the interest
- the nature of any risk exposure threatening the achievement of the specific objectives of stakeholders
- the way in which incentive structures align diverging interests

Stakeholders are characterised by:

- differing core competencies and competitive advantages in risk control (Lessard 1996).

The sources of such competitive advantage are: information asymmetries, differing influence over investment outcomes, and differing ability to diversify risks. This is often recognised for risk allocation in project financing (Lessard 1996: 54–56).

- a different perspective on risk.

Some are interested in the nature of risk as systematic or unsystematic, others in the financial leverage of the enterprise and still others in any uncertainty of net income (Miller and Bromiley 1990).

- different assets and assets of a varying degree of diversity.

Managers and workers often have a portfolio in which their human capital is by far and away the most important asset. Such stakeholders have made sunk investments in enterprise-specific knowledge which tie a disproportionate share of their future earnings to the fate of the firm (Miller 1998: 500). This can also be true of buyers, suppliers, alliance partners, other employees, even government and the local community, sometimes customers, particularly for intermediate goods. All these groups differ in this respect from shareholders. If the enterprise is considered a coalition of stakeholders, this inability to diversify becomes a major source of difference. It changes the role of managers in risk control, both with respect to their own position and that of other stakeholder groups. The managers can pay the stakeholders for their risk bearing or they can deliberately hedge or insure, if they are making investments which involve enough risk to upset the stakeholders.

- assets with exposure to differing types of risk and different vulnerabilities to failure of the enterprise.

Such differences require structuring of a project in a way which gives an acceptable distribution of risk. That distribution reflects the bargaining ability of the different stakeholders, which is exercised in imperfect markets. Stakeholders negotiate trade-offs which are acceptable to all and are compensated through distribution of the value created by an investment project for the risk to which they are exposed.

The structure of the enterprise

Most financial theory views an investment project as a mini-enterprise with a single owner who, providing all the finance, both owns and controls. The decision rule is straightforward – does the investment project create value for its owner? Once we move beyond a notional 'one project, one enterprise' situation we move into a more complex world. An enterprise can be organised in different ways depending on the nature of its core activities and purposes. 'For-profit' organisations can be a proprietorship or a partnership, in which ownership and control are fused: those who own, also manage. Alternatively, they might be mutual financial organisations which are owned by their customers, depositors or policy holders. These are fast disappearing, being converted into public corporations. More often the relevant organisations are public corporations, either open or closed.

The typical organisation is continuously adapting to a changing risk environment. Such a process may include the elimination of forms which involve a high level of risk for key stakeholder groups, notably but not only the shareowners. In most circumstances, the winning organisation in developed countries is the open corporation with common stock, and this is the focus of attention in this chapter.

The main feature distinguishing such organisational forms is the nature of any claims made on the enterprise. For most stakeholders, these claims are contained in contractual arrangements. For equity holders, as the residual claim holders this is not the case. A significant feature of the enterprise is whether, after fixed payoffs are made to suppliers and other contracted partners, the residual claims on the enterprise are restricted. If they are not, and if rights to the value created are freely alienable, the type of organisation is an open corporation with common stock. Unrestricted residual rights and the free alienability or marketability of such rights are two significant characteristics of such an organisational form. This requires both an appropriate body of enterprise law to validate the organisational form and an efficient capital market to ensure full marketability of shares. If there are restrictions on the enterprise, then it is a closed corporation.

Two issues are at the heart of risk control in the modern business enterprise – limited liability and bankruptcy.[1] The ultimate risk for most stakeholder groups is a failure of the enterprise. A failed investment can reduce the value of equity to nothing; greatly reduce the value of the debt held by creditors; lose both managers and workers their jobs; and deprive a local community of employment opportunities, government of tax revenue, suppliers of demand. Contracts will not be honoured. In theory, the shareholders are the first to suffer, losing any value to their ownership shares. Although in the event of a liquidation existing claims on the enterprise may be honoured, employees lose their jobs and suppliers future orders. There is a prioritisation of the obligations which the enterprise owes to particular creditor groups which is used as a base for distributing any remaining value, thereby distributing the impact of risk. In the event of bankruptcy, there are both rules about the degree of liability of the owners of the failed enterprise and rules for what must happen in order to resolve the bankruptcy.

Thus, an attempt to control risk is at the very core of the modern business enterprise. Limited liability is the result of an attempt to reduce the risk to which the owners of an enterprise are exposed, at the expense of other stakeholder groups, notably creditors. Just as in normal times different stakeholders bargain in the sharing of costs or returns so they also bargain in the distribution of risk for the bad times. Institutional structures help determine how that risk is distributed, by establishing the framework, both legal and conventional, in which bargaining occurs.

Various forms of liability have been tried. Before the modern era the basic reference liability was an unlimited one, in which the shareholder was potentially liable for the whole of any debt incurred by the enterprise. At the present, it is limited liability. There are other possibilities, such as an unlimited proportional liability, that is, if a shareholder owns 5% of the shares he/she is liable for 5% of any debt of the insolvent company. Another alternative would be the negotiation of contracts between shareholders and creditors which limit liability on an individual basis. In a situation of limited liability, the act of asking for contractual limited liability would be interpreted as a anticipation of serious trouble for the enterprise (Moss 2002: 82–83).

Under limited liability, owners of shares are only liable for the amount they have invested in the purchase of these shares and liable only for the period of time they own those shares. Limited liability is a legal device whose function is 'to shield the owners of corporations from personal liability in the event of corporate default' (Moss 2002: 53). It is possible to opt out of limited liability indirectly by the shareholder pledging personal security for any loan(s) received by the enterprise which he/she partially owns. Why is it so desirable to shift risk management from the owners to other creditors and not allow these various stakeholder groups to negotiate the transfer of risks themselves? The initial aim of limited liability, when first introduced during the nineteenth century, was to mobilise capital and induce additional investment, notably in areas of high risk where failure was common (Moss 2002: 57–58). Whether it did is difficult to answer because there is no real evidence showing a link between limited liability and economic performance (Moss 2002: 69), although the presumption is that it did.

The impact on investment depends on two opposing influences, one encouraging investment, the other discouraging it. Limited liability was designed to encourage a new inflow of equity funds from passive investors, who were now much less at risk of ruin. At the same time, limited liability raised the default risk for creditors who could no longer seize the personal assets of shareholders when an enterprise failed to honour its debts. As a consequence, a rational creditor would ask for a risk premium to be included in the rate of interest received, raising the cost of capital, which would tend to reduce the level of investment. In the words of Moss, 'The shareholder's maximum possible loss is capped at a much reduced level, while the creditor's probability of loss is simultaneously increased' (Moss 2002: 74).

The conventional argument that risk diminishes the supply of capital to investment is based on a tendency for investors to be risk averse. The distinctive combination of limited downside and unlimited upside which characterises stock market investment with limited liability, just as lotteries, explains its attractiveness. Moss (2002: 83) has argued that limited liability mimics an insurance policy in shifting a portion of default risk from shareholders to creditors. Typical of financial theorists, Doherty talks of the default put option created by this historical development, the ability of shareholders to pass the enterprise on to its creditors. Today, involuntary creditors, such as injured consumers or polluted communities, have such large potential claims on companies that the meaning of limited liability has been transformed.

From the perspective of an individual investment project, the implications of limited liability differ according to the size of the project relative to the size of the enterprise, how the project is to be financed, and the existing debt leverage of the enterprise. The weighted cost of capital is likely to rise, and sometimes dramatically, as enterprises have no choice but to use debt or additional equity to finance such a project, particularly where the project is large and the enterprise already highly geared.

Insolvency in conditions of unlimited liability means that an owner might lose all his/her assets, including earning capacity for the rest of his/her life or for a period necessary to pay off the debt. In order to avoid this situation it is possible to separate out activities with a particularly high risk into stand-alone companies, sometimes with a large part of any existing debt. Sometimes these are called special purpose vehicles. An individual can limit the impact of any particular failure to the relevant company. A rational risk control strategy might be to make this a consistent policy. There is therefore a tendency for enterprises operating in an environment of high risk and limited liability to be small. This limits the exposure or value at risk to a liability suit for professional or product damage. Some studies have shown widespread attempts in the USA to avoid liability for hazards and disease by shielding assets through divestiture of the relevant activities (Ringleb and Wiggins 1990).

Nevertheless, insolvency still represents a threat to both creditor and debtor, who can each initiate a bankruptcy. In order to ensure that an individual continues to make a contribution to economic life there needs to be a restriction on how bankruptcy affects an individual. The same applies to a company. It is illegal in most countries to operate a company which you know to be insolvent. The danger of insolvency, which might reflect a problem of scarce liquidity, could easily be compounded by a prisoner's dilemma situation in which there was a rush by creditors to secure their loans, and to refuse further credit critical to the continued operation of an enterprise. Herd or contagion effects are linked to such a loss of confidence. An otherwise viable enterprise might be brought down. It was partly to stop such a run that bankruptcy laws were enacted in the first place. In the words of Moss (2002:

135), 'Even apart from the discharge provision....., bankruptcy law represented an important risk management mechanism, dramatically reducing the risk of runs on cash-poor debtors as well as the risk to creditors of receiving less than their fair share from a failed enterprise.' A second aim was therefore to increase the recovery rate for creditors and diminish what banks call the loss given default (LGD).

Discharge is the important mechanism for debtors which shields them from considerable downside risk by forcible shifting it onto creditors. The original purpose of the promise of discharge from debt was to rectify an information asymmetry by persuading debtors to reveal their assets. Over time, this motive receded in importance. Bankruptcy laws are often passed in the aftermath of an economic crisis. Through limited liability and bankruptcy laws the aim is to encourage risk-averse savers to invest in risky ventures by providing them with an insurance against extreme loss (Moss 2002: 124) and by giving them a mechanism for release from bankruptcy. The first step in the latter mechanism was to free the debtor from the threat of imprisonment. Discharge from debts on the realisation of certain basic requirements, such as the loss of all current assets, serves the purpose of restoring the individual to business life. The bankrupt does not have to hazard his entire lifetime earning capacity on a particular venture. Risk is transferred from debtors to creditors. There is an ex ante benefit – the encouragement of individuals to undertake activities more hazardous than they would otherwise (moral hazard), and an ex post benefit – the avoidance of financial catastrophe in the event of bankruptcy. This might help the resurrection of failed entrepreneurs. The same argument can apply to the corporation itself, which under chapter 11 rules in the USA can remain in business while adjustments are made to restore its operations to solvency.

Bankruptcy costs are significant, consisting largely of legal and administrative costs. They impose a cost on any enterprise which goes into liquidation. The risk of insolvency partly comprises the risk of incurring these costs. They are regarded by financial theorists as a friction in the efficient operation of markets strong enough to justify risk management.

There is a connection between the two elements, limited liability and bankruptcy. It is often claimed that limited liability and bankruptcy laws allow inefficient investment decisions to be made. This is because the interests of two key stakeholder groups, creditors and owners, diverge. In the words of one commentator (White 1989: 138): 'Inefficient bankruptcy decisions and inefficient investment incentives appear to be the price society pays for limiting the liability of equity holders. From the standpoint of economic efficiency, no simple bankruptcy priority rule works as well as unlimited liability by the firm's owners.'

Value and risk distribution

Both the structure and the strategy of the enterprise define the different interests and roles of different stakeholder groups. The relevant issues are:

- how far decision making is decentralised
- what decisions are made locally
    who assesses a project's acceptability
    who makes the decision on whether to go ahead
    who monitors and controls the project
- how the enterprise is structured and how the local organisation fits into the broader organisation
- how a particular investment decision fits into the strategy of the enterprise as a whole
- what happens to the cash streams generated and to resulting profits

There may be two possible situations at the inception of an investment project:

- the investment is evaluated independently by the local decision makers on criteria which would apply to any domestic project
- the investment is assessed in the context of the overall strategy of the home enterprise

The dichotomy requires a consideration of how key stakeholders in an enterprise perceive risk, and how they respond to it. The different assets which constitute the resources of the enterprise create different exposures. Any stakeholder is exposing himself/herself both to part of the overall enterprise risk but more particularly to that risk as filtered to specific stakeholders. It creates exposures which differ according to the nature of the stakeholder involvement. The nature of the risk confronting various stakeholder groups and the owners differs markedly. Where there is a market relationship with those at risk the nature of the market contract, explicit or implicit, often reflects the risk level. For example, lower prices or higher wages can compensate the consumer or worker for bearing risk. If managers are the final arbiters of any investment decision, they have a strong interest in trying to keep the various stakeholder groups onside. The managers need to manage the stakeholders in order to make an investment successful.

What can be said about the distribution of value or of risk? The combination of purchased inputs and the value added by the enterprise creates the value realised in the final market. In theory that value is distributed in a way which reflects the opportunity costs of the relevant inputs as determined in competitive markets. The opportunity cost of any input is the lowest price which a marginal supplier would be prepared to accept for delivery of the input in a competitive market in which there are many rival suppliers. The distribution usually reflects markets which are less than perfectly competitive, the price being made rather than taken.

There is a choice between two strategies. The first is keep an arms length relationship with all suppliers, to enter only short-term contracts and to minimise the immediate costs of any inputs. The second strategy is to enter a closer, more long-term relationship which seeks to minimise the cost over a longer time horizon. The managers of the enterprise, wishing to keep the various stakeholder groups happy, might tend to the second strategy. In order to keep the groups supplying inputs happy it is helpful to provide a share of total value in excess of that suggested by the level of opportunity cost. There are a number of reasons for doing this:

The lack of a competitive context – there are seldom a large number of possible suppliers. The suppliers have asymmetric information in that insiders, those who already supply, have experienced a learning process which gives them an advantage over outsiders in quality, design or cost level. This creates significant switching costs.

The need for a longer time horizon. In the process of negotiation it may be important to create a long-term relationship, not a series of transitory, arms-length relationships. Such a relationship is not a zero-sum one, rather one in which both partners can benefit from the cooperation. There may be an exchange of information concerning strategy, specifically of technical and organisational knowledge about specific investment projects. Input suppliers can provide knowledge which improves the net cash stream of the investment.

The existence in a typical enterprise of 'organisational slack'. In the words of Buckley (1996: 3), 'Slack consist in payment to members of the coalition in excess of what is required to maintain the organization.' It also consists in resources which are not fully utilised. Such a strategy has positive implications for the enterprise. It is possible to allow in good times the development of organisational slack in the knowledge that in bad times this slack can be taken up. Pressure can be applied to suppliers to reduce costs when there is a particular need to do so.

The point in the life cycle reached. Profit levels vary during the life cycle of the enterprise's business units. They tend to be at their lowest at the beginning and the end of the life cycle. The risk tolerance of the enterprise varies according to its financial position. When profits are at a satisfactory 'above normal' level, particularly if there is a free cash flow, it is possible to be proactive rather than reactive in controlling risk. The scope for behaviour which keeps the stakeholder groups happy varies with the pressure on the profit level of the enterprise. When profit is low, there is a tendency to react slowly to stakeholder groups, doing the minimum to keep them happy. On the other hand, during adolescence and maturity, when profit levels are satisfactory, there is more inclination to keep such groups happy. At this stage in the life cycle, there may be more latitude in negotiating with contractual partners and giving them more of the value created by the relevant investment.

The importance of the different stakeholder groups varies according to where in the life cycle of the relevant product(s) the enterprise is. In its early life, the sources of finance are important. During the period of rapid expansion the relationship with suppliers and with workers is critical. Individual investments should be analysed with this in mind.

For all stakeholders the degree of the commitment required determines the degree of interest and the nature and level of risk. Each of the stakeholder groups, with an investment in the relationship at risk, wishes to mould that relationship to meet its own interests as effectively as possible. The risk increases with the degree of asymmetric investment, being greatest for those who have made the largest investment. Stakeholders are the possessors of knowledge not possessed by any other group. The greater is the degree of asymmetric information the greater is the bargaining strength of those who are in possession of that information. The ideal combination for a stakeholder group is large information and small investment. The smaller the number of partners within the groups dealing with the relevant enterprise and the greater the dependence of the enterprise on that group the smaller is the degree of risk for that group but the greater the risk for the enterprise.

All the groups work together to create economic value. Political value is also created, which can be turned into economic value. Political value comes from the advantage to be won by instituting a change in government policy or regulation in your own favour, or from the gaining of social legitimacy by managing important social issues in such a way as to win support for the enterprise and to enhance its reputation. Some of the stakeholders are more involved in this second network than the first. However, they will negotiate in a way which influences the distribution of economic value.

Ownership and control

Financial theory separates the decisions made by managers about whether to invest in productive facilities and those by investors (or really savers) over what financial assets to hold. The full separability of finance and investment, and therefore of ownership and control, holds only under certain unusual conditions. By contrast it is not difficult to see the divorce between ownership and control as a defining character-istic of modern business. There have been attempts to model the effect of the differing objectives of managers and owners (Marris 1964). Marris argued that the managers have a particular interest in growth, rather than profits, and in continuity of employment, avoiding takeovers, and keeping all creditors, including shareholders, happy. There is an obvious agency problem (Jagannathan and Meier 2002: part 6). 'Agency conflicts between the manager and the shareholders emerge because managers prefer to control large amount of capital. Managers have a desire to build empires as the private benefits increase with the size of the project or division they control' (Jagannathan and Meier 2002: 24).

The focus is on how the divorce affects the investment decision. In this divorce the managers and the owners are regarded as homo-geneous groups, whereas the managers can be divided into various groups – senior and junior managers, those with a significant owner-ship stake and those without, and the owners into those with a con-trolling interest, other large holders, often financial institutions, and the mass of ordinary retail share purchasers. Clearly these groups have different interests, a different degree of organisation, and a differing relationship to the process of investment decision making, including a different potential control over that process. The assumption here is an ownership group seeks to control through the board of directors, but that the senior management team tends in normal times to dominate the board, largely through executive directors. There may be a close and continuing relationship between the two groups. In normal times there is no attempt to directly control the managers, although there is a general oversight over strategy by the board on behalf of the owners.

This separation can be presented more formally. Fama and Jensen (1983: 3) have broken down the decision process, including that relating to investment, into four separate steps:

1. Initiation – the generation of new investment proposals,
2. Ratification – choice of which initiatives to implement,
3. Implementation – execution of ratified decisions,
4. Monitoring – oversight of performance.

They join initiation and implementation under the heading of 'decision management' and ratification and monitoring under 'decision control' with an assumption that the former process is allocated to managers and the latter to owners, represented by the board of directors. The governance system of an enterprise will determine exactly how these functions are shared between the two groups.

Financial theorists deal with this issue through agency theory (Jensen and Meckling 1976; Fama 1980). Even an enterprise with no debt, financed solely by external equity, has an agency problem, which arises because owners and managers, as principal and agent, have different interests and asymmetric information. It is difficult to devise an incentive structure which aligns the two stakeholder groups. Managers have a range of motivating interests including status, power, or position. These are expressed partly in non-pecuniary benefits, such as large offices, parking spots and company cars, and partly in larger objectives best served by the pursuit of size rather than profit. Where the two objectives diverge, managers favour the former over the latter. This may mean that there is a tendency to approve of more, larger and riskier, investment projects than would be the case if profit maximisation were the goal. The result may be the adoption of investment projects yielding a negative net present value or a return below the threshold level, or just appraised with overly-optimistic inputs. This can happen since the managers control the input of data needed for any appraisal. The asymmetry in information compounds the problem since it means that managers have the relevant information which owners do not possess. There is a tendency for executive directors to be in a stronger position than independent directors to know whether a particular project is being presented in a favourable light.

Agency costs take three principal forms:

- a loss of enterprise value resulting from poor decisions reflecting a failure to adequately manage the principal/agent relationship,
- the costs of equity holders monitoring the behaviour of their agents, including measurement costs and the costs of putting in control mechanisms to align the interests of various stakeholder groups, including compensation incentives, rules, and appraisal schemes,
- the cost incurred by agents in providing to principals a bond of good behaviour (holding shares or share options of the company might be regarded as such a bond).

There is one very significant constraint on the willingness of managers to take on low-return or risky projects since they are concerned with the possibility of losing their jobs. The average working life of a CEO is short. The employment of all senior managers is threatened by take-overs, by turnaround situations or simply by a change of CEO. An investment failure may precipitate one of these outcomes. The managers are deterred from making decisions which are likely to lead to these outcomes, including any action which reduces the value of the enterprise below a valuation ratio of one (Tobin's Q). Managers need to be circumspect in their behaviour; any blatantly self-serving action would reduce share prices and lead to scrutiny by shareholders or creditors.

One important issue, which highlights possible conflicts of interest, is what managers should do with a significant free cash flow. This cash flow is of great importance to the enterprise and its use a critical decision variable. There are three options:

- return it to the shareholders through dividend payments or buybacks
- use it to expand the enterprise, either
  - by projects internal to the enterprise, e.g. increased R&D
  - by acquisitions
- improve the position of various stakeholders and/or increase the degree of organisational slack

There is a tendency for managers to prefer to use free cash flows to expand the enterprise. In this situation the process of investment appraisal is reversed and managers use the system to confirm decisions they have already made for other reasons. This may be justified if the investment fits into a broader strategy for future growth.

By contrast, equity holders are deemed interested solely in the value of their ownership share, but receive this value as dividends, buybacks or as potential capital gains. Share values are normally a reflection of dividend or profit flows and their timing. The option of making payments to shareholders or of retention and reinvestment of profit can be viewed differently according to the time horizon of the shareholder. Some shareholders may be long-term holders of shares and sensitive to the nature of strategic investments. All owners dislike a loss of value to their shares. However, there is always the option of selling their shares and readjusting their portfolio of assets to suit their risk tolerance.

In a world of asymmetric information, changes in dividend payments act as a signalling device. A reduction in dividends may be seen as an admission of declining performance, just as an increase in dividends may be seen as an indication of an exhaustion of strategic ideas for future growth and therefore capital gains. The exact interpretation depends on the particular circumstances. It is necessary to look at the role of payout ratios as signalling devices as well as a means for distributing value.

Capital structure and risk: creditors and owners

The classical Modigliani-Miller approach is based on the notion that the capital structure of the firm is irrelevant to both value and decision making. There is an alternative view that there are different costs attached to the different sources of finance for an investment project – internal cash flows, debt and equity. Such an approach is implicit in the weighted average cost of capital in which the level of costs accords closely with the level of risk associated with different sources of funds. There is a different risk premium attached to each source of finance, although it may change with the riskiness of an investment project. One potent source of risk is asymmetrical information between insiders and outsiders, in this case the managers of investment projects and financial investors.

Financial structure and policy do make a difference to the capacity of the enterprise to raise finance. The cost rises as the level of risk rises for those who provide the finance. The weighted average cost of capital sees internal funds as the cheapest source of capital with an opportunity cost of the risk-free interest rate. Debt is the next most costly source, with an interest rate required which reflects the riskiness of a project, given the existing level of gearing of an enterprise. As riskiness and gearing rise so does the interest rate charged. The cost of equity considers only the market risk to which an enterprise is exposed, that is the risk of the particular asset, say shares in general, the risk specific to the relevant industry and that specific to a particular enterprise. The last is usually represented by the beta of the enterprise.

It is possible to interpret both debt and equity as claims on an enterprise taking the form of options. Equity is equivalent to a put option held by the shareholders on the underlying value of the enterprise, with an exercise price equal to the face value of the debt (Doherty 2000: 181). If the income from the enterprise falls below the interest paid, the option can be exercised by the equity holders, particularly if the enterprise becomes insolvent. The option is called the default put option. Debt is valued at its face value minus the value of the short position of a put option with an exercise price equal to the face value of the debt. For the creditors the more likely the exercise of this option, the greater the value of the put option to be subtracted and the higher the value of the put option for equity holders.

Those who purchase the debt of a company are interested in the debt leverage of the enterprise. The higher the level of debt relative to equity, the greater the risk that a failed investment will lead to the insolvency of the enterprise with its accompanying bankruptcy costs. In that situation, prospective debt holders seek a higher return to compensate for the higher risk. The greater the risk, as measured by the variance of prospective returns, and the greater the likelihood that this range of returns overlaps what is required to service the debt, suggesting that the enterprise might become insolvent, the more likely it is that managers will make risky investments whose downside falls on the creditors and whose upside is received by the equity holders. Prospective creditors, aware of this situation, will be unwilling to provide finance for investment projects which might be substituted by risky alternatives, certainly not at a price which the equity holders are willing to pay. This can lead to either insolvency or to significant underinvestment. The cost of debt rises with the level of leverage, reflecting the increasing level of risk confronting creditors. Consequently the same investment project may be viewed differently by enterprises with different capital structures and different sources of finance for the relevant project.

Although most attention has been focused on the two stakeholder relationships there are other stakeholder groups who, as important players, share the value created and risk generated by a particular investment. The risk for different stakeholders can be, and in perfect markets is, converted into a reward which compensates the stakeholder for the risk. This takes the form of a higher wage or a higher price paid for an input. The devising of an appropriate remuneration system for managers is more complicated than for other groups. All these additional costs are subsumed within the Xs which indicate the resulting net revenue streams. Unhappily, markets are not perfect and it is difficult to estimate the size of the appropriate 'loadings'; there is a risk that they themselves may be volatile.

The decision-making process

Risk influences the structuring of the decision-making process itself. Buckley has offered four different models of decision making – the rational, the bounded-rational, the political and the garbage can models (Buckley 1996: 3–11). Each of these approaches makes implicit assumptions about the amount of relevant information available, the ability of the decision makers to process this information and the influence of organisational structure on decision making.

Rationality

The usual capital budgeting approach sees the process as rational, concerned with a single objective, the maximisation of profit. The limited amount of uncertainty can be reduced to well-defined risk. There is a clear designation of who the decision makers are, although some tasks can be given to specialised groups. The process of decision making is a sequential one (Mintzberg, Raisinghani and Theoret 1976). These steps are: the recognition of an opportunity as a result of reading the environment, the articulation of the opportunity as a problem to be solved, i.e. by maximising its value, the search for relevant information, the definition of the specific available options, the assessment and evaluation of these options, the choice of the one which is optimal, authorisation of the choice within the context of the overall strategy, and finally implementation of the solution. This approach is best suited to routine decisions rather than significant investment decisions which are far from routine.

Bounded rationality

This approach admits that a wholly rational approach is impossible and/or undesirable (Simon 1955). All sorts of constraints operate to limit the processing of information – at the individual level, such as the cognitive, and at the organisational level, the 'political'.

The important bounds are:

incomplete information

a reactive rather than a proactive stance – search is often accidental a limited capacity to process information, both cognitive and organisational

a focus on a limited number of opportunities and options

the slow and accidental emergence of opportunities, problems and solutions

time pressures – the search process is always incomplete

incrementalism and disjointedness

the frequent use of intuition and judgement, often based on fragmented information

the prevalence of satisficing, i.e. seeking a satisfactory rather than a perfect solution – made necessary by the existence of multiple objectives

In the words of Buckley, 'The bounded-rational approach is appropriate for non-programmed [i.e. non-routine], complex and more disparate issues' (Buckley 1996: 6), i.e. foreign investment decisions.

Political

The political model highlights the existence of many stakeholders with an influence on decision making but differing interests. An enterprise consists of a coalition of stakeholders with different risk exposures and tolerances and different access to information (White 2004: 26–33). The tolerance of risk partly reflects differential familiarity with a risk environment. Governance issues arise in terms of the relationship between the various stakeholders, notably those making decisions, and owners, that is those responsible for areas in which risk can have an impact. It considers as relevant issues such as bargaining and negotiation; the championing of positions, projects or people and biases in decisions; opportunism – the use of guile and distortion, selective disclosure and withholding of information; the universality of conflict and of coalition building. Since these issues cannot be avoided they are factored into any decision-making process. The insertion of values into the present value formula is the result of a long political process.

The garbage can

This most nihilistic approach sees the process as inevitably anarchic. It involves problematic and undefined objectives, ambiguities of various kinds, but notably on the cause and effect of certain decisions, and the fluid participation of various individual or stakeholders in any decision making. Problems, choices and solutions are not linked in a rational way. Some problems are never solved, some solutions are never linked to a problem. Such a situation cannot continue for too long without the enterprise failing. There is an inflation of the uncertainty facing decision makers, a situation which can only be temporary.

The first and fourth situations are very unusual and largely irrelevant to investment decision making. The second and third can be combined in a realistic view of a world in which there is significant uncertainty. There is plenty of opportunity for the exercise by decision makers of a rationally constrained approach, which is the result of much negotiation and bargaining. An awareness of this does not preclude the attempt to live by sensible decision rules and the need to search for whatever information will help make a good decision.

Part III
The Different Types of Risk

> Breaking the risk construct into distinct exposures to multiple
> environmental contingencies allows for more precise specification
> of the relations between risks and strategies.
>
> (Miller 1998: 510)

There are a number of different types of risk relevant to an international investment project. The exposure to different risk types
creates risk environments which differ according to the nature of the
relevant risk events characterising them. In particular, these risk
environments differ significantly by sector of the economy or industry, and by country location. This section seeks to find a schema for
distinguishing such risk environments, which can serve as a template for the measurement of both generic and specific project risk.
It is easier to measure a 'systematic' generic risk than it is to measure
the specific risk of a single project. The section therefore moves from
the generic to the specific, from global, industry and country risk to
enterprise or project risk. The ultimate aim of the analysis, after the
achievement of a clear identification and measurement of risk, is
to see how that risk can be incorporated into the present value
formula. In the process, the analysis moves to a point at which there
are workable measures of risk which can be incorporated into an
international investment appraisal. An initial aim is to remove any
divergence in the use of the terminology used in identifying risk and
to establish a comprehensives and clear taxonomy, although it must
be accepted that this terminology is relevant to the FDI decision and
not necessarily to other decisions, such as those relating to portfolio
investment or to the making of loans.

In this section there are three chapters which deal in turn with:

- analysing the generic types of risk which have their source outside the enterprise, either at the global or industry level,
- estimating a generic measure of country risk as a preliminary to considering the ratio of country risk in home and host countries,
- focusing on enterprise and project risk, amalgams of risk which are both generic and specific to the enterprise, as a preliminary to assessing the level of project risk relative to generic host country risk.

8
The Context of Risk

> Many managers believe that uncertainty is a problem and should
> be avoided ...... We hold the opposite view. If your firm is prop-
> erly positioned, you can take advantage of uncertainty. Your
> strategic investments will be sheltered from its adverse effects
> while remaining exposed to its upside potential. Uncertainty will
> create value and take you to market leadership.
>
> (Amram and Kulatikala 1999: vii)

This chapter begins by explaining the difference between generic and
specific risk. It explores the nature of generic risk, concentrating particular attention on two types of generic risk, which are potentially
significant for enterprise or project risk, global and industry risk. It
argues that such risks are systematic enough to be considered separately. It produces comprehensive classifications of the two risk types
and indicates the steps necessary in the quantification of this risk and
its later incorporation into an investment appraisal.

There are six sections in this chapter:

- The first section emphasises the limited applicability of the conventional approach to risk for international investment projects and
  explores a different approach.
- The second section gives a definition of global risk – analysing how
  such risk differs from other types.
- In the third section there is a consideration of the varying
  perception of different types of global risk.
- The fourth section analyses who controls global risk, what mechanisms are used to do this, and what are the implications for an
  investment project.

- Section five explores the nature of industry risk, distinguishing it from other types of risk, and outlines a comprehensive classification of industry risk.
- In the final section there is an analysis of the components of industry risk.

The sources of generic risk

An international investment project is exposed to various types of risk, some specific to its international nature, some not. The present chapter begins an exploration of the relevant types of risk. International investment projects are subject to the usual types of risk to which any domestic project is exposed, and more. Two types are basic to the risk context of any enterprise undertaking an international project, industry and country risk. All products and services belong to a particular sector of the economy, or industry, although there may be a problem in defining in a consistent manner such an industry (see Kim and Mauborgne 2005: 6 for a discussion of the changes which have occurred between the Standard Industrial Classification Manual 1987 and the North American Industry Classification System 1998). The facilities for production and sale are also located in particular countries; this is inescapable. The enterprise is therefore bound to be exposed to these two types of generic risk, systematic risks, which affect, in a way which is qualitatively similar, all enterprises operating within a particular country or industry. There is a filtering process by which the generic risks generated at different levels affect the specific risk of the enterprise and its projects. The emphasis in this book is on the country risk environment because that is the risk most characteristic of FDI, but it does not ignore the other types of risk, which are discussed in this chapter.

The different risk types, and therefore risk environments, should be defined in a way which makes them independent of each other, but it is difficult to achieve this. No risk type can be considered in isolation, including country risk. There is a considerable overlap between the different risk types.

The approach adopted is to consider the sources of all risk, identifying and distinguishing the main types. The analysis avoids the conventional approach of generalising through the impact of all types of risk on a key performance indicator such as profit, shareholder returns or the value of a relevant share. It does not assume an integrated world stock market, which would allow the definition of country betas expressing the systematic nature of country risk. It does not assume that liquid markets exist everywhere nor does it assume that markets are efficient where they do exist, certainly not efficient in that they fail to incorporate significant information which is available to the enterprise.

The conventional approach to the incorporation of risk in the appraisal of an investment project also fuses the two stages, those of risk assessment and of project valuation. This analysis adopts a separate treatment of the sources of risk and focuses on an exploration of the types of risk-generating events, or risk-generating changes of behaviour, which characterise the relevant risk environments. It is appropriate to consider total risk, not just systematic risk for two main reasons:

- the enterprise is a coalition of stakeholders and any project, viewed as stand alone, has a similar network of linked stakeholders, most of whom do not have a diversified portfolio of assets,
- the enterprise is not able, or for good reasons often does not desire, to diversify its assets.

There are two sets of events with which the analysis deals – those which are relatively frequent but which have an impact which is manageable and those which are extreme, or lower-tail, events which are infrequent but which have a potentially large impact. Frequent events which occur in a predictable pattern are not a source of risk. In any distribution of probable outcomes those which lie within the accepted confidence level are sometimes regarded as expected and those which lie beyond that confidence level are unexpected. The dividing line between the two is somewhat arbitrary. However, the point is that the usual concentration on the variance or standard deviation of profit or share value as a measure of risk neglects an enormous amount of information which is directly relevant to the future performance of an investment project.

The 'expected' events are capable of being handled through the law of large numbers. Insurance companies usually have no difficulty in dealing with the normal every-day threats to life and property, which can be summarised in mortality tables. They can even deal with particular kinds of country risk. An increasing range of risk-generating events have been drawn within the fold of insurance and defined as expected in that they conform to a normal distribution of outcomes. The impact of extreme events, especially those which do not fit a normal distribution, reflects the amount of capital which is at risk as well as the frequency of such shocks.

No matter whether managers engage in actual risk management or not, markets are a good source of relevant information for investment appraisal, provided they are at least weakly efficient (Anderson and van Wincorp 2004). There are three ways in which the market puts a value on risk – firstly through implied risk spreads on international loan instruments, best shown by government loan prices (Merton 1974); and secondly, through insurance premiums charged by insurance agencies, such as OPIC or AFIC for political risk; and thirdly through the market for derivatives, which has the advantage of looking forward rather than backwards.

The first source, the risk spread, is of limited helpfulness to foreign direct investment since the spread measures sovereign or government risk, that is the creditworthiness of governments, which may bear little relationship to the riskiness of private investment projects. However, there is a link with country risk through government policy. It gives a first look at the role of government in any FDI decision. The second market source, insurance, is far from comprehensive in its coverage. Since the market for insurance is not perfect, the prices of insurance only give imperfect information on risk. Implicit in the insurance premiums charged is a view about the probability of certain risk-generating events. Again, this is information which is useful. Where well-developed futures markets exist and the source of the risk is price variability, the use of future prices can help, e.g. in appraising the value of an oil field or a gold mine. The existence of such information constitutes a starting point for any quantification. For most projects, there is no such relevant market. A view on future volatilities can be found if there are developed markets for debt, derivatives and risk contingencies of various kinds. The prices thrown up by such markets are a valuable source of relevant information on future expectations. They offer information on the market view of volatility (Bodie and Merton 1995), that is the riskiness which the market has factored into prices. The prices of futures, options and swaps and their insertion into the Black and Scholes formula allow the extraction of implied volatilities.

Because of the deficiencies of each of these three sources, it is better to assess the relevant risk directly. There is a need to focus on the risk environments relevant to specific investment projects. It is also necessary to consider all the sources of risk, not just in order to appraise accurately but also to make possible the mitigation, or reduction, of risk. There are many attempts to rate directly the country risk level of different economies, notably by rating agencies which specialise in the assessment of country risk. Such country risk indexes as the Euro-money Index are common. Some of these estimates are publicly available and are discussed in chapter 11. The approach adopted in such ratings is critical to any investment appraisal. The present chapter seeks to extend this approach to industry and global risk.

The problems discussed make it appropriate to separate fully the two stages in the incorporation of risk in the valuation of an investment project. The assessment of risk is treated as a separate procedure. The assessment, and quantification, of risk requires the completion of basic steps common to all types of risk:

- identification of the main components of each risk type,
- a breakdown of those components into sub-components, and even sub-subcomponents,
- at each level a weighting of the various elements,
- identification of any co-variance between the components,
- the selection of proxies which make possible a quantification of components,
- collection of the relevant information.

The identification, rigorous definition and weighting of risk components is a necessary preliminary to any attempt to measure either generic or specific risk.

The nature of global risk

Most prominent in general references to risk in the media and in popular work on risk is global risk. For various reasons, including the drama of the unfolding shocks associated with the terrorist attacks of September 11 2001 and the devastation wrought by the Asian tsunami on Boxing Day 2004, there is an increasing focus on those types of risk whose influence spills across international boundaries. There are, therefore, risk-generating events which can be described as global, covering all industries and all countries, and creating the potential for a type of overarching generic risk. Global risk is that risk which has a systematic tendency at the global level.

The associated events are referred to by a variety of names – catastrophes, disasters, crises, shocks. In this account, the generic term shock is used to cover all these events. To an economist a shock is exogenous to the particular model used to describe a relevant economic system. The other terms are used to describe events of an extreme kind, marked out by the magnitude of their potential impact – physical, financial or psychological. It is not difficult to accept a ranking by the magnitude of the relevant impact, running from crisis to disaster to catastrophe. Any particular threshold level chosen is arbitrary.

Global risk is in principle a problem everywhere. It is the perception of a threat, rather than the actual incidence or impact, which extends to the whole world. Some types of global risk affect particular regions or groups of industries, but not all. Shocks occur in particular places, but it is of their nature that they can occur in many places; there is a degree of randomness which characterises their occurrence, often more apparent than real. Perceived global threats reflect patterns of incidence of the related shocks. An earthquake, volcanic eruption or tsunami is more likely to occur on fault lines in certain parts of the world. At certain times of the year, Florida is likely to be threatened by hurricanes. Disease has particular epidemiological paths. Even in the case of war, it should be possible to predict where it will occur and how far it will extend. It is helpful to understand the causation of such shocks in order to understand their location.

There seems to have been an increase in the impact of catastrophes or disasters which qualify as global shocks. There is certainly an increased sensitivity to such risk. It is highly likely that the amount of global risk has increased. Whether this apparent increase in incidence is real or simply the result of an increasing impact, which results from more capital being at risk, is unclear. The accumulation of capital in all countries, but notably in developed countries, particularly the infrastructures necessary for modern economic activity, has created a hostage to bad fortune. A breakdown in the infrastructure can have dire effects on the operation of any business, whether it is the breakdown of the transport, communication or energy systems. Such infrastructure is threatened by a host of global shocks.

Global risk can be defined:

- by the locational range of the initial risk-generating event. In some cases, the location is a moving one. The event(s) or relevant behavioural change(s) might be located in regions covering more than one country, for example, a geological fault line or even the epidemiological lines of the spread of disease. Terrorism can occur anywhere, but is more likely to occur in certain parts of the world,
- by the scope of the exposure to particular kinds of shock. For example, some risk-generating events have their source outside the

national jurisdiction in which they have a significant impact. The location of significant impact may be uncertain. There may be a threat to many different regions. In an extreme case, the threat is universal, as with terrorist attacks, an epidemic disease such as AIDS or SARS or a computer virus. There are other types of shock which in certain circumstances become universal, e.g. war or economic depression,

- by the degree of impact on a relevant performance indicator at the highest level, which might be a key demographic indicator, the overall level of profit in a region, the rate of capital formation or even the GDP growth of the affected countries. A global shock might be defined as one which has a sufficiently large impact to make necessary international assistance,
- by the identity and location of the appropriate risk control agency. The nature of interdependence may make international cooperation not just desirable but critical to the containment of the impact. Many of these events are infrequent, but have a large impact when they occur. Global risk is the risk, which for various reasons cannot be dealt with at lower levels, but has to be handled by international agencies or with the cooperation of different governments.

The global risk environment comprises an increasing number of different sources, events or groups of related behavioural change which qualify as risk-generating. The source of such events differs – some have a natural provenance such as climatic shocks – drought or floods, others are of human making, including war or economic depression (White 1987 and 1992). Of the latter, some relate to the nature of technology, others to the operation of integrated markets, and others to the political aims of governments or other organised groups, including terrorist groups. In some cases, there is a mixture of natural and human causation. Some events generate pure risk such as fire, others have an upside as well as a downside; there may be positive climatic fluctuations which increase food production. Volcanic eruptions create fertile soil for the future. In few cases is it impossible to find some benefit resulting from the shock. Even a fire may clear away old buildings which are inappropriate to the new economy.

Global risk can take many different forms:

- an international depression such as the Great Depression of the 1930s, or even lesser events such as the Asian Economic Crisis of 1997 whose impact was limited largely to developing countries.

Potentially there are significant contagion or herd effects which cause an initial crisis to spread and to enlarge its impact into a disaster or catastrophe:
- war or civil unrest which spills across international frontiers;
- terrorist attacks of various kinds;
- natural catastrophes, some linked to global climatic change, but affecting broad areas of the world such as earthquakes, volcanic eruptions, storms (typhoons, hurricanes or cyclones), floods and tsunamis. Some are less dramatic such as drought. Climatic shocks sometimes accumulate into famine. Human action, it is argued, through global warming has increased the incidence of such climatic shocks although the degree to which this is true is contentious;
- computer viruses;
- disease of various types – epidemics such as AIDS or SARS, epizootics such as foot and mouth and mad cow disease or plant diseases such as phylloxera or rust (smut). These are traditionally of great importance, e.g. outbreaks of plague such as the Black Death, the onset of disease among unprotected populations such as those in the Americas before white settlement or periodic outbreaks of influenza such as the Spanish flu which after World War I killed more people than the war itself.

Any typology of global risk seeks to identify independent components and then the sub-components which comprise these components (see Figure 8.1).

There are three main difficulties associated with exploring the nature and implications of such shocks, using global risk as a model for the other types of risk:

- predicting their incidence

Frequency decreases with the size of impact. Because these shocks are infrequent and the records insufficiently long to test the probability of occurrence, they are difficult to predict. It has become increasingly important, but much more difficult, to be able to predict that frequency, which usually requires a sophisticated understanding of causation. There is considerable effort being invested in improving the predictive capacity of the relevant organisations researching in this area.

- understanding their causation

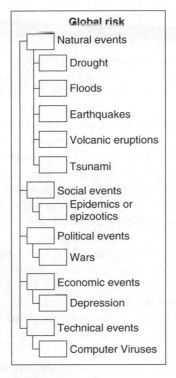

Figure 8.1 A typology of global risk

This is important because it makes possible prediction. There are still arguments about the causation of such prominent events as the Great Depression. Disease mutates and it is unclear why disease sometimes becomes epidemic, even among populations which have an acquired immunity. Forecasting volcanic eruptions is not easy, but there are geological explanations.

• anticipating their impact

This reflects exposure which changes with the nature of the assets at risk, but shocks have a greater impact on the unprepared and those without the resources to combat the shock. It is necessary to identify and value these assets. The build up of infrastructure and of capital investment in developed countries increases the potential exposure, while at the same time their capacity to mitigate such risk has increased.

The perception of global risk

Global risk-generating events are more visible, often more dramatic than other events, and certainly more talked about and analysed. It is not difficult to follow in news broadcasts the path of a hurricane in the Caribbean. The bunching of such events can colour attitudes in a particular time period, influencing the way in which risk is perceived. They influence the level of tolerance to such events, sometimes transitorily. The degree of risk tolerance is linked with the perception of the riskiness of the environment, as revealed by events such as the terrorist attacks of September 11 2001 or the Asian tsunami of Boxing Day, 2004. It is reasonable to consider the psychological impact of the events generating global risk and to assume that tolerance reflects the incidence of risk-generating events and the nature of the relevant risk environments. The level of risk aversion may be linked to particular kinds of events but is more general. In other words, such dramatic events may sensitise decision makers to all types of risk, some apparently unconnected with the relevant one. Risk aversion is influenced by ignorance, with the result that the same risk environment can look very different to different people. There may also be a differing impact from particular events, some events having a particularly intense influence.

There are a number of possibilities of the impact of global risk for a particular international investment project:

- no impact on key decision makers in the area of investment, whether on attitudes or behaviour. The events may be deemed to be irrelevant or any impact of such low probability that it can be ignored. The additional costs are regarded as trivial,
- an impact, but only temporary since the events themselves are infrequent. For a period of time, there may be a perceptible change of attitude and this might translate into a change of behaviour, for example, a greater concern with and commitment of resources to risk assessment, but the status quo ante soon reasserts itself,
- a long term continuing impact such as lower levels of aggregate FDI or the emergence of new and different patterns of flow of FDI, which may bypass areas perceived as high risk in favour of areas seen as low risk. The country risk premium added to the normal discount rate in investment appraisal may increase, and significantly for some areas of the world. These changes may or may not be linked to other significant changes in cost levels.

The negative effects of such uncertainties are filtered to the enterprise in different ways.

- imposing direct costs on the enterprise and/or reducing revenues. Production may be interrupted or there may be costs involved in undertaking measures of risk mitigation, some imposed on the enterprise, some voluntarily taken up,
- imposing indirect costs on the enterprise, e.g. the costs of increased security at airports, which fall on the airlines and on those who buy services from the airlines, or the costs of dealing with absenteeism as a result of sickness. The cost of an early warning system for tsunamis may also be factored in,
- initiating a change in attitudes, in particular, changing the perception of risk by raising the level of risk aversion and therefore the likelihood of an avoidance response. For example, banking crises are often followed by long periods of very circumspect lending by the survivors. Prudential checks become much more rigorous,
- changing behavioural patterns such as the design and operation of control systems, including the way an investment is appraised and the resources committed to such an appraisal,
- eliciting a strategic response which changes both the existing strategy and the structure of the relevant enterprise, notably the organisational or capital structure. This kind of response is premised on the possibility of a repetition of the shock. Such strategic responses may give the relevant enterprises a temporary competitive advantage but, if successful, might cause imitation by competitors.

The incorporation of global risk

Any independent action taken by decision makers within an enterprise to mitigate such risk might be insufficient. Such action might have to be supplemented by intervention by government or some other body which brings together the separate enterprises affected by the risk in a coordinated effort. It is possible to 'avoid' most risks, but not global risk. Even in the case of global risk, this might mean a persistent tendency to avoid certain parts of the world, which are perceived as high risk areas, at least during periods of threat. FDI inflows into Africa are usually as low as 1% level of the aggregate for the world as a whole.

There are methods of mitigating risk which can be successful, provided they are carried out by all the affected players. There may be virtuous and vicious circles involved, in that avoidance increases the cost for those who do not avoid. There are problems which have been described as interdependent security (IDS) problems (Kunreuther 2003, Kunreuther, Michel-Kerjan and Porter 2003). The issue is whether it pays an individual player to take action to control a source of risk, since for that individual the private costs might exceed the private benefits. Such problems relate to a number of the different threats, in particular to security against terrorist attack, to protection against computer viruses or against disease.

How far should an individual airline, an individual computer user or possible disease victim take action to protect himself/herself against such a threat? The relevant mitigating actions involve a host of behaviours including baggage screening, virus protection or immunisation. The incentive to take such action depends on whether others are likely to take similar action. It is markedly less helpful for one airline to check baggage if it is receiving baggage from other airlines which is unchecked. Such a situation may render any checks of little advantage. The destruction of Flight 103 of PanAm in 1988, the Locherbie disaster, was caused by a bag put onto a Malta Airlines flight at Gozo, Malta, flown to Frankfurt and then on to London where it was transferred to the PanAm flight. Opportunism might dictate that one airline steals a march on the others by being cursory in it security checks – costs are lowered, at least in the short term.

The risk faced by one player depends on the actions of other players. It is possible, if decisions are made by individuals in isolation from each other, to have underinvestment in finding a solution to the problems created by the event. This may mean that there must be cooperation; some industry body or government has to take action to coordinate the appropriate risk control. The adoption of action by one or a few risk mitigators may tip others into similar action. There are sometimes cascade effects, with one positive action following another in rapid succession. It may be enough for the initiators to concentrate on opinion leaders who provide the model for others to follow.

Global shocks can put insurance companies under risk since the size of the associated claims makes the insurance beyond their ability to handle. The risk is broken up into apparently manageable shares – shared horizontally and/or divided into separate vertical tranches. Even reinsurers find some risk too large to manage. During the 1980s and 1990s there has been a series of major shocks which have reduced the ability of reinsurers to cope with the situation. These shocks controverted the expectations of the insurers concerning the frequency of the relevant events. The concentration of impact caused enormous stress for both insurers and reinsurers. As a consequence, the supply of reinsurance was reduced just at the time when the demand for insurance and, therefore, for reinsurance increased. A lot of work has gone into improving the ability of the industry to predict the incidence of shocks. If reinsurance becomes more profitable, a simple solution in an efficient market is for new reinsurers to establish themselves and to raise capital on the market.

Reinsurance has proved inadequate to the task, particularly because it generates too much moral hazard, that is, it removes the incentive to mitigate. Because of moral hazard, insurers underwrite risks they should not and are overly generous in meeting claims. A range of other instruments such as catastrophe bonds have been devised to deal with this problem, at the same time encouraging mitigation and managing the risk which remains (Doherty 2000: chap. 18). A catastrophe bond acts as a form of insurance if a certain specified event(s) occurs.

Global risk is more a potential than an actual problem for international investment projects, but it increases the sensitivity to risk and therefore the aversion to other types of risk.

The nature and classification of industry risk

Industry risk is sometimes described as if it were no more than the market risk which manifests itself through price movements, although this comprises only part of the type of risk systematic to an industry. Even if the term market risk were used in a broad catch-all manner there would still be a need to analyse its relevant components and sub-components in order to anticipate the unexpected. The market situation can change in an unpredictable way, reflecting changes in demand or supply conditions, which in their turn reflect other changes. There are many specific events or behavioural changes which are confined in their influence to one industrial sector. This is obvious in the case of most changes in technology, government regulation, competitive conditions or consumer tastes. Almost by definition insiders within an industry are rather better at anticipating these changes than players in the financial market who derive their information from insiders.

Industry risk can be defined as 'the potential negative consequences for a key performance indicator, or strategic target(s), of an unanticipated change in the environment specific to a particular industry.' Industry risk can be considered systematic in that all enterprises within that sector are exposed to the same kind of risk. Industry risk arises from factors specific to a particular industry which might vary in an unexpected way. Such a variation in conditions can refer to either the supply or demand sides and their underlying elements, or to the context in which both demand and supply manifest themselves.

A prerequisite for dealing with the nature of such risk is to describe the industry environment. An industry consists in the enterprises which sell a group of related products for which the price elasticity of substitution is high, and enterprises in other parts of the economy closely linked as suppliers or complementors to the production or sale of such products. The products are regarded as substitutes for each other by the consumer. Such enterprises are often, but not always, selling on international markets.

It is possible to take Miller's classification as a starting point for an acceptable classification of industry risk. Components are significant independent risk factors.

Miller aspired to be comprehensive and to separate industry risk from general or enterprise risk. Although Miller's (1992) industry uncertainties provide the initial foundation for an acceptable characterisation, there are a number of desirable adjustments. First, there are two significant omissions from his classification:

- the nature of the product or the relevant product processes characteristic of the industry, including transportation,
- the nature of the rules of the game which determine how the main players behave in a particular industry.

The former raises safety and liability issues for those engaged in the production, transport or consumption of the relevant product, and for those who live near the production or transport facilities. There may be the danger of personal harm which results from the nature of the product. The area of shared harm might be large, as the Chernobyl disaster showed. This component of industry risk is rising in importance. Asbestos, smoking, silicon breast implants have all been sources of harm to workers, consumers or passive bystanders. It is not uncommon in developed countries for an environmental audit to be necessary before a significant project is implemented in order to reveal such sources of potential harm. A sensible enterprise may self-regulate before a problem emerges. The increasing focus on harm and the greater willingness of courts to find liability and to award large damages has a twofold effect on costs – to raise the initial investment costs to take account of the need to satisfy the regulatory authorities and minimise the danger of relevant accidents, and to raise operational costs where the project needs to be modified to meet the regulatory requirements.

The second component includes standards adopted within the industry by an industry association, even informally where there is a clear industry leader, and/or the regulations which government introduces to determine how the industry is to operate. The latter reflects the former. Sometimes, the standard emerges from the micro decisions of individual suppliers and customers without any guidance from above, as a natural result of competition. Often, the first mover or innovator has the advantage of setting such standards. Sometimes, there is uncertainty for a considerable period of time.

Another modification to the Miller classification is needed. Technological uncertainty, not really a part of competitive uncertainties, justifies a separate component.

A full amended list therefore includes six main components:

- Product nature uncertainties
- Input uncertainties
- Product market uncertainties
- Competitive uncertainties
- Technological uncertainties
- Regulatory uncertainties

This component list includes all areas in which significant independent risk factors are relevant. The following categorisation, as shown in Figure 8.2, breaks the components into sub-components.

The components of industry risk

The analysis explores the nature of the separate items, discussing in general terms what proxies exist for a quantification of industry risk.

Product nature risks

The first component relates to the nature of the product and the way in which it is consumed, produced or transported. There are hazards which are inherent in the nature of the product. Most products carry an element of danger, but some are very dangerous. For example, the occurrence of a nuclear accident such as that which occurred at Three Mile Island or Chernobyl, is sufficient to cause a major avoidance response. Certain stakeholder groups are most affected. The use of the product may damage those in close proximity without key personnel being aware of any danger. In this case the problem is ignorance, which gives rise to what has been called 'long-tailed risk'. It is long-tailed in two senses, that

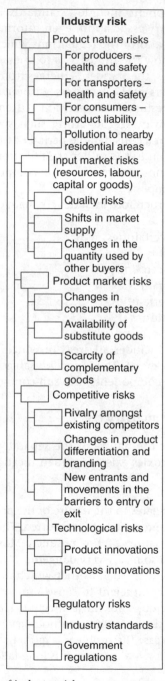

Figure 8.2   A typology of industry risk

its occurrence is infrequent and also that there is a significant separation in time between the causative exposure and the resulting harm. Workers or the local community may be totally unaware of the hazards involved even if there is a public literature showing that research has identified possible harm. Even with accurate knowledge of the consequences of a failure to mitigate, there may be accidents. It is sometimes too expensive to remove the most dangerous of activities from the dense populations exposed to the associated accidents.

This is a component of industry risk which is rapidly rising in importance. The nature of product or production process may expose the enterprise to product liability actions or to accusations of pollution. In the nineteenth century courts tended to favour the defendant over the plaintiff whereas in the twentieth century there was a change in focus with protection being given to those damaged (Scheiber 1971, 1972–3, 1973, 1980 and 1981). Courts are increasingly willing not only to find the defendants guilty but to impose fines and compensation costs which are large. The oil spill of the Exxon Valdes, the chemical explosion at Bhopal or the ravages of asbestos are good examples of the problem. Single accidents of a significant magnitude can seriously jeopardise the financial viability of an airline through the loss of reputation. Many smaller accidents can accumulate into a major impact, as with breast implants.

Class actions magnify the impact. The implications of this kind of risk can be either domestic or international. An oil spill threatens a wide area. The dangers of smoking or asbestos are the same all over the world. International cigarette companies or miners are vulnerable to action taken by those harmed anywhere in the world.

There are two kinds of cost – direct costs which result from the need to clean up or to compensate those damaged by an accident and indirect costs, which result from a loss of reputation; potential customers are deterred from consuming the product for an unknown period of time by the loss of reputation. In principle, it is possible to insure against the former, but difficult to do so against the latter.

There are two ways of dealing with the problem – a mitigation policy which reduces the possibility of such damage or a management policy which gives the enterprise cover against the losses arising from the action of individuals damaged by such hazards. The former is preferable to the latter in that it avoids the loss of reputation. Avoiding such costs is closely associated with the notion of corporate social responsibility. It is also a matter of considering the enterprise as a network of stakeholder groups who can be damaged in the ways indicated above.

The next two sub-components relate to the supply side. Both can change in unpredicted ways or at an unanticipated pace, thus creating risk.

Technological risks

These risks result from the impact of unforeseen difficulties in implementing the technical change involved in the introduction of a new product or group of products, or the introduction of a new process to produce or deliver an existing product.

The speed of technical change reflects the point in the life cycle of the relevant product or industry. If the product or industry is young, it is difficult to predict the direction which technical change might take, or the speed with which the new technology will be taken up. Whether it is taken up quickly depends on whether there are first mover advantages which might persuade an enterprise to lead the way and incur the additional development costs which fall on the pioneer. Strategy hinges on whether there are first mover advantages to leading the way in technology or whether it is better to wait and allow others to bear the initial costs of developing and mastering a new technology. There is considerable strategic risk in such situations since it is impossible to know what others will do. To some degree there is an attempt to pre-empt others. Will Boeing follow Airbus's lead in developing the A380 or other mobile operators Hutchison's in introducing the third generation mobile technology? There is a degree of path dependence in the choice of attributes of any new product and even in the nature of the technology itself. Small events, or apparently trivial circumstances, can sway a decision in favour of a particular variant of a technology. There is a learning process which implies very different rates of productivity increase implicit in different technological variants. Only the technology actually adopted realises this learning. In some industries, the rate of technical change is high and unpredictable, in others slow and more predictable.

Input costs

Input risk takes the shape of unexpected changes in the availability, quality and price of inputs. This relates to what is required for production, such as equipment, components or intermediate goods, and to the labour and capital required for operations to commence and continue. The degree of vertical integration of the relevant economic activities determines how far inputs need to be purchased in the market and how far they are under the control of the relevant enterprise. Difficulties can arise from unexpected changes in the supply or demand conditions for any given input.

There are two sub-components relating to the demand side.

Product market risks

Product market risks take a number of different forms – the impact of unanticipated changes in consumer taste, changes in the availability of goods which are in some way substitutes for the relevant product, and problems in the supply of a complementary good. Such unexpected changes can reduce the demand for a particular product and, therefore, the price. Some product areas are particularly susceptible to such changes of taste.

An unforeseen intensity of competition

The second demand side factor refers to the level of competition from other enterprises and to the advent of new competitors. In any oligopolistic or imperfectly competitive market, there is always a degree of indeterminateness in the way in which competitions manifests itself. The price level or the number of competitors may differ although these two factors are interconnected. The smaller the number of competitors, the higher tends to be the price. Such an outcome may reflect an initial strategy of keeping the price down in order to discourage new entrants. A tendency to reap the maximum profits from an early monopoly of supply encourages new entry and imitation. Prices fall to a level below what they otherwise would have been. There is considerable path dependence in the evolution of most markets for consumer products. Michael Porter's analysis of the forces of competition is relevant in this context, in particular his discussion of the barriers to entry. The higher such barriers, the lower is the likely intensity of competition.

The influence of unpredicted changes in regulations or standards

Finally there is any change in the 'rules of the game' – a change in government regulation, a change in industry standards or the emergence of a dominant standard setter. Some of this is formal, much is informal. The process by which the rules of the game emerge is of particular importance in the early history of a product or an industry. There may be rival technologies and both production and consumption methods are poorly understood. The strategic action of the competitive leaders will be important in determining these. The role of government or quasi-government intervention is often important where the product is potentially dangerous or has a particular significance nationally.

9
Country Risk

> ....firms engaging in international production are at a disad-
> vantage compared with local firms (Buckley 1996: 114). ...the
> great puzzle about FDI remains. Why do it at all?
>
> (Buckley 1996: 110)

This chapter examines the nature of country risk as a type of systematic risk which, like industry risk, extends beyond a single enterprise,
in this case to the enterprises which operate within the jurisdiction of a
particular country. National frontiers are among the most clearly
demarcated boundaries which exist in the economic and political
world. No part of the world is outside a national jurisdiction. It is
obvious who holds sovereignty and is responsible for the law and policies which operate in a particular country. Risk arises from unanticipated change in such policies. The aim of this chapter is to establish
a template for a measure of generic country risk.

   There are six sections in the chapter:

- The first section considers the nature of country risk.
- In the second section there is an identification of the important elements of country risk.
- Section three identifies how the sub-components might be
  classified within groups constituting the components making up
  country risk.
- Section four sets out a comprehensive country risk taxonomy.
- The fifth section looks at the issues of weighting and finding proxies
  for components in a quantitative country risk index.
- The final section analyses the way in which a quantitative index of
  country risk might influence the investment decision.

The nature of country risk

By far the most important risk context for FDI is the country environment. This reflects the continuing importance of the nation state as the chief political unit in the world and the role of the government of such a nation state as a purposeful actor developing a strategy to achieve the objectives which give it legitimacy. It is easy in an era of so-called 'globalisation' to play down the role of national governments, but there is considerable evidence that the prime loyalty of many citizens is national and that governments continue to have much scope for pursuing independent policies of various kinds. Any government creates an environment of both opportunity and risk for an enterprise considering an investment project within its jurisdiction.

Put simply, country risk is the unanticipated 'downside' variability in a key performance indicator, or significant strategic target, which results from engaging in international business transactions with an inevitable exposure to the performance and policies of a sovereign country other than the home country. It is, therefore, the risk which attaches to international business transactions as a consequence of the existence of national boundaries, i.e. separate countries, for example the consequent existence of separate currencies and separate sovereignties. One way to express this is that governments devise strategies in the context of which corporate strategies must be made. Inevitably government policies influence the enterprise and its performance, much more than the reverse is true. Country risk arises from the interaction of strategies formulated and implemented by the relevant enterprise and the relevant country government. This interaction occurs within a political, economic, financial and cultural context which is often alien to the foreign investor. The problem in the political area may be ignorance of what the host government is likely to do. Country risk brings in the government as a critical strategic player.

Political risk is therefore a particularly important component, perhaps the most important component, of country risk. Buckley defines political risk as 'the exposure to a change in value of an investment or cash position resultant upon government action' (Buckley 1996: 321). This is too restrictive. Consistent with the definitions of risk already given in chapter 3, political risk can be defined as the negative impact on a key performance indicator or a strategic target relevant to an investment, of an unanticipated change in the political environment of the host country, whatever its nature – a regime change, a policy change or an increase in political turbulence. Political risk includes elements of political instability, government policy change uncertainty, comprising everything from expropriation to tax changes, and social instability uncertainty.

The effectiveness of any government in exercising political sovereignty differs according to the degree of legitimacy of the government and its effectiveness in both framing and implementing policies. It is critical that government can exercise what is sometimes called 'infrastructural power', the power to implement relevant policies (White 1987). Both legitimacy and effectiveness are threatened by an inability to implement policy. The degree of stability of policy depends partly on such infrastructural power and differs from country to country. In this context, it is easy to understand reference to failed states: states lacking the infrastructures necessary for the successful implementation of key policies.

A critical part of the infrastructure is the legal system which influences the nature of political risk. Law needs to be predictable and not simply the result of administrative whim. The rule of law, covering action by government itself, can protect the enterprise from the extremes of risk such as the arbitrary seizure of capital in its many guises often referred to as expropriation (Brewer 1985). Some commentators think of expropriation, interpreted broadly, as the major source of political risk.

Most enterprises are not large enough to have a significant influence on government strategy. Some do, particularly, if they are in their turn backed by a powerful home government. Negotiation with government is one response to political risk, a critical form of risk mitigation (see chapter 12) The responses of international enterprises to government action are unlikely to cause a further reaction unless their commitment of resources is largely relative to the host economy. The responses of a group of enterprises, if they are similar, may have such an influence. The context is a complex and dynamic one of action, response and further reaction by the relevant players.

In the normal run of events, any government impinges on the enterprise through various policies. These policies establish the political context in which an enterprise operates. The key issue is how far that context is less predictable when it is foreign. There is a need to predict the political conditions in a host country for the time period of the investment (Haner 1979: 18). These conditions include the nature of all relevant policies. Some policies are obviously relevant, for example fiscal, monetary or commercial policies since they affect directly the cost streams of an investment project. A policy such as exchange control can have multiple effects on costs. Other policies are more indirect in their impact, including foreign policy or policy on social welfare. Such policies, even in the absence of exchange controls, influence the value of the exchange rate, whose level is vital to the maintenance of international competitiveness and the remittance of profits. They might involve the establishment of tax rates and labour costs relevant to the enterprise and to the revenue and cost streams generated by any investment project, or change the cost of capital, if the enterprise is resorting to local sources of capital.

It is often argued that globalisation has reduced the scope for independent policy making, that conformity to the rules of the international game, the 'golden straitjacket', leaves little room for the unexpected; policies conform to a general pattern. This is much less true than usually asserted. The imposition of the Washington consensus on debtor nations does restrict the scope for independent policy, but in the absence of a crisis it is unlikely that such pressure is brought to bear.

Political risk of this kind is so characteristic of country risk that for some it alone constitutes country risk. However, it is possible to make an a priori conceptualisation of the country risk environment into four distinct segments – political, economic, financial and cultural. Political legitimacy and economic performance are closely linked. Economic performance differs markedly from country to country, both in the rate of sustained economic development and in vulnerability to cyclical fluctuations. Most governments measure their economic success by the performance of the economy, principally by levels and rates of growth of GDP per head of population, compared with others or past performance in the relevant economy. The focus of interest in risk analysis is the unanticipated change of performance, which might reflect a number of unfortunate conjunctures – movement from one stage of modern economic development to another: a sudden crisis with a significant deterioration in economic performance, attributable to a deterioration of a relevant environment, either internal or external or a failure of policy; or even a particularly severe downturn in the business cycle (Gangemi et al. 2000: 267–8).

Some economic contexts are very favourable, others much less so. In some countries, the internal market is growing rapidly. The productivity of labour and other factors of production is also improving and reducing costs. Where these are occurring, the exchange rate may reflect a persistent upgrading in the value of the currency. It pays to receive revenue streams in such an appreciating currency. The existence of a multiplicity of exchange rates, reflecting the existence of a multiplicity of currencies, particularly in the context of floating rates, constitutes another kind of risk, one which cannot be fully managed by hedging since FDI usually involves investment beyond the short term.

Most financial theorists are more familiar with the financial risk environment which is focused on the creditworthiness of those engaged in business transactions. Sovereign risk, the creditworthiness of government, is an element of country risk. Often, this is shown by the interest rate spread on similar debt instruments. Credit risk is a well-established type of risk, very important for financial institutions and for any transactions in the money market. Again the risk arises from events which are unanticipated, for example a default or a risk migration, that is the re-rating of a relevant institution or country into lower rating category. For some, this is the only kind of risk, but this is to miss most of the risk relevant to FDI.

For completeness, it is necessary to consider the cultural risk environment, that is the risk which arises from ignorance of another culture and the unexpected discovery of behavioural patterns which imposes a cost on the relevant enterprise. Corruption or nepotism are both difficult to define and often difficult to anticipate. Strictly speaking, risk consists in an unexpected rise in the level of corruption.

The definition of political risk can be extended to cover each of these environments – economic, financial and cultural with the substitution of one word. It is true that such environments overlap in their influence on international investment decisions. It is impossible to fully separate these risk sources, but highly desirable to try to separate them and to be fully aware of the differences.

The account above has assumed that the national unit is the key defining unit for FDI. There is also a possibility that countries can be grouped by the nature and level of the country risk which characterises them. If this were the case, the natural unit would not be the nation state but some grouping which might be regional or reflect some characteristic other than proximity, such as level of development, common heritage or even a cultural feature such as language or religion. It is interesting to identify such groupings, clusters of countries exposed to risk in a similar way with close FDI links, as will be noted in chapter 12. This defines the context of policy making rather than the nature of that policy. However, governments share characteristics with their countries. Both content and process of policy making reflect the cultures.

The sub components of country risk

It is useful to start from the risk elements which form the basis of the broader components described above. It is important to identify those sub-components which are likely to have an influence on decision making and candidates for inclusion in any definition of risk. There are a number of problems in doing this:

- the fragmentary nature of most previous analysis, which in individual cases refers to only certain risk elements and only some of the sub-components. Each commentator has his/her own preference for risk types. The aim in this analysis is a comprehensive coverage. It is to identify those sub-components most frequently referred to by all theorists or practitioners,
- the use of different terminology. The summary requires some degree of editing in so far as the sources use different terminologies. This is true of all three sources of relevant information – theorists of risk and of FDI, agencies rating such risk and the managers making the relevant decisions. The terminology used is intended to reflect an all-embracing approach, in that it includes all the potentially significant elements.

There has been a long debate on the relevant country risk components. It is not difficult to collect a list of such items by simply reading one day's newspaper, or if a comprehensive approach is required, reading newspapers from a range of different countries over a period of time. It is possible to short-circuit this effort. There are two possible starting sources for a list of sub-components relevant to country risk.

One is previous theoretical work done. The criteria for inclusion in such a list of reference theorists are threefold:

- the theorist aspires to being comprehensive
- the analysis is oriented to FDI and not to other decisions
- the work has often been cited and continues to be cited

The result is a listing of 16 different authorities whose work was mined for a listing of sub-components.

The second source is the practice of ten rating agencies (Erb et al. 1996a, b). The components identified as relevant in country risk assessment by the various rating agencies are sometimes differently described.

The tables on the following pages summarise the inclusions from these two sources. The first table analyses the 16 significant theoretical sources and summarises the elements discussed.

Table 9.1 Country risk sub-components from previous research

Variable	Root 1968	Stobaugh 1969	Robock 1971	Boddewyn & Cracco 1972a, b	Green 1972	Knudsen 1974	Van Agtmael 1976	Bradley 1977	Rummel & Heenan 1978	Kobrin 1979	Haner 1979	Nagy 1979	Hashmi & Guvenli 1992	Miller 1992	Walo 1998	Meldrum 1999
Changes of government	X				X		X				X	X		X		X
Political instability	X	X	X		X		X				X	X		X		X
External insecurity	X	X			X		X		X		X	X		X		
Internal insecurity	X	X			X		X		X							
Armed conflicts	X		X		X		X		X					X	X	
Kidnappings and extortion														X		
Breakdown of law & order			X	X												
Acts of terrorism											X		X	X		
Competing political philosophies	X	X	X													
Policy discontinuity		X	X					X			X	X	X	X	X	X
Slowdown in economic growth						X						X	X			X
Deficit in current account of balance of payments												X				X
Fluctuations in foreign exchange rates		X								X	X					X
High inflation rates		X							X	X		X		X	X	X
Fluctuations in interest rates										X	X	X		X		X
Currency devaluations												X				

Table 9.1 Country risk sub-components from previous research – *continued*

Variable	Root 1968	Stobaugh 1969	Robock 1971	Boddewyn & Cracco 1972a, b	Green 1972	Knudsen 1974	Van Agtmael 1976	Bradley 1977	Rummel & Heenan 1978	Kobrin 1979	Haner 1979	Nagy 1979	Hashmi & Guvenli 1992	Miller 1992	Wafo 1998	Meldrum 1999
Diminished ability to borrow												X				X
Infrastructural deficiencies																
Bureaucratic delays																
Restrictions/difficulties in access to credit and capital markets		X														
Vulnerability in credit ratings									X			X	X			X
Ignorance of patterns of business behaviour																
Language barriers											X					
Ethnic/religious tensions											X					
Corruption and nepotism																
Different negotiating styles																

Source: Compiled for the research.

153

Table 9.2   **Country risk sub-components from rating agencies**

Variables	BOA	BERI	CRIS	EIU	EURO	II	S&P	PRS ICRG	PRS COPL	MOODY
Changes of government	X	X	X	X	X	X				
Political instability	X	X	X	X	X	X	X	X	X	
External insecurity	X	X	X	X	X					
Internal insecurity	X	X	X	X	X					
Armed conflicts	X	X	X	X						
Kidnappings and extortion	X	X								
Breakdown of law & order – Present	X	X								
Acts of terrorism	X	X	X							
Competing political philosophies	X	X	X	X	X					
Policy discontinuity	X	X	X	X	X	X	X	X		
Slowdown in economic growth	X	X	X	X	X	X	X	X	X	X
Deficit in current account of balance of payments	X	X	X	X	X	X	X	X		
Fluctuations in foreign exchange rates	X	X	X	X	X	X				
High inflation rates	X	X	X	X						
Fluctuations in interest rates	X	X	X							
Currency devaluations	X									
Diminished ability to borrow	X	X	X	X	X	X	X			
Deficient infrastructure	X	X	X							
Bureaucratic delays	X	X	X	X	X					
Restriction/difficulties in access to credit and capital markets	X	X	X	X	X	X				
Vulnerability in credit ratings	X	X	X	X	X					
Ignorance of patterns of business behaviour	X									
Language barriers – Present	X	X								
Ethnic/religious tensions	X	X	X	X	X					
Corruption and nepotism	X	X	X							
Differences in negotiation styles	X									

Note: BoA: Bank of America World Information Services
BERI: Business Environment Risk Intelligence
CRIS: Control Risks Information Services
EIU: Economist Intelligence Unit
EURO: Euro-money magazine
II: Institutional Investor magazine
Moody: Moody's Investor Services
PRS-CORS: Political Risk Services: Coplin-O'Leary Rating System
PRS-ICRG: Political Risk Services: International Country Risk Guide
S&P: Standard & Poor's Rating Group
Source: Compiled for the research.

The second table carries out the same operation for the 10 rating agencies. Consideration of the two lists gives 26 sub-components. The next task is to group these sub-components. The simplest classification, often adopted in the literature (Moosa 2002: chapter five), is to have a twofold grouping, political and economic. This leaves a number of sub-components difficult to place. Several of these are cultural factors. It is also reasonable to consider a separate heading for financial sub-components. The sub-components have therefore been classified under four specific component headings – political, economic, financial or cultural risk. The following section considers each of the sub-components in turn, grouped within the different categories. It goes further and seeks to group the sub-components into groups within the four component classes. It also notes the existence of sub-sub-components.

The components of country risk

In this section the sub-components are grouped under the broader component headings.

Political risk

It is possible to group the sub-components of political risk into three different sources of relevant change – political instability such as inter-actions with other states, e.g. war being its most extreme manifestation, or changes of regime, whether through elections or more violent means; social instability, including attacks on the legitimacy of a particular regime from within – riots, strikes and the like – in the extreme case a loss of legitimacy on the part of the government; and finally, deliberate changes of policy by government in areas relevant to the business enterprise, usually as a result of pressure from key interest groups. In developed democratic states, there is often little unexpected change since there is a consensus between government and opposition in most policy areas, and any significant change is flagged with a mandate sought at the next election. In other states, there may be much more instability.

All the sub-components relevant to political risk are listed, with an indication of the numbers of references by theorists and by rating agencies respectively.

- Change of government including democratic changes through elections, coup d'etats, and revolutions (7,6).

The issues are twofold – the degree of legitimacy in the transfer of power and whether a successor government retains existing policies regarding FDI.

A new government may adopt unanticipated policies different from those its predecessor adopted. Radical shifts in political leadership create political risk for investors, in that a new government may unilaterally announce measures that restrict the future profitability of foreign operations. In order to reduce expenditures and increase revenues, a government may not service the country's debts or even expropriate foreign assets. If the government in power is irresponsible and not competent to solve the problems of the country, themselves already the cause of the change of government, the political risk to FDI may be high.

* Political instability, resulting from factional rivalries, regional conflict, imbalances of power within the ruling group, and coercive measures by government directed at certain groups (9,9).

Such political instability can seriously damage the operating environment for business and represents a potential risk to both personnel and property. In an extreme case there may be a breakdown in law and order. Workers may not turn up for work. Distribution systems may close down. Normal production or consumption routines are seriously disturbed.

* External insecurity, including the danger of wars, invasions, and foreign-inspired disorders (8,5)

External threats may lead to an unstable political environment. Nagy (1979) argues that the wars and disorders have the following negative effects: they make a significant drain on a country's resources; often paralyse production on a large scale and over a long period; substantially destroy productive capacities; and impair the availability of entrepreneurial, managerial and technical expertise. The impact of the external threat depends on the degree of resistance and the duration of any hostilities.

* Internal insecurity, including a high level of criminal activity and social conflict, sometimes resulting from job insecurity and high unemployment (6,5)

When fractionalisation of a society degenerates into the repression of a regional group or of the lowest or poorest class, a risk to political stability can arise (Kennedy 1987). A low level of security, with high level of criminal activities and unemployment, can constitute a serious hazard to companies wishing to undertake investment in such countries. Foreign business people become prime targets for robbery, burglary, car theft and extortion by armed criminals.

- Armed conflicts including internal rebellions and civil war (9,4)

This is an extreme form of political instability and it can create a high level of internal insecurity, generating unpredictable outcomes. Such conflict happens when tensions are high, antagonisms deep and the government is weak and unable to control the relevant hostile groups (Nagy 1979), or when one strong group refuses to accept the legitimacy of the government. Foreign companies operating in a country experiencing internal rebellions or civil wars are at a high risk of being attacked and having their business operations interrupted.

- Kidnappings and extortion (1,2)

Politically-motivated kidnappings and extortion may occur in a host country when multinational enterprises conduct foreign direct investment operations. They can pose threats to foreign nationals, including business executives, and their families.

- Breakdown of law and order (1,2)

This breakdown may result from a high level of criminal activity or a deteriorating system of law enforcement, or a combination of both.

- Acts of terrorism (2,3)

Individual terrorists may attack business facilities or personnel, or a vital part of the infrastructure.

- Competing political philosophies, including nationalism, and dependence on an outside major power (8,5)

Boddewyn and Cracco (1972a, b) focus on nationalism as a major concern for MNEs. Nagy (1979) argues nationalism is often inherent in the philosophy of the host government, which is sometimes expressed in the threat of a take-over of foreign enterprises. Through various types of pressure the government induces foreign owners to

relinquish control to nationals. In the international political community, there are various ideological groupings, although the divisions
are not as strong as during the Cold War. Re-jigging of such alliances
is as threatening as the alliances themselves.

* Policy discontinuity (10,8)

Changes which disfavour FDI may relate to many policy areas. The
most obvious may involve a restriction on foreign ownership of relevant assets, limitations on international payment – through currency
inconvertibility or blockage of profit transfers, restraints on political
relationship with the foreign country, constraints on the establishment of business ties in the host economies, unfavourable investment
incentives, and a mandatory turnover of the assets to domestic ownership – through native empowerment. The host country government
may impose a repudiation of contractual obligations, expropriation
without compensation, restrict imports or exports, significantly raise
relevant taxes, or introduce restrictions on the nature and level of the
foreign firms' productive operations and/or profit.

There is an overlapping between many of these individual elements.
Some are broad enough to include others as special cases.

Economic risk

The second most important component is economic risk, arising
from unexpected changes in the economic context of an investment
project. Again it is possible to place the sub-components into larger
groups. The main sub-component groupings are performance uncertainties – rates of economic growth and the like; context uncertainties – comprising mainly prices in different markets, including
the price of foreign exchange (often referred to under the heading
transfer risk); and infrastructural uncertainties.

There are nine items in this broad grouping:

* Long-run slowdown of economic growth, including at worst a
  sustained deterioration in the level of GDP per capita (3,10)

The growth of GDP per head, the usual measure of a country's economic performance (Alon and Martin 1998), may slow for a variety of
reasons – a decline in the level of inputs and their effective use, including a fall in domestic fixed investment, a decline in the marginal productivity of that investment, a reduction in the intensity of use of the

labour force or a decline in the growth of labour productivity (Nagy 1979). Green (1972) shows how economic stress has an adverse impact on an individual corporation's performance.

• Deficit in current account of the balance of payments (1,8)

Balance of payment problems arise from a movement in either the current or the capital account, often the former followed closely by the latter. The former may initially result from a terms of trade shock or from the maintenance of an over-valued currency. If the balance of payments on the current account is negative, it may indicate uncompetitiveness in the economic operations of a country and may result in a build up in debt which generates an outward flow of interest payments. There may be difficulties revolving around the servicing of debt. Such circumstances may signal that policy is likely to change, with repatriation restrictions or tariff increases as countries seek to gain hard currency. Foreign direct investors are also concerned with the risk of currency inconvertibility as host governments react to a trade deficit and seek to restore currency stability. The experience of Argentina in 2001 illustrates these dangers. Intervention by the International Monetary Fund may force a change of policy which in the short term damages foreign companies.

• Persistent depreciation of the exchange rate (5,6)

The real exchange rate, which reflects both the nominal exchange rate and price movements, can measure the competitiveness of an economy. If prices are tending to rise faster than those of competitors, the exchange rate may deteriorate persistently. A poor performance in the rate of productivity increases compounds, both the inflationary and the exchange rate problem. Such a deterioration in the exchange rate can accelerate the inflation of prices, so that it becomes cumulative – a vicious circle. The real problem is volatility and unexpected change. Problems arise with a continuing but uneven depreciation (Stobaugh 1969; Kobrin 1979; and Meldrum 1999), since the value of a foreign investment project in foreign currency falls in a discontinuous fashion.

• High inflation rates (5,4)

The inflation rate can be regarded as an indicator of the quality of a country's economic management, notably if it moves beyond a modest rate of 3 to 4% (Oxelheim and Wihlborg 1987). The higher the inflation rate, the lower the country's economic prospects. Rummel and Heenan (1978) argue that rates of inflation above 100% are sure indicators of trouble. An accelerating rate of inflation is a significant threat. Once the momentum of an accelerating rate is established hyperinflation is a real possibility.

* A significant increase in interest rates (3,3)

When credit becomes scarce, its price rises, and in extreme circumstances, the rise is dramatic. Borrowing becomes very expensive. Should a foreign company need a loan to finance its operations it finds its costs have risen significantly (Meldrum 1999). Moreover, high interest rates reduce the level of demand by discouraging investment, and in some cases even consumption.

* Currency fluctuations (1,1)

A currency fluctuation occurs either when the currency is floating and its parity is changing, under the impact of market forces, or when with a fixed rate it is induced by policy action (Nagy 1979). Even small changes can be a problem if the value of the currency of the home country is moving in the opposite direction to that of the host country. The possibility of abrupt changes in relative value can create an environment antithetical to FDI or foreign transactions in general.

* Diminished ability to borrow abroad (2,7)

Serious economic problems are indicated by difficulty for a country in borrowing abroad. A country's inability to borrow is shown by an attempt at debt rescheduling which pushes repayment to a later date. In some circumstances, the host country's total burden of external debt is too high for the level of exports to support and a moratorium or a rescheduling is inevitable. A government can find itself unable to roll over existing debts. A low level of host country external reserves and a high degree of debt overextension may create an unfavourable investment climate for FDI operations (Nagy 1979).

* Infrastructure deficiencies (0,3)

Miller (1992) highlights as potential problems inadequate provision of public services and facilities by the host country. There may be unanticipated power cuts, breakdowns in communication or even shortages of water, an increasing problem in many countries. Such inadequacies may have serious negative implications for investment productivity, forcing the reallocation of some investment funds to an improvement in infrastructure.

- Bureaucratic delays (0,5)

Approvals and the adherence to regulation often involve unexpected delays, both to the construction of new facilities and the operation of existing ones. The way in which particular regulations are administered may be a source of risk. There may be a deliberate halt or slowdown in foreign managerial and technical transfers imposed by relevant governmental institutions.

Financial risk

Financial risk comprises unpredicted changes in creditworthiness, including sovereign risk, both the danger of default and an unexpected increase in the size of the loss given default. This is of less relevance to FDI than often thought, except where there is portfolio investment linked with the direct investment. Creditworthiness is of indirect relevance in that it may indicate a starting point for a risk premium for a particular country. An unexpected fall in creditworthiness may be associated with two outcomes in particular:

- Restriction/difficulties in access to credit and the capital market (2,6)

Availability is as important as price. In some circumstances, it may be impossible to borrow at all. The liquidity of foreign subsidiaries may be threatened by such restrictions (Stobaugh 1969 and Hashmi and Guvenli 1992).

- Vulnerability in credit rating (3,5)

A country's creditworthiness indicates how easily a country can get loans at a reasonable cost, if at all. A country's credit rating may also show how well the host country is able to attract or generate other types of capital to finance a firm's day-to-day operations (Rummel and Heenan 1978). A low rating, one less than the conventional investment level, and/or a highly fluctuating rating, describes a risky and unstable operational environment for the country's financial institutions and therefore for foreign enterprises undertaking FDI (Nagy 1979).

Cultural risk

Misunderstanding the influence of specific cultures on the patterns of business behaviour, including selling, consuming and negotiation, is another source of risk. The two main sub-components are transaction cost uncertainties which arise because of nepotism, corruption or excessive bureaucratisation, and negotiation uncertainties, which arise from ignorance of how to interpret what is offered.

- Ignorance of the patterns of business behaviour (0,1)

When MNEs do business overseas they have to live with a degree of risk deriving from ignorance of the host countries' culture combined with significant differences in business behaviour (Dunn 1983).

- Language barriers (1,2)

The same words do not have the same meaning in different languages. This may lead to basic misunderstandings. It is difficult to communicate effectively even if there are translators. Understanding high context communication may be a particular problem.

- Ethnic/religious tensions (1,5)

The world is divided by major religions, which have their own sub-divisions. Some of the bitterest conflict in the world is based on religious difference. Huntington (1996) projected religion as a focal point of future conflict. Kennedy (1987) argued that the higher the diversity of the population, the more likely it is that the demand of some groups will not be met. Examples of countries that suffer from internal fractionalisation include India, Israel, Ireland, the Republic of Congo, South Africa and Indonesia. Green (1972) argues that ethnic and religious conflict can have as an outcome an irregular turnover of government.

- Corruption and nepotism (0,3)

What is defined as corruption differs from one society to another. The payment of bribes imposes an additional cost on international business. It is often difficult to employ the most suitable candidate for a job because of nepotism. Rent-seeking behaviour creates significant uncertainty about cost levels.

- Differences in negotiating styles (0,1)

Different cultural perspectives affect the way in which negotiations are conducted in different countries. Such negotiations can have unexpected outcomes. For firms engaging in overseas investment, there is the issue of when to use Western or to use local rules.

The conceptual framework of country risk

On the basis of the analysis above it is possible to define three levels of components of country risk and therefore to break that risk into components, sub-components and sub-sub-components. The latter distinction is based partly on the number of references by experts and rating agencies in the analysis above, but also on the nature of some elements as special cases of the broader elements, that is significant potential overlapping. Not all the elements referred to above are of equal standing.

The figure on the following page summarises the conceptual framework of country risk, providing a full taxonomy. It is consistent with the work of Miller (1992), criticisms of that work (Werner and Brouthers 1996; Shrader et al. 2000) and with the 26 sub-components identified above.

Assessment: weighting and the use of quantitative proxies

The aim of the present exercise is to provide a template for measuring country risk, a check list of components which should be weighted to provide a country risk score. The main aim is to develop the means to estimate a generic country risk rating for all countries, including in the appraisal of any particular investment project that of both home and host countries. It is common to score risk out of 100. There are advantages in having an exact score, not the least of which is that it is easy to estimate a ratio of host to home country risk. Although the scoring may indicate an illusory degree of precision, such a scale helps in the measurement of risk and its incorporation into an investment appraisal. Rating indexes differ according to whether a higher score means more or less risk. The Euro-money index indicates a higher risk by a lower score, whereas Moosa (2002) is strongly in favour of a scale which rises with the level of risk. This is logical since the focus is on risk. From the perspective of such a ratio, it is better to have a scale which rises with the level of risk. This is easily achieved by subtracting the score from 100.

In all cases, it is better to avoid redundancy. If possible, there should be a single indicator for each sub-component. In the case of qualitative factors, the use of the Delphi method allows the judgements of experts

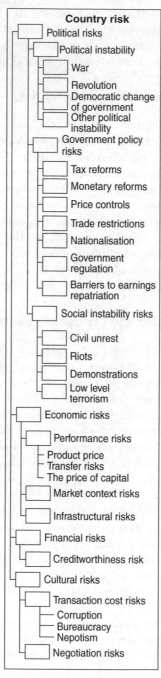

Figure 9.1   A typology of country risk

to be given a quantitative form. For economic or financial risk it is not difficult to find quantitative indicators; the important issue is choice of an appropriate indicator. There should be a good theoretical justification for each components of country risk which can then be scored out of hundred. This requires a weighting of the relevant sub-components. The weightings, rather like price weightings in measures of output, may change as the risk environments change and the sensitivity to those environments of decision makers also changes. In theory, there should be an occasional re-weighting of different components, but there is much advantage in stable weights.

In the case of an obvious overlapping between different sub-components, or even components, the elements having a significant correlation need to be fused. It is necessary to define the level of correlation between components beyond which this should occur. Where the correlation is negative, that is where one risk factor offsets another, this needs to be taken into account in an explicit way. In other words, the components are not simply additive as the account above implicitly assumes.

The country risk exposure of international investment projects

A generic country risk rating is a good starting point for an assessment of the risk relevant to a particular international project. It is an attempt to measure the risk which is systematic within any country, notably a potential host country. In order to make such a measure, it is necessary to apply a common set of weights to the components for all countries. The home and host countries are the ones most relevant to an investment decision and therefore the ratio between the relevant generic risk ratings is likely to be of great interest.

As will be shown in the next chapter, there is probably no universal system of rating relevant to all investment projects: even the rating agencies differ in their willingness to use a single quantitative index with a single set of weights. In practice, the weighting may be specific to a particular kind of investment in a particular kind of country. Rating agencies allow for this. It may be necessary not just to differentiate by groups of countries or even by country but to differentiate by the nature of the assets exposed to risk. It is better to do this after the estimation of generic country risk. This is a matter to be considered in the estimation of specific risk.

It is clear that certain risk components are likely to be a consistently more significant source of risk than others in groups of countries with significant common characteristics, such as the level of economic development. For example, it is highly likely that political component is more important in developing countries and the economic component in developed countries. There is a often a focus on the investment made by the enterprises of developed countries in developing or undeveloped countries. There is also an interesting literature on a concept parallel to that of country risk, country vulnerability, and the construction of a vulnerability index relevant to small countries (Chander 1996; Briguglio 1997; Atkins, Mazzi and Ramlogan 1998; and United Nations (1997). The literature relates in particular to small island countries. It shows a much higher level of vulnerability of small countries as against large countries. It measures the level of output variability and seeks the reasons for this in three main elements – economic exposure, usually measured by export dependency and export diversification; remoteness and insularity; and proneness to environmental events and hazards, i.e. natural shocks (Atkins, Mazzi and Ramlogan 1998; chapter 6).

There are three problems which need to be addressed. The first relates to what is being measured. There is some disagreement in the literature over whether the analysis is concerned with possible deviations from what is expected or with overall variability, whatever the expectations (Miller 1998: 507–508). Sensible approaches deal only with the unanticipated changes in variables (Gangemi et al. 2000: 267–8). The country risk index should be a measure of the risk of the unexpected happening, notably when it results in a downside impact. There are alternative measures for the unexpected – the relative level of the risk index for the different countries in which a project might be located, the change in such an index over time for one particular country, or the migration of the index from one level of risk to another, that is a significant shift in the perceived riskiness of a country (Nordal 2001: 80). The possibility of the latter two events occurring should be incorporated in the level of the country risk index. The possibility of a major change in the relevant risk level must be taken into account.

A second problem is that all types of risk depend for their impact on context; in that sense, risk is of its nature specific. While it is true that a whole host of environmental factors influence the 'risk intensity factor' (Clarke 1997), that is, the context either heightens or lessens particular threats depending on its nature, only when this environment changes significantly and unexpectedly can such changes themselves be a source of risk. While expected change can never be a source of risk, such a change, although contextual, can increase the vulnerability to particular kinds of risk, while not itself constituting a risk-generating event. Again this is something which must be addressed in the assessment of specific risk.

A third issue is even more significant. With country risk and all other types of risk it is important to consider the degree to which it is possible to mitigate risk. One significant advantage of the check list approach is that it shows where this might be possible and where it will produce the largest results. Given the importance of learning it may be that the potential for mitigation is much larger than often thought. Learning is also dynamic in that it occurs continuously. It is therefore necessary to separate the outcome of learning from any risk analysis. Chapter 11 pays particular attention to this issue.

10
Enterprise and Project Risk

> Despite its importance to economic growth and market struc-
> ture, the investment behaviour of firms, industries, and coun-
> tries remains poorly understood.
>
> (Pindyck 1991: 1110)

The final chapter in this section returns to the enterprise level and to
the components/sub-components of enterprise risk, and through enterprise risk to project risk. The focus of any decision maker is the total risk
which confronts the enterprise and which is relevant to the investment
decision under analysis. Any enterprise in making an investment decision is faced by two different kinds of risk, the element of generic or
systematic risk filtered from higher levels, considered in the previous
two chapters, and the element of risk specific to the enterprise. Whatever the exact source the broader types of risk impinge on the enterprise
or project in highly specific ways.

The implication of the analysis is that the template for risk, not just
the values fed into the formula, differs from one enterprise to another
and from one project to another. The combination of risk environments and therefore components and sub-components to which the
enterprise is exposed differs from one enterprise to another for a whole
range of reasons. Each situation is unique. The implications for any
particular project and its evaluation are the same, that there must
be allowance made for the uniqueness of the circumstances. This is the
reason why specific risk differs from generic risk and merits a separate
treatment.

There are six sections in this chapter:

• The first section discusses the nature of both enterprise and project risk.

- In the second section there is an analysis of the unsystematic risk specific to the enterprise and how to classify such risk.
- In the third section the notion of the risk filter is introduced, indicating the way in which the higher levels of systematic risk influence the risk exposure of the enterprise.
- Section four presents an overall classification of risk and considers the way in which the different types of risk interact with each other.
- In the fifth section there is a discussion of possible groupings of projects or enterprises which experience similar risk contexts.
- The final section begins the integration of risk measures into the appraisal of an investment project.

The nature of enterprise and project risk

The aim of this chapter is to examine the nature of project risk. It does this in the context of enterprise risk, that is of risk which is specific to the enterprise. Such risk takes two forms – the risk which arises only at the enterprise level and the risk which is filtered down to the enterprise from higher levels. Core enterprise risk can be defined as 'the potential negative impact on a key performance indicator of an enterprise, or the performance of a strategic target, arising from unanticipated events and/or changes of behaviours which are specific and internal to that enterprise'. The second kind of risk arises outside the enterprise, but interacts with the internal risk to help shape the overall risk environment. The definition of the relevant risk changes to 'the potential negative impact on a key performance indicator of an enterprise, or the performance of a strategic target, arising from unexpected events or behavioural changes which are specific but external to the enterprise'. The source could be either country or industry risk, even global risk. The problem is the interaction or overlapping between these different types of risk.

The enterprise has built a set of resources, capabilities and competencies which assist it to identify, assess, measure and respond to the relevant risk, mitigating that risk where appropriate. The level of risk affects the valuation of the enterprise. These considerations also apply at the level of the project. Any enterprise consists of a set of projects at various stages of development. In the words of one commentator, 'the firm can be thought of as a portfolio of projects or assets' (Rogers 2002: 12). In a simple additive world, it is just a matter of adding up all the present values created by the net income streams generated by the projects or assets linked to them. If the streams generated by one project can be valued, the aggregate can be valued. The aim of any strategy is to maximise the value created by all the projects. The sum of the parts may be greater than that of the individual units. Projects by extending the range of assets available to the enterprise to be used as inputs in other projects increase the overall value of the enterprise. Introducing a new project can have an impact on the value of other existing projects, and of course future projects. It is necessary to take account of this interdependency.

The problems of identifying and measuring risk multiply as we move from generic risk to the risk specific to a particular project.

- Overlapping and interdependencies become more common. These increase with the range of risk types to be dealt with, including both industry risk and the risk specific to the enterprise and its projects.
- It is necessary to consider possible diversification benefits, since any project can reduce risk in a portfolio of projects whereas standing on its own it may have a higher risk than is actually the case, as part of a portfolio.

There is no choice at this level except to make an in-depth qualitative assessment of project risk with the aim of estimating a ratio of the relevant risk to that generic to a particular country (or for that matter to a particular industry). The relevant question is, is this project riskier than the comparison of the host country to home country generic risk suggests? The project risk ratio may be greater or less than one. For example, the diversification benefits and positive effects of overlapping may outweigh any tendency for a wider range of risk types to increase the ratio. The ratio may therefore be significantly less than one.

Any project brings its own set of risks with it but they are experienced in the context of existing enterprise risk. Two main issues are raised in this chapter:

- how is it possible to conceptualise the relevant risk environment which has an impact on a given investment project? How is it possible to do this in a way which makes easier the estimation of a ratio of project to generic country risk?
- are there patterns of risk exposure which allow us to group enterprises, or even investment projects, according to the nature of their risk environments, or according to their risk ratios?

A conceptual framework of enterprise risk

First, it is necessary to consider a taxonomy of enterprise risk, that is the range of components which constitute enterprise risk. The figure below summarises the framework of specific enterprise risk, without consideration of the risk filtered from higher levels. Once more Miller (1992) is an initial source for an appropriate classification. His classification is modified to take account of other treatments in the relevant literature. As the figure suggests there are three different components of 'core' enterprise risk – the operational, financial and behavioural components. These are defined in such a way as to make this risk specific to the enterprise, comprising all aspects of the operation of an enterprise; however, the template deliberately minimises the overlap with the types of risk already discussed, notably industry risk.

The nature of the enterprise determines the risk components. For example, for a bank or credit institution credit risk is an obvious and important component of operational risk. In this case, creditworthiness is an attribute of the service or product provided by the bank. The creditworthiness of the bank is itself an issue relevant to those borrowing from the bank. Even more important for an enterprise is its ability to borrow, both in terms of availability of funds and the price of those funds. The credit rating of an enterprise is an important determinant of the cost of its capital and indirectly of the price of its shares. There is an enormous literature on credit risk and a whole range of different ways of measuring such risk.

The first component, operational risk, can be broken down into various sub-components – labour, input supply risk, and production risk. The first refers to the problems posed by a possible change in the attitudes and morale of the enterprise's labour force. These may be manifested through a sudden onset of strikes or the appearance of poor labour morale causing a high rate of absenteeism or labour turnover. The motivation of the labour force is a critical element in determining both productivity levels and changes in those levels over time. The capacity of the enterprise to innovate and keep ahead of its competitors reflects the empowerment of its labour force. This applies at all levels of the enterprise. Risk arises from an unexpected and unanticipated change in that labour context, which might result from a change in the aims of the trade unions operating within the enterprise or from the reaction of workers to a change in government legislation relating to working conditions. It might even be a reaction to a change of strategy formulated by the managers.

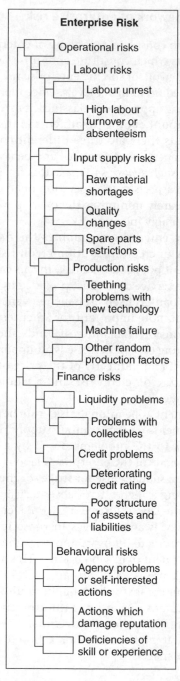

Figure 10.1   A typology of enterprise risk

The second operational item refers to both qualitative and quantitative problems with the supply of raw materials, components or even necessary equipment. This refers to the situation of specific suppliers. A supplier can get into difficulties for a host of reasons outside the control and even knowledge of the relevant enterprise. Often it is argued that vertical integration allows control over such suppliers and a reduction in this kind of risk. There are industry supply problems and problems of supply specific to the relevant enterprise.

The third operational item refers to the technological problems which arise when new technology is introduced, although technological difficulties also arise when existing equipment fails. The latter is probably more unusual than the former. It is impossible to anticipate all the problems created by the application of a new technology. Teething problems are very common. The individual capacity of enterprises to master particular technologies varies. The residual sub-component has particular reference to services which have different operational modes from manufacture and in which the operational items have a different role.

The financial risk component can be broken down into two main components – liquidity and credit risk, but with the latter viewed from the perspective of the borrowing enterprise. It comprises those difficulties which arise from either a limited supply of liquid assets to meet immediate obligations or from a limited ability to borrow, often worsened by the existing structure of assets and liabilities. A change in market liquidity, that is the ability to convert certain assets into cash, may be the source of the trouble. Much of the analysis of risk in the existing literature focuses on these elements. Liquidity risk is commonly separated out as an independent risk type.

The final component comprises agency problems, actions which can damage reputation or actions which reflect a lack of experience in the labour force, notably the managers of the enterprise. They arise because it is impossible to anticipate the way in which specific conflicts of interest arise between different stakeholder groups. There is a continuous process of negotiation over the distribution of both risk and value to these groups. Whatever is done gives signals to all the stakeholders concerning the economic health of the enterprise. Not all contingencies can be anticipated, nor can the response to such contingencies by the relevant stakeholder groups. Some actions involve sudden changes in reputation.

Each of these components of risk affects an enterprise in a different way. They reflect the nature of the organisation, its history and current personnel. They are for that reasons highly idiosyncratic. The same exercise can be carried out for any project undertaken by the relevant enterprise. An enterprise, unless it is a conglomerate, has core activities and core products. Any project is likely to be in the core area. The taxonomy discussed above is directly relevant to any such project. The situation is more complicated for a conglomerate, since the relative importance of different elements in the taxonomy is likely to differ from business unit to business unit.

The conceptual framework of all risk

The analysis of the last three chapters can be incorporated into a single diagram which shows a comprehensive framework for dealing with the different types of risk which confront an enterprise and which are relevant to any investment decisions made by the decision makers in that enterprise. This could be considered as a check list of what components might be relevant in any overall risk assessment. The diagram also shows how risk at higher levels is filtered down into risk at the enterprise level.

There are a number of implications which can be drawn from the analysis above:

- the diagram shows clearly that risk is a complex notion, one not easily reduced to a simple treatment
- it also reveals that any categorisation implicitly downplays overlapping, or co-variance
- that the risk is highly specific to particular enterprises and to particular times

However risk is defined, there is considerable overlapping both vertically, between different levels of risk, and horizontally, between different types and components of risk. The risk environment, with associated co-variances in its various components, is unique to a particular enterprise and to a particular project.

The work of this book is based on rejection of the notion that environmental uncertainty is a single, uni-dimensional construct. Managers perceive their environments to consist of distinct components of risk (Miller 1993: 699), as the analysis above emphasises, but which levels are the most important in individual cases varies. It is possible that perceptions differ from manager to manager according to their own experience, their functional area or even according to differing national tolerances of ambiguity (Miller 1993: 696).

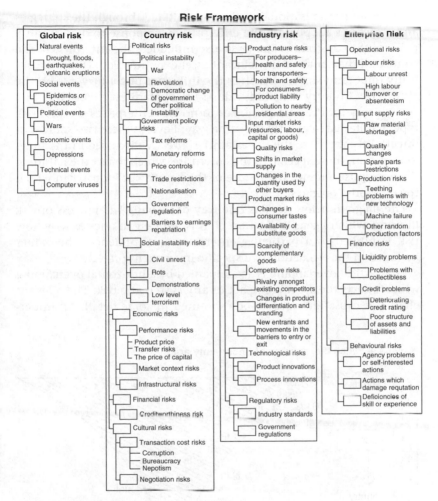

Figure 10.2 A typology of investment risk
Source: Compiled for the research

The risk filter

The most difficult element in the categorisation of enterprise risk, the external risk arising from global, country and industry uncertainties, affects the enterprise filtered through various constraints and contexts. In particular, there are the constraints on investment decision making already discussed, notably those which are cognitive or informational, strategic and organisational. Risk comes filtered through the strategies and structures adopted by the enterprise in response to opportunity, risk and the constraints. Such risk also influences the enterprise in the context of the nature of the relevant asset exposure. For FDI this is critically important since it involves the influence of country risk on the enterprise. Country risk, and industry risk, manifest themselves in a specific way for the enterprise. For in no two enterprises is either risk type manifested in exactly the same way. Beyond these two sources of uncertainty there are the uncertainties already discussed in the previous section, those specific to the enterprise, which reflect the nature of the enterprise and not the nature of the country or industry in which the enterprise operates.

The diagram below depicts one way of viewing the process of risk filtering, which likens it to a funnel. It is not easy to trace exactly how risk is filtered to a particular enterprise and influences the values included in the evaluation of a specific investment project.

The vertical overlapping is accompanied by a horizontal overlapping which affects the specific impact of any systematic risk. The relevant chains of causation need to be examined in some detail. An under-

Levels at which the sources of uncertainty arise

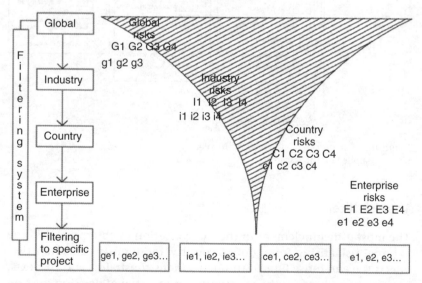

Figure 10.3   The filtering process
Source: Compiled for the research, adapted from Torre and Neckar, 1988.

standing of causation improves both the identification and assessment of risk. This is an interesting focus for further research.

Country risk is divided into the four components (the big C's) and each component is divided into sub-components (the small c's) and in their turn each of these is divided into sub-sub-components (the cc's). The same applies to both global and industry risk. The different kinds of risk are filtered to specific enterprises as highly specific risk elements – global enterprise (i.e. with an appropriate number), industry enterprise (i.e. with an appropriate number) and country enterprise (i.e. with an appropriate number). The general becomes the specific in a process of disaggregation. The filtering can be continued to the level of a project.

Different patterns of risk

A qualitative in-depth assessment of project risk reveals the weightings of relevant components and sub-components. A check list may familiarise the decision makers with the kind of risk factors which need to be considered but the weightings follow from the specific circumstances of a given investment – the time and place of a specific project. Any weighting may vary from enterprise to enterprise and from investment project to investment project. This is inevitable since the influence of mitigation will vary from enterprise to enterprise. The aim is to adjust any generic country score according to the nature of the project by asking:

- Is the project directed at sales on the local market or at generating exports?
- What is the nature of the assets which might be at risk? Are they tangible and therefore vulnerable or are they intangible?
- Which stakeholders are threatened by country risk?
- Are there natural risk hedges, e.g. assets and liabilities, or incomes and costs designated in the same currency? What scope is there for mitigation in general?

The answer to such questions builds up a profile of the risk to which an investment project exposes the enterprise. It is wise to consider the assets which are at risk and help define the exposure. A tangible asset which is immobile, conspicuous and easy to codify, such as a mine or a hydro power station, is much more vulnerable than an intangible asset which is mobile, difficult to identify and impossible to fully codify, such as the ability to brand a product or the ability to relate new technology to specific circumstances, as in developing new software. It is important also to consider the identity of the stakeholders and the nature of their interests in the project. Risk sensitivity of the managers is an issue which should be separated as much as possible.

A particular risk environment creates a differing risk exposure. The patterns of risk exposure differ markedly from enterprise to enterprise, and therefore from project to project. The way in which sources of risk combine differs from enterprise to enterprise. It is also the case that the assets created and exploited in any investment project differ markedly. Therefore, exposure reflects a number of different factors:

- the nature of the activities pursued and the assets required to support those activities,
- the size of an investment and its prominence or visibility,
- the speed of change, and volatility in that rate of change, in a given sector of the economy,
- the degree of competition, both within the host economy and from outside that economy,
- the nature of the host economy – is it developed or not? Is it developing and how fast is it developing?
- the degree of familiarity decision makers have with a particular economy.

These factors influence the relevant mix of risk types and the mix of components within those risk types. The analysis below discusses in more detail these issues one by one. The stress is very much on the international aspect of FDI.

The nature of activities and assets

Any enterprise is identified by the nature of its main activities and of the assets which support those activities. There are features of the assets which are important in influencing the nature of the risk exposure and the level of any relevant risk.

- The distinction between tangible and intangible assets. The assets of any enterprise are a mixture of tangible and intangible resources. Such resources define the potential capabilities of the enterprise and together with strategy its core competencies. Risk threatens the value of these resources in different ways according to the nature of the resources.

- The mobility or immobility of the assets. Those assets which are immobile are much more vulnerable. It is impossible to move a mineral deposit and very difficult to move a factory once it is constructed. However, most enterprise-specific assets are mobile.
- The ability to codify the assets, that is to spell out in detail exactly in what the assets consist.
- The marketability of the assets, meaning the marketability of the assets outside the host country.
- The appropriability of the assets and who owns the assets. Some assets are of their nature appropriable, others have the characteristics of a common good.

One way of classifying the risk is by sector of the economy. Clearly, the characterisation of the relevant products or services in terms of the assets which are critical inputs differs markedly from sector to sector. It is much easier for an enterprise to mitigate core risk, since the enterprise has a competitive advantage in certain activities and significant insider knowledge about associated risk factors. If insider knowledge is the main asset it is difficult to expropriate that asset.

Size of commitment

There is a non-linearity in the vulnerability to risk related to size of commitment, whether measured by the size of investment or by some other indicator such as total sales. There is a threshold both in the level of activity of an enterprise and in the size of any individual project beyond which both become visible and a potential target for negative actions, notably by government and those associated with government. Offsetting this is the fact that the bigger is an enterprise, the greater is its negotiating strength; it has more financial clout and a greater ability to mobilise the home government in its defence.

Certainly, large enterprises devote many more resources to risk assessment and are much more likely to have a formal risk assessment function (Fan 2004). This is probably just as much because they have access to larger resources than smaller enterprises, as because they are more vulnerable. It is highly likely that they have a greater incentive to commit those resources because of the prominence of their investment. They may also have an added incentive to find a partner, hence the importance of joint ventures.

Rates of change and cycles

Uncertainty arises from the possibility of unanticipated change. Any unanticipated change creates risk. It is paradoxical that the rapid rate of economic change which underpins economic development itself creates risk. Such change always occurs in an unstable way, often in surges. Technical change creates new capital but destroys the old. Risk is the other side of the coin to opportunity. Uncertainty and risk are inherent in economies or sectors of an economy which display a capacity for significant innovation. The more rapid the rate of change, the greater the risk inherent in the process of change and the greater the need to control that risk. It is never possible to predict the exact rate of change.

Exposure to risk is the result of a path dependent process specific to an enterprise. Modern economies see the rapid rise and fall of different products. Risk fluctuates according to the place in the product cycle at which a particular product has arrived. The rise and fall of different products is linked with that of different industries. There is always a new economy emerging, but the rate of emergence is not fully fore-seen. Industries also change their nature. Technical change is never easily predicted for the rapidly growing new sectors of the economy. Just as industries rise and fall, so does the performance of different economies. This is best shown by the behaviour of rates of growth of GDP over time. Economic performance is sometimes closely linked with political risk.

Degrees of intensity of competition

Depending on the competitive structure of an industry there is likely to be significant strategic risk, which follows from the interaction of the different players operating in the relevant markets. The size of the players at the global level has tended to increase. Even to protect their own domestic markets it is often necessary for the large multinational players to have an international presence. If foreign economies are open to competition, then it is difficult to avoid a high degree of risk.

Strategies can differ. In some cases, there are distinct advantages in being first with an investment, a situation which reduces the value of the option to delay. There are significant first-mover advantages. Many enterprises try to get into new and potentially important markets ahead of other players. There is a race to be first. In some cases, the enterprises entering a new market are prepared to make losses for a lengthy period of time. In other cases, it is perceived by important players as better to wait. There are significant first-mover disadvantages. The market share achieved will reflect the strategy adopted and the revenue stream will reflect the market share. If all players try to enter simultaneously, then the risk level is high. Market shares may be low and loss-making common. The beer industry in China is a good case. Since there is an indeterminateness about the responses of other strategic players, the revenue and cost streams depend critically on the responses made in particular circumstances: they cannot be predicted with any exactness. These considerations are even more important at the international level.

It is true that a step up in the level of globalisation increases for a period of time the intensity of competition, although the iron law of oligopoly will almost certainly reassert itself in the future. For a period there may be an increase in the number of players and even an acceleration in the rate of innovation in an industry.

Developed and developing countries

It is reasonable to assume that some parts of the world are markedly and persistently riskier than others. The estimates of rating agencies such as Euro-money show very pronounced differences in the perceived level of country risk and in the stability of those perceived levels of risk (see chapter 11). Those which fall at the extreme of a high risk rating and/or extreme volatility in such rating are infrequently the recipients of FDI.

On the assumption that any weighting of country risk is likely to elevate political risk as the most important component of country risk, the strength and role of government becomes important. In the absence of the infrastructure supporting market activity the role of the government is accentuated. In the end it is true that, in the words of one commentator, 'Political risk is the restraining force in the foreign investment process while return on investment is the driving force.' In undeveloped countries, the return is likely to be low unless the project is a resource or energy project, but it is also true that the government is likely to be weaker and more fickle. Therefore, developing countries are likely to be characterised by more threatening risk environments, with a mix of the political to the economic component of country risk which is greater than in less risky countries. By contrast, in developed countries often ruled by a strong element of consensus, political risk is less important than economic risk. To some degree, this is reinforced by the nature of investments in developing and undeveloped countries which often take the form of resources projects with highly visible and vulnerable assets. They can be confiscated easily or have high levels of

tax imposed on them. Because they are more visible and more immobile they are much more vulnerable, particularly to governments
seeking additional sources of revenue and to rent-seeking activity on
the part of individuals using the government for private purposes.

It is not simply a matter of the level of development. Countries also
sustain very different rates of economic development. Those growing
quickly have certain advantages. Growth generates tax revenue and
also weakens the tendency to rent-seeking behaviour by allowing all to
share in the incremental income generated by development. Any divergence in growth rates is relevant to the level of risk. A significant but
stable growth rate is good for risk. A high but fluctuating growth rate
can cause problems. It has a negative consequence in causing expectations not to be realised. Any change of pace affects the level of risk, for
example markets do not develop in the way expected. Those countries
which are growing rapidly often attract investment which is made in
expectation of, and in advance of, market growth.

The implication of this analysis is that it is highly likely that there
are clusters of countries with similar risk levels and clusters of enterprises operating in the same sectors of the economy with similar asset
exposures. This is reinforced by the following feature.

Familiarity with different economies

There are various sources of familiarity. It is almost invariably true that
decision makers fear the unknown. The more they know about risks
the less they have to fear. The most obvious source of familiarity is a
previous project which is located in the country under consideration
for a new project. A long history of previous activity in a host economy
usually means a comprehensive familiarity with institutions and
behavioural patterns. The experience of having gone through the same
process of evaluation before certainly helps the assessment of risk. It
enables the decision makers to be much more confident of the nature
of the risk profile of the relevant country. Geographical proximity is
another aspect of familiarity (gradient theories of trade and investment
explain a significant part of that trade or investment – see Helliwell),
but much more important is a shared cultural background which itself
may result from a shared history and a shared language.

This stress on familiarity usually implies considerable insider information and a greater ability to mitigate risk, if only by negotiating
with government and key local organisations. Just as an enterprise may
have a competitive advantage in certain industrial activities it may also
have a competitive advantage in operating in certain economies.

How to quantify enterprise and project risk

This section has established a way of classifying the different kinds of risk to which any foreign investment project is exposed; there is a clear typology or taxonomy of all the different types of risk, including country risk. Such a classification should help in the description and analysis of relevant risk environments and eventually in the measurement of the risk found in those environments. It provides the basis for a check list of relevant components for both generic risk, such as country risk, and the specific risk associated with a particular international investment project. This is the first step necessary in the incorporation of risk in the valuation of any project and in the elaboration of a decision rule on making such an investment.

There are two significant results of the analysis so far. Firstly, there is a means of calculating a generic risk measure, whether for country or for industry risk. In the case of international business, the generic measure most commonly referred to and used is that of country risk. In other work, the focus might be on industry risk. It is possible to estimate an ordinal measure which can be used to indicate the relative generic country risk level between the host and the home countries, although there exists no absolute measuring unit. It is possible to make a relative measure of the country risk in the relevant economies.

Secondly, there is also a means for measuring the risk specific to a particular project. This is more complicated than estimation of a generic country risk level. The taxonomy, and therefore the check list, is much broader. It includes the influence of industry risk. Such an estimate requires an in-depth qualitative assessment. This is a necessary preliminary to estimating the ratio of project risk to generic risk for an international project. It is not difficult to see a relationship of this kind as beta like, in other words to see the former as related to the latter. A particular project for a given enterprise may involve more or less risk than the generic level for the host country. However, it is not based on market returns as a conventional beta analysis is, although any information provided by the market may be useful in making this estimate. It is probably better not to confuse the issue by using the beta term. Conventionally, the divergence between specific project risk and generic risk is measured in the home, not the host country. This is because it is likely that markets are more developed in the home country, but it is a mistake.

There are areas of omission. The analysis tells us nothing about the risk tolerances of the decision makers, nor does it distinguish carefully between the risk exposures and tolerances of different stakeholders – in other words, whose risk tolerance is the critical one. It does not consider in any depth what assets are at risk and how this might affect the measurement. Quite rightly, it sees these issues as separate from the main analysis, although they should all be part of a proper in-depth assessment of project risk.

There are a number of significant problems which need to be addressed after the identification and classification of the different types of risk and before it is possible to indicate how the evaluation of an investment project might proceed. The first is to ask the relationship between a generic measure of country risk and a measure of project risk. The first applies to any investment in a particular country. The second is highly specific. In the latter case it is reasonable to ask how far it is possible, and even desirable, to move beyond an in-depth qualitative assessment of a particular project, in which there are elements which need to be considered separately and then weighed against each other. There is no doubt that this assessment is time consuming and expensive. It cannot be repeated frequently. Given the complexity of the risk environments described above, it is likely to demand the full-time activity of a group of specialists over a period of months rather than weeks. This leaves unanswered the problem of review of a project after its implementation or of monitoring the risk level to which that project is exposed in later years. The key issue is how far the assessment needs to be up-dated in the later monitoring of projects which have already been approved. Can the generic risk measure be used for such a monitoring purpose?

It is also interesting how far the assessment is useful in the assessment of other projects. There are advantages in pooling such knowledge and in extending an expertise in this area. Since it is necessary to compare the relevant project, both with other projects and to assess the changing standing of the project as circumstances change over time, it is clearly preferable both to quantify and to reduce the assessment to a single measure which makes risk a comparative indicator, one which can be included neatly in any investment project evaluation. The emphasis is on comparison, so the assessments need to be carried out consistently.

A second associated problem is that this need for quantification requires the analyst to find proxies which provide a quantitative measure of all the relevant components and sub-components, which often of their nature have qualitative characteristics. It is better to apply this at the level of sub-components or sub-sub-components, the more specific they are the better. Once quantification is achieved at the lowest level the estimates can be aggregated to yield quantification at the higher levels. This may require the use of more formal techniques to identify relevant proxies, such as multivariate regression analysis. Such analysis considers a number of such proxies simultaneously, indicating which proxies are better at explaining the pattern of FDI flows. This analysis does not offer the final word since it is somewhat circular in its reasoning. The modelling is itself difficult. Economic risk lends itself most easily to this approach since it offers a large number of such quantitative indicators. Difficulties arise for political risk which is least amenable to quantitative analysis. The simplest technique is to use the Delphi method in which a group of experts on the political environment is asked to indicate the level of a particular component of risk on a scale which allows them to convert qualitative statements into quantitative ones, such as the Likert scale.

The third problem is to tackle the issue of weighting and how such weights might be estimated. Such weights can be common for the generic measures of different countries but may still change over time as the perception of risk itself changes. It is better to try to maintain a consistent set of weights for as long as possible. However, they will differ from enterprise to enterprise, and from project to project. The advantage of retaining a separation of the different elements is that it highlights the nature of any trade off which must be made; increasing risk in one area may diminish it in another. At all levels in the analysis there is a need for such weighting.

Regression analysis can give a clear indication of the relative significance of individual elements. However, the significance almost certainly changes over time and often in unexpected ways. It might be possible at the aggregate level to use multivariate regression analysis to derive weights which can be attached to different determinants of FDI, including country risk. By re-jigging according to a changing overall index, a best fit could be achieved, but the accuracy of the weightings depends on the specification of the other determinants. An alternative is to use survey information if it is available, that is information on how the decision makers themselves rate the importance of different elements. However, this raises the question – how do you recognise an optimum? Do managers make correct decisions on weighting? Does the market do this implicitly in a way which can be used to estimate weightings?

There are a number of different approaches to the quantification of risk. One is to use past data on the flows of FDI to test the predictive ability of any index of country risk. The whole process would involve a sophisticated and time-consuming process of iteration, improving in a qualitative manner the country risk index by re-jigging the weights at different levels and continuously testing and retesting the new index against actual flows of FDI. This is a lengthy process. Its major weakness is that it assumes that decision makers operate with a rational view about the choices they face, and that implicit in the actual flows is accurate information about the risk level. There is no reason why this should be so.

As the analysis above has shown, it is difficult to come up with a full quantification of the different types of risk. Having achieved such a quantification, it is difficult to weight the different types of risk and to adjust accordingly the values that go into the present value formula. Ideally, it is desirable to reduce everything to one formula, that is, to adjust the values put into the present value formula according to the level of risk. It is better to separate the two problems: the measure of country risk or project risk and the incorporation of that measure into the present value formula. The first task is difficult enough without fusing it with the even more difficult task of valuing a project.

An alternative approach is to have a different quantification for returns and for risk and to allow the managers to make a choice based on the trade-off between the two, according to their risk tolerance. After all, whatever method is used, there is an implicit trade-off, or in the case of the real options approach the establishment of an equivalence between a risk-free outcome and a risky one. In the end, this is what probably happens, but it is helpful to provide as much explicit information as possible.

Part IV

Responses to Risk and the Determinants of FDI

> Despite its importance to economic growth and market structure, the investment behaviour of firms, industries, and countries remains poorly understood.
>
> (Pindyck 1991: 1110)

There are two parts to this section of the book. The first chapter shows how to appraise an international investment project decision. The evaluation of decision rules and measurement systems for FDI requires a treatment different from that given to financial or portfolio investment. The FDI decision is viewed in the context of all the elements which influence the decision-making process and the potential success of any investment project. On the one hand these elements include the financial perspective, the strategic perspective, and the organisational perspective, on the other the relevant risk environments and the various opportunities for profit.

The analysis goes on to summarise the implications of the decision – making process for understanding the way in which country risk and the level and pattern of FDI interact at the macro level. If the influence of risk on the individual investment decision has been correctly understood, that influence will be reflected in the overall level of FDI, its movement over both the short and the medium to long term, and its pattern of distribution between countries or regions. The second chapter therefore considers; firstly, the way in which FDI has grown over time, fluctuates with the business cycle and is distributed between different countries, and secondly, explores possible explanations of these macro patterns, notably with the help of country risk.

11
Responses to Risk

> The aim is to establish a structure for decision-making that produces good decisions, or improved decisions, defined in a suitable way, based on a realistic view of how people can act in practice.
>
> (Aven 2003: 96)

The aim of the chapter is to show how an investment project can be appraised, taking into account all the complexities of decision making. Most of the book has been devoted to placing the investment decision in its appropriate contexts, and in delineating how to identify and conceptualise the various risk environments which confront decision makers. This chapter starts by considering the two stages required in incorporating risk into the valuation of an investment project, quantification of country risk and valuation of an investment project. It brings together the different approaches – financial, strategic and organisational, and the different risk environments, culminating in the statement of an expanded net present value formula and how to determine the inputs into such a formula.

There are six sections in this chapter:

- The first section considers two steps necessary for establishing the relationship between risk and the valuation of an investment project.
- Section two takes a financial perspective, showing how the present value formula might be adjusted to incorporate the various kinds of risk.
- In the third section there is a discussion of alternative approaches and the nature of a solution.

- The fourth section takes a strategic perspective, discussing risk control as part of the general strategy of the enterprise.
- The fifth section takes an organisational perspective, summarising how to incorporate the risk exposure of all stakeholders and strategic risk.
- The sixth reviews the expanded net present value formula.

The quantification of risk and valuation of an investment project

There are two stages in the incorporation of risk in the appraisal of an international investment project:

- developing a typology of the risk types relevant to a project (Miller 1992: Lessard 1996), whether it relates to country risk, some other risk type, or a combination of different risk types, and measuring the relevant risk level. This has been explored in chapters 8, 9 and 10,
- determining what adjustment should be made to the estimation of present value in order to allow for the risk confronting a specific project. The relevant analysis was begun in chapter 5.

The first has been more frequently attempted than the second, on which there is little relevant work (for exceptions see Miller 1998, Nordal 2001, Lessard 1996, Damodaran 2003). There are different approaches to linking the two stages:

- use an integrated method of valuation combining the two stages in one quantitative approach, which is what the international capital assets pricing model seeks to do,
- use separate quantitative measures for assessing risk and estimating a net present value but a qualitative technique for translating the former into the latter; probably the most common approach adopted in various forms in the work of Miller, Damodaran, Nordal and Lessard,
- use a combination of the quantitative and qualitative, most often the former for investment appraisal and latter for country risk; inevitable if it is impossible to quantify project risk,
- use an integrated qualitative approach specific to a particular project; this is the typical approach advocated by strategy theorists who see projects as part of a broader whole.

The attempt to reconcile the general and the specific has led to the adoption of two perspectives which have caused confusion in investment appraisal. The first is the focus on an enterprise rather than a project (Damodaran 2003). The second is the adoption of the financial investor perspective, rather than that of other important stakeholder groups, notably the senior managers directly responsible for the key 'real' investment decisions.

How to incorporate risk into an investment valuation

The mechanisms for incorporating risk into investment appraisal are three: adjust the discount rate, modify the cash flows, and/or add separate terms to the conventional net present value formula. Some commentators accept adjustment of the discount rate as the only legitimate way of taking account of country risk (Damodaran 2003). Analysis is then concentrated on how to select the discount rate, in theory a rate which varies from period to period according to the level of risk. Usually the relevant discount rate is taken to be the weighted average cost of capital.

The simplest assumption is that the enterprise is an all-equity enterprise and the project a stand alone one which is like a simple owner-controlled enterprise. The capital asset pricing model provides one means for the inclusion of risk in the cost of equity (Dumas 1993). Any asset (project), in a world of co-variation any portfolio containing such an asset, must yield an expected return greater than the risk-free return, plus a risk premium which compensates for systematic risk. The risk-free interest rate is sometimes defined as different for separate countries (Moosa 2002: 207–210), but this threatens to incorporate in the risk-free return an allowance for risk. There are two main elements in such a risk premium.

- a systematic market risk premium which is the excess return expected of that class of asset (Buckley 1996: chapter 4), relative to a risk-free return (usually taken as the rate for a New York treasury bill),
- a systematic enterprise-specific element, which reflects the degree to which the return moves with the market, or more precisely, the co-variance of a particular asset's return with respect to the market return, divided by the variance of the market return. It might increase or reduce the systematic market risk premium. The asset or portfolio beta is usually estimated from past data on returns or alternatively from any real characteristics deemed to impart a persistent and measurable divergence from the market level.

With an integrated world market the exercise would stop here. The market premium would be a world premium and the beta could be a country beta, which indicates the degree to which the country market diverges from the world market.

There are two problems with the analysis so far. The market risk premium suggested by the theory diverges badly from the actual premiums implicit in historical returns. There is considerable debate about this and a growing literature discussing the reasons for the divergence. Estimating the betas has its own difficulties. The beta could be estimated in the usual way or be a function of the numerous economic, political and financial variables discussed in the previous section of the book. The aim is to avoid redundancy so that sometimes there is an argument for only one significant variable, such as a trade weighted index (Gangemi et al. 2000: 260 and 274).

Unhappily there are significant limitations on the integration of the capital markets of the world, and it is unclear what a proxy for a world market should be, but the Morgan Stanley Capital International global stock index is often used for this purpose (Gangemi et al. 2000: 269). Most commentators reject the use of this model, some modifying it to take account of segmented markets.

It is necessary to add two risk elements:

- any non-systematic asset-specific risk independent of the behaviour of the market, which is not usually included in the risk premium since it is assumed that it can be managed away by diversification of assets,
- any risk arising from the international destination of an investment, that is country risk. Notionally it might be the divergence in returns of the relevant country market from the world market premium. Dumas (1993) extends the beta concept to include foreign exchange risk, seen as the core element of country risk. In his analysis there are separate betas to cover market risk and currency exposure risk. Multiple regression analysis allows simultaneous estimation of both.

The analysis sometimes reaches the unexpected conclusion that there is no reason to apply a higher discount rate to international projects than to domestic projects. 'At the very least .... when evaluating prospective foreign investments, executives of multinational firms should seriously question the use of a risk premium to account for the added political and economic risk of overseas operations' (Shapiro 1985b: 564). Most country risk is seen as unsystematic risk which should have no influence on discount rates since it is dealt with by diversification. If world markets are integrated, international projects add to both the number and independence of assets in a portfolio available to financial investors and make risk reduction by diversification easier to achieve. If the markets are segmented, they add to the range of choice indirectly through the ability of financial investors to make investments in the shares of multinational enterprises engaged in FDI. This is an oversimplification of the situation.

In such analysis the relevant 'market' premium is the typical risk premium of the home country, including an allowance for an enterprise or project beta, plus a specific but controversial allowance for country risk in the host country. It can be estimated in different ways.

The first approach uses past data to estimate a historical country risk premium. This is done either from country bond interest (default) spreads, or from a relative volatility measure. The former reflects a view of country risk as credit, or more specifically sovereign, risk in which a country is likened to an enterprise with a variable gearing ratio. The higher its debt level relative to GDP, the higher is the level of country risk, since it threatens higher interest rates, a greater likelihood of default and a decline in the relevant exchange rate (Gangemi et al. 2000: 260 and 264).

The latter can be either the relative standard deviations of returns in the home and host country markets or the debt spread multiplied by the relative standard deviation of returns for equity relative to debt in the host country. However, this is inadequate since the spread on bonds only takes into account the creditworthiness of government, not other aspects of country risk. The first and the second approaches can be melded together to give a fuller accounting (bond interest spread plus or times the relative standard deviation of equity returns).

The second approach is to use the implied premiums yielded by equity prices in current capital markets. The valuation of an enterprise reflects a notional dividend stream discounted at an implied return with the growth rate of future dividends subtracted. If there is adequate data on values, on dividend streams and their growth, an implied discount rate can be estimated. The advantage of such an approach, compared with the first approach, is that it looks forward rather than backwards.

This approach makes allowance for the divergence of enterprise experience from general market experience, but not for the divergence of project experience. It assumes all enterprises are exposed only to generic country risk. It does not make allowance for the way in which such risk is filtered to the enterprise and to the project. It is possible to introduce a concept parallel to the beta, a lambda, defined by a regression of the returns on the relevant stock on a government bond of the relevant country, or on any other measure of country risk (Damodaran 2003).

There are a number of general difficulties with these approaches.

- stability of the relevant elements

The usefulness of the analysis rests on the stability of the relevant betas and of the elements which determine the betas. One critical aspect of risk is the way in which returns move, as markets react to risk-generating events; the betas may not have stable annual values. For example, the beta for Australia over the period 1974 to 1994 is about 0.5, but rose dramatically to almost 4 at the time of the stock market crash in 1987 (Gangemi et al. 2000: 269–272). Even without the crash it moved in a way which involved outliers well below the average and well above the average (Gangemi et al. 2000: 272–274). A significant aspect of risk is proneness to a change in the level of risk itself.

For most indexes there is stability for low-risk developed and high-risk undeveloped economies, but marked instability for higher risk developing countries (Euro-money).This is reinforced by the absence of liquid markets in developing countries and of price and return data adequate to make the necessary calculations.

- estimating project betas

Valuation in the stock market is for the set of linked projects which make up the enterprise, rather than for an individual project. The same applies to the estimation of a beta or a lambda. It is necessary to adjust the enterprise beta for a specific project, often done on the basis of the beta for an enterprise with a single business unit closest to the project area.

There are two ways of estimating the beta for an international project (Lessard 1996: 58):

The direct way – regressing the returns on local shares against those on the home-market portfolio, and then adjusting for any significant differences in debt leverage for a particular project. Any gains or losses from debt financing can be included as a separate term in the conventional present value formula.

The indirect way – estimating the beta of the project relative to the local market portfolio (that is, the beta of a comparable home country project) and multiplying the result by a country beta. The country beta is often regarded as the product of the relative volatility of home and host markets and the correlation of the changes in value with the benchmark portfolio (Lessard 1996: 60). The use of the latter means that the potential to diversify where country risk is independent reduces the risk premium.

This is correct only if there is no correlation between the risk exposures of the project and of the benchmark home portfolio. This is likely to be true for developing economies where the market co-variance with any developed economy is likely to be small, but not for developed economies. For developing countries, even if relative volatility is very high, this is offset by the weak correlation in market performance between home and host countries which means that such country betas are generally low. For developed countries the volatility is less but the correlation stronger.

- the enterprise as a coalition of stakeholders and the incorporation of unsystematic risk

Many problems of the CAPM analysis follow from the assumption that the aim of any investment project is to maximise the value of the enterprise for its owners. This simple maximand fuses the problems of financial and physical assets, but investing in physical assets is not the same as investing in financial facilities. 'Buyers, suppliers, alliance partners, managers, and employees have sunk investments in firm-specific knowledge which tie a disproportionate share of their future earnings to the fate of the firm' (Miller 1998: 500). The portfolios of such stakeholders cannot be diverse, particularly government, which has the most domestically-focused portfolio (Miller op. cit.: 500).

There is also a problem where for some reason the owners do not hold a diverse portfolio. If shareholders cannot diversify in the way desired by CAPM, an enterprise should acquire a portfolio of unrelated assets, since any non-systematic risk will be diversified away by a careful choice of assets, provided that the portfolio is large enough. For example, it should sell its products in different countries. Whether country risk can be diversified away depends on how far the risk is regarded as unsystematic and whether there are enough countries to build an appropriate portfolio.

It is sensible to start with the assumption that in most periods country risk is unsystematic, but that it is impossible to create a large enough portfolio of independently performing assets, for the same reason that enterprises are often encouraged to focus on the core activities in which they have a competitive advantage. Diversification has costs which are often ignored and which limit how far it can go. Where it does occur and has a significant influence on the risk level, it should be taken into account.

Unsystematic risk affects the performance of an enterprise in a significant way, i.e. both profits and the achievement of strategic targets, and has an impact on its stakeholders, whose behaviour in turn affects the performance of the relevant enterprise. If it cannot, perhaps should not, be diversified away, non-systematic risk influences the value of the enterprise. There is always a competitive advantage in mitigating non-systematic risk, which allows the enterprise to make above-normal profits. The value of an investment project in the enterprise's area of competence is likely to be greater than for other enterprises operating outside that area (the first chapter of Culp 2001).

• a failure to take account of the different risk types in the valuation

The CAPM approach does not take into account all types of risk and does not consider how risk which arises at the industry or country level is filtered down to the project. It focuses solely on imperfect markets and reflects their imperfections. The fusion of risk assessment and valuation of the project obscures how risk influences decision making. It is critical to consider the source of risk and to examine all the relevant components in country risk, tracing the way in which they have an impact on the performance of the enterprise through a specific project.

Alternative approaches and a solution

There are three alternative approaches which offer possible solutions to these problems.

The first, *arbitrage pricing theory,* resting on the putative existence of efficient markets, argues that the CAPM beta is too narrow a measure of risk. It broadens the approach, recognising the existence of different risk factors which affect the valuation of a project. The relevant issues are:

• how to measure a relevant risk factor

The core difficulty in assessing the influence of risk is what proxies to use for the risk factors and how to weight them relative to each other and to other factors influencing the success of a project. The previous three chapters have set out a full taxonomy of risk and discussed how to produce a quantitative measure.

• how to estimate the relevant betas

These estimates provide a means of estimating hedge or delta ratios, which indicate the elasticities of enterprise value with respect to each independent risk factor (Miller 1998: 506–507), and can be used to compare projects, for example the same project in different locations, or to estimate the impact of a change in risk on a project. There are significant weaknesses in this approach. There may be no continuous trading in the relevant asset and an illiquid market, which means that any price is arbitrary. For most investment projects there is no marketable asset which directly reflects the value of the project – a proxy has to be found. It is not the value of the enterprise. This kind of analysis also looks backwards and does not allow for future changes in the betas (Nordal 2001: 6).

The formula for the change in the value of an enterprise or project is written:

$$= \beta 1(\text{risk factor } 1) + \beta 2(\text{risk factor } 2) \ldots + \beta N(\text{risk factor } N)$$

or it can be modified so that the formula for the expected return is:

$$= rf + p1b1(\text{first risk factor}) + p2b2 \text{ (second risk factor)} \ldots + pnBn$$
(final risk factor)

where the p's are risk premiums or market prices of risk (often written as Rm – Rf/ σm), the expected excess return above the risk-free rate when the relevant b = 1 and all other b's = 0.

and the b's are sensitivity coefficients, indicating the average response of the project return to an unexpected change in the relevant factor, holding all the other factors constant. They are rather like weights for individual risk factors.

• how to take account of co-variance between the risk factors

A significant degree of co-variance between the factors complicates the analysis considerably, but suggests that the assessment of country risk should be carried out in an integrated manner.

For those critical of both the CAPM and the APV approaches there is a second approach, which simplifies the decision rule as:

Max. $Vf = \sum Vi - P(\sigma)$

where Vf is the value of the firm, Vi the present value of each of the firm's divisions, strategic units or projects, and $P(\sigma)$ is a penalty factor representing the impact of total risk on the present value of relevant cash flows generated by the project. This approach is more realistic since it incorporates unsystematic risk, but how do you estimate the penalty excess? It can be viewed as a notional impact on cash streams which can be put together from the impact of the risk factors, designated by the b's above. There is still a problem of measurement.

The *real options* approach, sometimes called the contingent valuation approach, is a third approach to incorporating risk into an investment appraisal (Dixit and Pindyck 1994). It is also based on arbitrage theory and is tied to market valuations, in an attempt to minimise what is called basis risk, the failure of a particular market value to relate to the project under consideration. The higher the level of uncertainty and the greater the irreversible part of the investment, the greater is the opportunity cost of carrying out the investment at the current time. Such a cost can be added to the investment cost.

In such an approach the movement of the value of an investment is often represented by the equation:

$dV/V = \sigma dt + \sigma dt + dq$

where V is the value of the investment

There are two kinds of uncertainty. The variance parameter σ represents 'the day-to-day variation in the investment value' (Vonnegut 2000: 85), whereas the jump process, q, (the Poisson process), represents generally anticipated but specifically untimed 'major shifts in policy or economic structure', which are infrequent. This allow consideration of instability in key risk elements. The shock has a mean arrival time of λ, but the arrival date is only known stochastically. This will shift the value of the investment by a % factor π with probability π. In other words:

$$dq = \begin{cases} 0 \text{ with probability: } (1 - \lambda)dt \\ \theta \text{ with probability: } \pi\lambda dt \\ - \theta \text{ with probability: } (1 - \pi)\lambda dt \end{cases}$$

The model shows that the decision rule must be amended to say, invest if:

$$V > \text{or} = [\beta/\beta - 1] \, I$$

As β increases the rule converges on the usual decision rule, $V > \text{or} =$ I. The larger the uncertainty, the smaller is β and the larger is $\beta/\beta - 1$. β is in inverse relationship to σ, λ, θ and/or π, all elements of uncertainty. Greater uncertainty increases the opportunity cost of investing now rather than waiting. With any reasonable values the hurdle of net present value, multiplied by the opportunity cost factor, is twice the conventional hurdle (Dixit and Pindyck 1994: 153). This approach shows that it is much more difficult to justify immediate implementation of an investment project than the net present value formula suggests. It is also much more difficult to make a decisive rejection.

One significant weakness of this approach is what Mandron has called 'dumb scenario-forecasting' (Mandron 2000: 140), prompting him to continue '...the RO model does not in any way help identify specific plausible scenarios, corresponding cash flows and appropriate decisions: all are theoretically taken account of through the choice of a particular statistical process (e.g. a geometric Brownian motion), but none can be separately identified.' (Mandron op. cit.: 15). In the interests of retaining an equilibrium approach, the use of such stochastic models throws away much information about future scenarios. A thorough scenario building approach is a critical prerequisite to any successful investment project appraisal, providing the basis for estimating realistic net cash streams.

There are two main ways of valuing financial, and therefore real, options (Amram and Kulatilaka 1999 and Trigeorgis 1996). The binomial method is the more general and flexible in its applicability. The second method, Black-Scholes formula, is a special case of the binomial (see endnote). The binomial uses discrete time periods, allows adjustment for 'leakages', that is carrying costs or convenience yields on the underlying asset, and allows for American options, which can be exercised at any time, rather than just at maturation.

There are three main steps in the valuation:

establish the payoffs at maturity to the investment decision
establish a replicating or tracking portfolio for the option, one which always yields a risk-free return equal to that of the option, or, putting

this differently, combines the tracking portfolio and the option to form a hedge position which yields a certain risk-free return

update the hedge position frequently

Uncertainty takes the form of a 'cone of uncertainty', a range of values for future streams of income, translated into two possible extreme outcomes for each time period. For each outcome, there is a payoff which equals the future stream of income minus the investment cost.

Imagine a situation in which the binomial path can be mapped in the following way for two periods. The same principle applies for any number of periods, although the lattice is more intricate. The investment cost is K and the value of the underlying asset, S, can either rise by u or fall by d.

$$Su$$
$$S$$
$$Sd$$

The possible payoffs from the exercise of the option are $Cu = \max(uS - K, O)$ and $Cd = \max(dS - K, O)$. A risk-free bond offers a return of R per period, $(1 + r^f)$ in a situation where there are no arbitrage opportunities $u > R > d$. The method could be simplified by assuming a zero interest rate.

A replicating portfolio can be constructed, with x dollars worth of the underlying asset and b dollars worth of the bond, which yields the same payoffs as the investment. The term x is the value of the underlying asset multiplied by the hedge ratio. The hedge ratio is commonly known as delta in the finance literature: it is the change in the value of the option due to a small change in the value of the underlying asset (in other words, the spread of option payoffs as a ratio of the difference in values of the underlying asset). It allows quantification of the required sensitivity of the tracking portfolio to changes in outcomes, and the type and number of securities needed to update the tracking portfolio. The term b is the sum required to finance the change in the investment, in other words the value of the issue of bonds at a level appropriate for each period. The leverage differs from period to period, i.e. the proportion of the purchase funded by borrowing. The hedge position is in each period self-financing.

The value of the portfolio will increase over the relevant period in the following way:

from	x + b	to	ux + Rb
from	x + b	to	dx + Rb

Since the portfolio must duplicate the payoffs to the option

$$ux + Rb = Cu$$
and $$dx + Rb = Cd$$

which could be written, if the stress is on the hedging of the option:

$$Rb = ux - Cu$$
$$Rb = dx - Cd$$

There are two equations and two unknowns, so it is easy to solve for both x, the hedging ratio, and for b, the borrowings.

$$x = Cu - Cd/ u - d$$
$$b = Cu - ux/R = uCd - dCu/R(u - d)$$

Therefore, the value of the portfolio and of the call option is:

$$x + b = Cu - Cd/u - d + uCd - dCu/ R(u - d)$$

or rearranging terms:

$$= 1/R\{(R - d)/(u - d). Cu + (u - R)/(u - d).Cd$$

Simplifying by letting $(R - d)/(u - d) = q$
and therefore $1 - q = (u - R)/(u - d)$ {since the last term $= 1 - (R - d)/(u - d)$}

$$C = 1/R(qCu + (1 - q)Cd)$$

q and $1 - q$ can be regarded as risk-free probabilities since the option and the replicating portfolio offer the same payoff; they are not the subjective probabilities held by managers concerning the likelihood of future outcomes.[1] The analysis is a risk-neutral approach to valuation, based on risk-neutral probabilities which ensure the outcome is a risk-free return. This approach breaks away from direct dependence on the actual probabilities of outcomes and avoids the use of expected returns and evaluation of the degree of risk aversion, and therefore the need to estimate a risk premium.

The analysis can be extended to more than two periods. Note that the hedge ratio and the borrowing will be different in each period. The procedure is to move backwards, from later valuations to earlier values, moving from the final outcomes to successively value the options in each preceding time period through to the initial period. The tracking portfolio can be valued directly or the risk-neutral probabilities used to do so. The result is a value for the option which can be added to the conventional net present value (for an example from the pharmaceutical industry see Appendix 2).

The solution

A good solution involves the use of all three techniques, but in an appropriate way, which reflects the particularities of investment projects. The first is to modify cash streams, which requires the careful choice of an appropriate scenario with its associated cash streams. It is important to follow any signals which indicate whether the chosen scenario is being realised. The more unsystematic or idiosyncratic is risk, the more important it is to incorporate its influence in the cash streams, using where necessary sensitivity analysis and the Monte Carlo method. It is sometimes argued that cash flows should be adjusted to take account of unsystematic risk whereas the discount rate be adjusted to take account of systematic risk, what Lessard (1996: 59) calls market co-variance risk. Since it is assumed that nearly all the risk is unsystematic it is sometimes argued that there should be no risk premium for the international nature of a project (Nordal 2001: 18). In this case, all the unsystematic risk should be reflected in cash streams, but not in discount rates, which are adjusted solely for systematic risk. It is important to avoid double counting.

Both realised and planned interdependencies, that is links with existing or future projects, are also best dealt with through ensuring that the net benefit and cost streams are incremental ones, that is the difference between the streams for the enterprise as a whole before and after the project is implemented. If diverse stakeholders are paid for their risk bearing role this is also reflected in cash streams e.g. discounts to buyers, improved compensation packages for management and employees, and premium prices to suppliers (Miller op. cit.: 500). The risk for most stakeholders is dealt with in this way. Much of the stakeholder risk is already incorporated into the relevant cash streams. If risk arises through ignorance or unfamiliarity with the prospective host country it is better to make allowance through the cash streams for a learning effect (Lessard 1996: 59 and 62). The cash streams can be adjusted to take account of the likely rate of learning.

The second technique is to adjust the discount rate. It is sensible to start with the equity market risk premium of the home country, which might be adjusted for specific enterprise or project risk, although it is better to do this for the host country. In two further steps, this is first multiplied by the ratio of generic country risk for host and home country, and then, by the ratio of project risk to the host-country country risk. The second adjustment takes into account the way in which country risk is filtered through the enterprise to the project in the host country. A full in-depth assessment of the risk relating to a particular project, compared with the country level, should be used as a basis for estimating the relevant adjustment ratio.

Once the risk-adjusted discount rate is known, it is still possible to convert the raw cash streams into certainty-equivalent cash streams by multiplying by an appropriate factor, which in theory should differ from period to period according to the risk level. This method has the advantage of separating the discount for time from the discount for risk (Moosa 2002: 122), but it further complicates the analysis for decision makers and is considered unnecessary.

The third technique is to add terms to the conventional net present value formula for:

i.   the value of options, for flexibility, that is, waiting, expanding, contracting or abandoning, and growth, where investment is organised in a staged sequence, realising that these are not additive (Trigeorgis 1996),

ii. strategic effects following from the possible strategic responses of other players, which include the positive value of the commitment necessary for first mover advantage and the negative value of erosion of competitive advantage by the entry of competitors (Smit and Trigeorgis 2004),

iii. the value of any financial arrangements, such as the tax benefits of favourable loans; or depreciation allowances (Buckley 1996).

The strategic context

A strategic appraisal of any investment project is a necessary part of a general appraisal. If the interdependencies between enterprise projects are large, which is likely in any enterprise which concentrates on its core business, the role of any project can only be appraised in the context of the strategy as a whole. Any strategy, which is by nature emergent, comprises different stages in the process of decision making, all relevant to investment appraisal:

• the identification of relevant investment projects, including all variants,

- placement of a particular project within the overall strategy of the firm, with the existence and scale of any interdependencies with other projects and their cash streams specified,
- indication of the relevant scenarios influencing the outcome for any project and collection of data relevant to forecasting all the revenue and cost streams relevant to different scenarios and to any other project dependent on the outcome of this project,
- analysis of the nature and viability of the project, including its variants and stages, in terms of its present value, modified to take account of its strategic value – its impact on other projects, competitors and stakeholders,
- decision on whether to go ahead or not, on the basis of the project's impact on the achievement of strategic targets,
- implementation of the investment with allowance for variation of cost streams as a result of learning and changes in the relevant environments,
- continued monitoring of the investment with a repetition of the appraisal, taking account of any change in interdependencies, but allowing for both sunk costs and any termination value.

A step-like process moves the perspective of the project from broad strategy to an individual investment project and back. The process of disaggregation is echoed within the project. It is possible to break up any major investment project into a large number of smaller projects, which may relate to different functions, processes or activities. Any decisions might be decentralised in an attempt to empower and motivate employees at all levels of an enterprise to choose the most effective option consistent with a strategy which includes this investment project. This process of iteration comprises small investments at the lowest level which improve the efficiency of a project, the results of learning by doing emerging steadily over time. The process by which information about the interdependencies is passed down, and information on small improvements is passed up is an important part of the articulation and implementation of good strategy.

The decision-making process, stakeholders and risk

Two issues arise at the organisational level – the nature of the decision-making process and the role of different stakeholders. At the core of any enterprise strategy are investment projects at different points in their life, from the earliest and most inchoate of ideas to a fully-functioning facility. How the enterprise is structured to incorporate these projects will influence the way in which new projects are appraised and reappraised, including how regularly this might occur. In recent years it has become usual to organise an enterprise into business units which have different strategies, sometimes within a matrix organisation (White 2004: 437). Decentralisation of decision making and empowerment of individuals are both important.

Highly relevant is the context of strategy making and the establishment of structures embracing various stakeholder groups, including the setting of the rules of the game by government and other rule makers, who themselves respond to risk. Since the risk environment for each of the stakeholder groups differs it is important to understand how this impinges on investment decision making. The bargaining relating to the distribution of the relevant risk and value created determines which activities are being promoted or which 'losers' are being protected. In what circumstances are enterprises risk tolerant or risk averse and what is the role of different stakeholders at different points in the life cycle of a product or enterprise?

The formulation of any investment decision should be set in the context of an appropriate risk control strategy. Controlling risk has three main levels of relevance (Aven 2003: 127):

- a specific policy of risk control

Such a policy includes the various activities involved in risk assessment – identification, analysis, and measurement, including the devising of an information strategy specifically designed to cope with the risk confronting a particular investment. The policy also comprises the four main responses to risk by senior managers – avoidance, mitigation, management and retention (see chapter 11).

- an awareness of risk

This is what is called by Aven a precautionary strategy. Such a policy would include a continuous policy of implicit rather than explicit mitigation, and is the basis of what is now called enterprise risk management (ERM). It consists of a constant reading and monitoring of that environment for risk at all levels of the enterprise, an information strategy broader than simply trying to put numbers to the various components of country risk.

- a stakeholder-oriented strategy of risk control

This is what Aven has called a discursive strategy and includes any measures which build confidence and trustworthiness among those having dealings with the enterprise, thus raising the reputation of the enterprise. It may mean:

• an all-round orientation to reduce uncertainty, such as the involvement of stakeholder groups in regular scenario building in an attempt to persuade all to look ahead,
• involvement of all affected people in significant decision making, their empowerment in processes for deliberation on the articulation and implementation of strategy,
• a perpetual seeking for new mechanisms of accountability and transparency for any decisions made and their outcomes.

Both risk and the investment evaluation should be placed in a broader context than is commonly done.

The adjusted present value approach

The intention of this book is prescriptive, but prescriptive within the confines of the existing business world. The second best shows that in a world where no optimal equivalencies are satisfied the satisfaction of one does not guarantee an improvement in the overall situation (Lipsey and Lancaster 1955/6). This does not mean that a second best does not exist and/or cannot be defined (Morrison 1965). The aim of the current analysis is to indicate how good decisions can be made in the world that actually exists.

There are two possible approaches. The first is narrow and tries to include all relevant material in the one present value formula. The second is broader and recognises the limitations of a narrow perspective. The same contrast between narrow and broad approaches is reflected in contrasting attitudes to risk control. There are two possible ways to use risk analysis to support decision making (Aven 2003: 97):

i.   Establish an optimisation model of the decision-making process and choose the alternative which maximises (minimises) some specified criterion.
ii. See decision making as a process of formal risk and decision analyses to provide decision support, followed by an informal managerial judgement and review process in a decision.

An example of 1 is a simple rule to make an investment if the net present value is positive or exceeds some threshold level. The analysis in this book has shown that it is appropriate to make at least three adjustments to the present value formula in order to include all relevant elements in an appraisal:

- to allow for uncertainty as a positive factor
- to allow for a strategic perspective where a project has an impact on the operation of other projects
- to allow for the strategic responses of other players
- to allow for risk to stakeholders other than the owners, notably but not only the managers

Unless the formula is modified in an acceptable way to take account of these other elements, such a simple rule should not be followed. Already these adjustments involve taking a broad strategic approach. It is not appropriate to see the issue purely as an optimisation problem. The approach of the book opts for ii, viewing i as a special case of ii.

The use of the present value formula should never be a mechanical exercise which ignores margins of error and difficulties of accurate measurement. The formula is an input which provides support for a decision, but not for a hard recommendation. The enterprise must make a decision on how many resources it commits to the process of investment project appraisal.

Table 11.1 The investment decision process

Emergence of decision problem – decision alternatives		Stakeholder values, goals
	Analysis and evaluation Risk analysis and decision analysis	
Evaluation of opportunity and risk environments		Managerial review and judgement Decision

The formula is written in the following way:

The value of a project = its conventional net present value + the value of any options attached to the project – the negative impact on other stakeholders of risk created by the project for them +/– any strategic effect of the response of other players (in so far as it is not already included in cash streams).

The conventional present value formula is expanded to include in the relevant cash streams the effect of interdependencies with existing projects, the cost of risk borne by various stakeholders and resulting from the action of other players. The last three terms capture the strategic importance of a project.

12
The Behaviour of FDI

These developments {rapid expansion of cross-border banking and finance} enhance the process whereby an excess of savings over investment in one country finds an appropriate outlet in another........ They thereby improve the worldwide allocation of scarce capital and, in the process, engender a huge increase in risk dispersion and hedging opportunities.

But there is still evidence of less than full arbitrage of risk adjusted rates of return on a worldwide basis. This suggests the potential for a far larger world financial system than currently exists. If we can resist protectionist pressures in our societies in the financial arena as well as in the interchange of goods and services, we can look forward to the benefits of the international division of labour on a much larger scale in the 21st century.

Alan Greenspan, Chair, US Federal Reserve Board
(Remarks, 15th Annual Monetary Conference of the
Cato Institute, Washington, DC, 14 Oct 1997, quoted by
Bryan and Rafferty 1999: 16, from http://www.afr.com.au/
content971022/verbatim/verbatim1.html.)

As a preliminary to the macro analysis of the relationship between FDI and risk there is a review of how decision makers respond to risk and how this affects FDI flows. This is followed by an analysis of attempts by rating agencies to measure country risk in order to discover a usable index. There are two other major themes to this chapter. The first is a profile of changing aggregate FDI stocks and flows. The chapter looks at the dramatic way in which FDI has grown over the recent past and its potential for further growth. It considers the way in which FDI fluctuates, whether there are regular cycles and of what length, and how far obvious shocks disturb such regular fluctuations. Finally, it analyses the geographical pattern of flows.

The second theme is the causation of FDI. There are many alternative explanations of why FDI occurs at all, which reflect the fact that the determination of FDI is highly complex. There is no uni-causal explanation; the determination is multi-causal and highly specific, unique to each country. There is a brief exploration of the most important determinants. The significance of risk is argued, both for the level of investment, whether domestic or foreign, and for the location of that investment. Domestic and foreign investments are substitutes, just as differing destinations are substitutes, since the output of the former can be exported in order to serve the same market.

There are six sections in this chapter:

- The first section considers the responses to risk which occur at the micro level and their general implications for aggregate flows of FDI.
- In the second section there is a review of the country risk rating agencies in order to choose a reliable index.
- In the third section there is a brief review of movements in the level of FDI and the pattern of fluctuations in the inflow of FDI.
- Section four considers the main directions of flow of FDI relative to the level of country risk in the host countries.
- The fifth section considers the tendency to clustering in the flows of FDI.
- The final section reviews the role of risk as a causative element in what happens to FDI.

Micro investment decisions and their macro consequences

Miller (1992: 321) laments the lack of analysis of responses to risk. He separates financial risk management from strategic management responses to risk, arguing that financial techniques reduce corporate exposure to particular risks without changing the strategy. This is what is called risk management in this book. In the absence of an appropriate financial instrument strategic action is seen as necessary. However, there may be a deliberate decision not to use a financial instrument, even if it exists; the risk exposure is retained. He indicates five 'generic' responses to environmental uncertainties – avoidance, control, co-operation, imitation, and flexibility, which all involve strategic action. On a modified classification, which does not make the distinction between financial and strategic in the same way, there are four possible responses.

- avoidance – the abstention from an activity, such as entry into a market or a country as too risky. This avoidance response may be forced on the relevant decision maker, e.g. by government regulation, or it may be entirely voluntary,
- retention – there is a deliberate intention to accept a risk exposure. A decision may be made to invest in a country despite a high level of country risk, because of familiarity with that country and/or an offsetting return,
- management – the sharing or redistribution of risk through shifting, voluntary or involuntary, or spreading, usually involuntary; here there is no reduction in the level of risk, but simply a redistribution of a fixed risk among a larger number of players. There are various possibilities. Risk management can be done:
  - commercially, through hedging or insurance. For example a foreign exchange risk might be managed through the market for futures or options
  - through a strategic alliance or cooperation of some kind. An influential joint venture partner, who can negotiate with government in order to mitigate political risk, might be found
  - through government action, action by quasi-government bodies or by industry associations
- mitigation – this involves a reduction in the level of risk which can be achieved in many different ways.

The distinction between risk management and risk mitigation is not as clear cut as it might be. Diversification reduces the level of risk involved in holding a portfolio of assets without decreasing the risk in holding any individual asset. For that reason, it is better to regard diversification as a risk management, not a risk mitigation mechanism, but the distinction is not as clear as it might be.

It is possible to reorganise Miller's categories, integrating financial responses into the overall schema. There are omissions. Cooperation is a form of risk control which is rising in importance. Negotiation with government or with other relevant organisations and enterprises is another response to risk. Negotiation involves both management and mitigation, and both the development of credible commitment and the avoidance of the opportunism which arises because of asymmetries of information and/or investment. On the other hand, control, imitation and flexibility are examples of mitigation. The full list of risk responses becomes:

Table 12.1   The risk responses

Risk avoidance
   Divestment and closure, both permanent and temporary (if the risk level suddenly rises)
   Delayed entry into a new country, market or industrial sector – deliberate waiting
   Deliberate choice of low risk niches

Risk management
   Commercial
      hedging
      insurance
   Cooperative
      long-term contracts with suppliers or customers
      voluntary restraint of competition
      strategic alliances, including joint ventures
      franchising agreements
      licensing and subcontracting agreements
      participation in consortia
      interlocking directorates and cross-ownership (keiretsu and chaebol- like arrangements)
      inter-firm personnel flows
   Government intervention

Risk mitigation (safety policy)
   Control
      political activities, including negotiation with governments to gain a credible commitment
      horizontal integration – acquisitions and mergers to gain market power
      exchange of threats, including signalling ability
      vertical integration
   Imitation of the successful
      imitation of best-practice technologies (second mover advantages)
      following other firms into new markets
      copying and merging with locals
   Flexibility
      Diversification
         of product
         of place of production
         of markets
         of suppliers
         of capital sources
      Operational flexibility
         flexible input sourcing
         flexible output mix
         flexible workforce size
         flexible workforce skills
         flexible plants and equipment (particularly as regards scale)
         multinational production
         protective and defensive techniques

Retention

Retention is a failure to cover existing risk. It is what is left after the completion of mitigation and management. For activities in which an enterprise has core competencies and a competitive advantage there may be good reasons for retention of what others regard as a high level of risk.

Often the level of risk determines the 'generic' risk response. The higher the level of risk, the more likely is an avoidance response. The likelihood of avoidance rises with the degree of risk aversion of the relevant decision makers. Many textbooks on risk concentrate on risk management, as if the only issue is how far to manage risk and what mechanisms to use in doing so. There is both a limit to the amount of risk which can be managed and alternatives to managing risk, notably retention, avoidance and mitigation. In some cases, risk mitigation can reduce risk levels to a 'manageable' level. The mitigation responses must be tailored to the nature of the relevant risk factors, as must the mix of mitigation and management. The risk responses can be used in combination. However, a complete coverage of risk removes the incentive to engage in mitigation, a situation otherwise known as moral hazard. Risk management and risk mitigation are seen as in contradiction.

There are two direct links between the micro and macro levels of analysis.

- any explanation of macro flows of FDI must take account of country risk as one of its determinants. There is reason to believe that the average level of risk, particularly country risk, has kept aggregate world FDI much lower than it might have been, given the expectations of most commentators,
- an appropriate awareness of risk, with a significant risk mitigation and management, assists in promoting FDI. Appropriate responses reduce risk exposure and raise the flow of FDI.

This chapter shifts the main focus of interest to the aggregate flows of FDI. The focus is on flows since risk has a more obvious impact on flows than stocks. FDI flows reflect a large number of individual investment project decisions. It is useful to pause and to ask, how might we expect the level, behaviour and pattern of FDI inflows be linked to the level, behaviour and pattern of country risk?

There are six major implications of this analysis.

- Given a significant level of country risk the level of FDI inflow will be lower than expected, that is, with no country risk. The higher the risk, the lower the FDI inflow.
- If the average level of country risk has fallen over the mid or long term, and it is not difficult to establish an a priori case that this is the case, the level of FDI is likely to rise. The faster the fall in country risk, the faster the rise in FDI.
- Given that in many economies the level of country risk fluctuates over time, often in line with the business cycle, it is likely that short-term fluctuations in country risk are correlated with short-term fluctuations in FDI flows.
- That the level and volatility of country risk in a particular country is in inverse relationship with the level of economic development of the relevant country.
- That the level of FDI inflows have an inverse relationship with the level of country risk. The higher is the level of country risk in a country, and the more volatile that level, the lower the inflow of FDI, and vice versa.
- If developed countries have consistently lower and much more stable levels of country risk than developing countries and if familiarity with a host country reinforces the impact of country risk by dissipating the ignorance associated with that country risk, there are likely to be clusters of countries linked by FDI flows.

Each of these implications will be briefly considered in the context of the empirical data on FDI over the recent past.

The rating agencies

There are few attempts to consider the movement of country risk levels over time, whether at the world or at regional levels. Haque, Mathieson and Mark (1997: 12). have put the ratings for Euro-money (from 1982), Institutional Investor (from 1980) and the Economic Intelligence Unit (1989) on a single graph for the period from 1980 to 1993. The impression is of an increase in risk, notably for Africa, Latin America and the Caribbean. The most marked increase is during the debt crisis of the first half of the 1980s. After that, all regions hold their own, except Africa, with Europe showing a distinct improvement. In the latter part of the 1990s, at least until 1997 and the Asian Economic Crisis, there is a general reduction in risk.

For two reasons, it is impossible to prove a general reduction. First, there is no absolute measure of aggregate risk. The ratings of agencies serves two purposes, to indicate changes over time in risk levels for particular countries and to indicate comparative risk levels for countries at a given moment of time. The aim is not to show a change in the overall level of country risk throughout the world.

The factors increasing country risk include:

- the movement from a regime of fixed to one of floating exchange rates
- an increased sensitivity to certain global events, notably terrorist attacks, epidemic disease and natural disasters
- the accumulation in most countries, but notably developed and developing countries, of considerable assets vulnerable to various types of risk

Factors reducing risk include:

- an improvement in communications
- the spread of economic development, notably the Asian economic miracle
- a change in attitude of most governments, promoting an inflow of FDI, rather than inhibiting it
- a greater ability to mitigate country risk, notably political risk, through multilateral institutions
- a greater ability to manage risk, through various financial derivatives, leading to a redistribution of risk away from the enterprises investing

At the country level there are many agencies prepared to assess a country risk level for all countries. The formulas used and the components included in such formulas differ from agency to agency, but the activity of these agencies show that there is a general perception that country risk is a significant factor in determining patterns of FDI inflow. The aim of this section to choose a measure of country risk which might be used to illustrate the nature of the relationship between country risk and FDI inflows.

In considering the rating agencies, the focus is mainly on a generic index which traces changes in the level of country risk which can help in the monitoring of risk at any time in the life of a project (Reisen and von Maltzan 1998). The generic country risk rating is capable of giving an alarm signal alerting managers to a significant change of situation.

By contrast an in-depth qualitative assessment of specific project risk takes full account of the uniqueness of each project and is time consuming and expensive.

Another distinction can be made between general and specific criteria for evaluating the agencies. There are general criteria which any rating system should satisfy: comprehensiveness, continuity and transparency (Haque, Mathleson and Mark 1997). The different rating systems differ markedly in these three respects:

- whether the system covers all of the world with a degree of accuracy likely to be the same whatever the country. There is in practice considerable specialisation in risk rating (Fan 2004). For example, some rating agencies are better at measuring risk for developed countries, others for developing countries,
- for what the period indices have existed, revealing their robustness, or ability to retain validity over a significant period. The relevant question is whether the system has a track record on which a judgement of its strengths and weaknesses can be based,
- whether the system of estimation is open to review. Many ratings are only available on payment. Others may be public but may not reveal the source of relevant data or the way in which this data is processed. Resorting to experts using the Delphi method often conceals the basis on which such experts make their assessments. Without transparency, it is unclear why a system performs well or not.

Most agencies attempt to cover all countries and industries. The quality of coverage is only as good as the data used and this varies. A significant number have 'form' over a reasonable number of years, certainly enough to mean that they are testable. Few of them are fully transparent, revealing exactly how the indices are put together. The International Country Risk Guide (ICRG), Euro-money and the Institutional Investor score well on the last criterion. Unfortunately, all rating agencies tend to be weakest in their transparency on political risk, the most important component of country risk.

It is desirable to reduce all the elements of country risk to one synthetic index. The formulas used to produce a single index are usually complex, unfortunately often unclear in detail and lacking a standard approach. Some of the rating agencies produce a scalar or cardinal measure, others an ordinal measure. The scalar measure aims for a precision which is illusory. The index can take the form of a score out of

100 or of a ranking according to a letter scale, usually of about ten steps (Japan Centre for International Finance 2001). The ordinal measure is more honest in its attempt to compare the countries similar in risk rating. The cardinal measurements is really ordinal since there is no absolute unit of measurement.

The specific criteria refer to three different aspects of a rating system, which involve the choice of

- components, that is the main classifications, such as political, financial, economic and cultural risk. This includes whether the index refers to current conditions or the possibility of a specific risk-generating event, such as expropriation, occurring (Nordal 2001: 7),
- sub-components which are included in the broader components, often much larger than the number of components,
- the weighting system used to measure the contribution of each component or sub-component to the overall index.

It is necessary to distinguish between sub-components and the proxies used to measure their level.

Table 12.2 shows that the rating agencies use many different components and sub-components. There is a broad agreement in making a split between political, economic and financial risk. There is obviously an overlap between economic and financial components and even between political and the other components. The number of sub-components is very large, in some cases reaching as high as 30 individual items. The number of sub-components indicates the complexity of the problem. It also indicates uncertainty about definition and sometimes an implicit assumption, the more the better. On the other hand, there is redundancy in that certain sub-components vary together. Weightings of different components differ significantly from system to system. Many rating agencies are reluctant to indicate what the weightings are, probably for reasons of confidentiality and to avoid too close a scrutiny of their method of construction. It is difficult to achieve a standard approach. There is a marked lack of clear and systematic justifications for what the rating agencies do.

One problem of the rating agencies is a bias in favour of quantifiable and against qualitative elements. This results in an under-weighting of qualitative elements such as political risks as against quantitative elements such as economic and financial indicators, including debt levels. It is tempting for the rating agencies to rely upon assessments of credit-worthiness. The methods of quantification often lack a comprehensive theoretical underpinning (Meldrum 1999). Most of the rating systems underestimate the importance of political risk, which is accorded at most a 50% weighting by ICRG or 25% by the Euro-money index, although in the first case there are items included under different component headings by other rating agencies.

Table 12.2 shows that the source of relevant inputs varies from published data to survey results, both superficially objective and easily evaluated, and the much more subjective expert panels and staff analysis. No agency uses four, the most used are two.

Those who support a positive role for the rating agencies must argue that general monitoring has a role as significant as the in-depth qualitative analysis related to a specific project (Nordal 2001).

The most frequently cited index is the Euro-money index (Moosa 2002: chapter 5), since it meets the general requirements of comprehensiveness, continuity and transparency. It is the one best suited for direct rather than portfolio investment, although it still carries an obvious legacy of a creditworthiness assessment. There is no assumption that managers use this index more than others. There is one significant problem with the Euro-money index. The estimate for political risk is not fully transparent. In an assessment tailored to direct investment, the weighting of 25% might be considered too low since political risk probably exceeds economic risk in importance, certainly for developing countries. A weighting of 50% might be more appropriate. This would increase the weighting of a component whose basis of estimation is unclear. It might be appropriate to reduce the creditworthiness elements to a 10% weighting, and to weight political risk and economic risk on a 50/40 basis. This would seem to fit better the nature of country risk, and the responses of risk managers (see Fan 2004 for one survey of managerial attitudes).

Stevens (1997) argues that the Euro-money Index does not represent a comprehensive treatment of country risk assessment, since it tends to neglect political risk (Stevens 1997: 78–79), and that it is not a good source to use in assessing an unfamiliar country's economic conditions. His sample included nine countries (Brazil, Poland, Indonesia, Bolivia, Mexico, Nigeria, Portugal, Haiti, and China), representing low to medium income levels, in a cross-sectional selection of various regions of the world for 1983 to 1991. He used regression and correlation analysis to test the relationship between foreign direct investment and the economic and market factors contained in the Euro-money assessment, notably those relating to creditworthiness. The study has shown a mixed result. Some of the variables show high correlations for

Table 12.2 Methodologies of country ratings agencies

Index Subcomponents	Country Risk Rating Agencies (Index Provider)									
	BoA	BERI	CRIS	EIU MY	EURO	II	S&P COPL	PRS: ICRG	PRS	MOODY
Index Type	Ordinal	Scalar	Ordinal	Scalar	Scalar	Scalar	Ordinal	Scalar	Scalar	Ordinal
Political and Policy		Qual		Qual	Qual	Qual	Quant/Qual		Qual	Qual
Financial	Quart				Quant	Qual		Quant/Qual	Quant/Qual	Quan-
Economic	Quant	Quant		Quant	Quant	Qual	Quant		Quant/Qual	Quant/Qual
Operations		Quant/Qual								
Remittances and Repatriation of Capital		Quant/Qual								
Security			Qual							
Lending & Trade				Quant/Qual						
Export								Quant/Qual		
Direct Investment								Quant/Qual		

Table 12.2 Methodologies of country ratings agencies – *continued*

Index Subcomponents	Country Risk Rating Agencies (Index Provider)									
	BoA	BERI	CRIS	EIU MY	EURO	II	S&P COPL	PRS: ICRG	PRS	MOODY
Data Sources										
Expert Panel		X						X		
Survey						X				
Staff Analysis			X	X	X		X		X	X
Published Data	X	X		X	X		X	X	X	X

Note: BoA: Bank of America World Information Services
 BERI: Business Environment Risk Intelligence
 CRIS: Control Risks Information Services
 EIU: Economist Intelligence Unit
 EURO: Euro-money magazine,
 II: Institutional Investor magazine
 Moody: Moody's Investor Services,
 PRS-CORS: Political Risk Services: Coplin-O'Leary Rating System
 PRS-ICRG: Political Risk Services: International Country Risk Guide
 S&P: Standard & Poor's Rating Group
 Quant: Quantitative
 Qual: Qualitative

Sources: Fan 2004.

a few of the countries, for example the level of gross domestic product. But those same variables show weak or low correlations for the majority of the countries. Ramcharran (1999a, b) has produced a much more positive result, but using the index differently. The sample is much larger, 26 developing countries from all over the world. He limits his attention to the political and economic components of the Euro-money index and to the years 1992–1994, excluding the factors which represent creditworthiness. Employing cross section data and regression analysis, he discovered a negative relationship between FDI and an increase in political risk and a positive relationship in terms of economic performance. He claims the model could forecast FDI flows.

This evaluation of the Euro-money index, while indicating an index vulnerable to a number of criticisms, is sufficiently favourable to make it a valid approximation of differences in country risk levels. The present study does not require the subtlety of an in-depth study, simply seeking to establish significant differences in the level of risk among countries.

The level and fluctuations in FDI

The following two sections deal with the implications of previous analysis of the movements in FDI discussed at the beginning of the chapter.

- The level of FDI is much lower than might be expected, which is seen by eyeballing the relevant statistics on the share of capital formation accounted for by foreign investment.

Persisting weaknesses of the statistical base are indicated by the divergence between the two ratios, which should be equal. The data indicate that at the height of the business cycle, in 2000, only one fifth of capital formation and at the bottom of a mild recession, in 2002, only about one eighth of capital formation is accounted for by

Table 12.3   FDI flows as % of Gross
Fixed Capital Formation

World	1991–96	2000	2002
Outflow	4.4	20.8	12.2
Inflow	5.0	18.3	13.6

Source: UNCTAD 2003: Annex Table B5.

Table 12.4   Levels of FDI
(in billions of $US, rounded to the nearest 100 million)

	World	Developed	Developing	Least Developed	
1991–6 av.	254.3	154.6	91.5	1.7	
1997–2001 av.	892.8	655.7	213.8	4.6	
	1997	1998	1999	2000	2001	2002
World	481.9	686.0	1,079.1	1,393	823.8	651.2
Developed	269.7	472.3	824.6	1,120.5	589.4	460.3
Developing	193.2	191.3	229.3	246.1	209.4	162.1
Least Developed	3.4	4.6	6.0	3.4	5.6	5.2

Source: UNCTAD 2003, Annex Table B1.

international investment, by any standards low figures. However, this is a decided improvement on the early 1990s when the proportion was as low as one twentieth. There is already strong initial support for a home country bias (see chapter 4).

- The level of FDI has increased enormously over the last ten to fifteen years, mainly since the debt crisis of the early 1980s which reduced the flow of portfolio investment. It has increased faster than the growth of trade (Thomsen 2000: 3). In 2002 the world stock of FDI reached $7.1 trillion, up by over ten times since 1980 (UNCTAD 2002: 23). In 2002, there were as many as 64,000 multinational enterprises with 870,000 affiliates.

Most FDI inflows go to developed countries. The disparity is greater for outflows. The inflows into developed countries have increased faster than those into less developed. The inflow into the developed countries rose by about 4.5 times between the two five year periods, whereas that into developing countries rose by 2.3 and into the least developed by 2.7.

- The extent of the fluctuations in FDI is shown by the downturn in 2001 and 2002 (UNCTAD 2003). In 2001, FDI was down 41%, and in 2002 down a further 21%. The result was that in 2002 FDI was just half what it had been at the previous peak in 1999, although still more than double the average level of the first half of the 1990s.

This is the last and most dramatic of four downturns since 1970 (UNCTAD 2003, Box 1.2: 16). Previous downturns occurred in the mid-1970s, and both the early 1980s and early 1990s. In 1976, FDI fell by 21%, in 1982 and 1983 by an annual average of 14%, in 1991 by 24%. The annual average fall in the recent recession is 31%. These are significant falls, but more than matched by the recoveries. Each fall followed either a decline in the rate of growth of world GDP or a recession. The behaviour of FDI flows is therefore highly cyclical.

The distribution of FDI

Where does FDI go?

* It is interesting to note the close relationship between the inflow of FDI and the level of development.

Levels of FDI outflow are much higher for developed countries than for less developed but the higher rates of inflow are also significant. In both ownership and location, the developed world accounts for two thirds of world FDI inflow stocks and nine tenths of outflow stocks (UNCTAD 2003: 23).

The picture confirms that presented in Dunning's theory of the stages of development in FDI flows (Narula 1996: chap. 1; Dunning and Narula 1996: chap 1). The least developed countries are at stage one or stage two during which those countries generate no outflow and almost no inflow of FDI. Only in the second stage do they begin to attract a significant inflow of FDI, although often linked either to natural resource projects or to import substitution. There is still little outward flow except towards the end of stage 2. Typical developing

Table 12.5   FDI flows as a % of GFCF by level of development

	1991–96	2000	2002
Developed countries			
In	3.7	22.9	12.3
Out	5.7	22.4	15.6
Developing countries			
In	6.5	14.6	10.5
Out	2.9	6.2	4.6
Least developed countries			
In	5.2	5.9	6.6
Out	0.6	0.6	0.3

Source: as above.

countries are at stages three and four when net inflow reaches its maximum. Outflow begins to pick up at stage four as developing countries began to produce their own multinational enterprises and to invest in other countries, still at stages 1 and 2. By the end of stage 4, outflows exceed inflows by a significant amount.

The developed countries represent stage 5 when outflow and inflow are closely matched, although there is a tendency in developed countries for outward flows to exceed inward. Individual countries may be biased towards either net inflow or outflows, but among the developed OECD countries the net givers and receivers are evenly balanced (Thomsen 2000: 7). For example, Australia is traditionally a net importer of FDI and Japan a net exporter. It might also be that the predominance of inflows or of outflows alternates for one country.

The differences in risk rating between developed and developing or undeveloped countries are significant. Developed countries consistently rate in the lowest risk groups and display a stability of rating which is striking. By contrast, developing countries are characterised by high levels of risk, but levels which are also unstable. There are obvious contagion or herd effects which might affect a geographical contiguous group, such as Latin American countries after the financial crisis in Argentina in 2001, or all developing countries after the Asian Economic Crisis in 1997.

Although a successful transition from developing country to developed country status is still unusual, it does happen. In the process, the level of country risk of the relevant countries comes down, stimulating an inflow of FDI. The Asian economic miracle is one obvious example of such a transition with the rising importance of FDI in a number of Asian economies.

- If the level of country risk was the only factor determining the pattern of inflow of FDI into different countries, it would be easy to rank the countries according to country risk and FDI per head and to observe an exact correspondence. This is not the case for a number of reasons:

other factors are at work determining FDI inflows, for example the deregulation of markets and removal of barriers to the flow of capital,

levels of country risk are unstable and the instability varies from country to country,

differences in the level of country risk within groups of similar countries, i.e. with comparable levels of GDP per head or similar economic structures, are insignificant and ranking can change without much movement of the risk level,

FDI inflows are often unstable because of a lumpiness in the size of relevant investment projects, including large acquisitions of foreign companies,

there are exceptional factors which influence the engagement of particular countries in the international economy, e.g. the closure of the Japanese economy to FDI.

As has been argued in chapter 4, the level of FDI is lower than might be expected because of a home country bias reflecting both a higher riskiness of investment made outside the domestic economy and an aversion to such risk. The pattern as well as the level of FDI is affected by country risk. The outflows of FDI are not distributed randomly or evenly throughout the world. There is a notable concentration of inward flows on countries with low risk ratings and high output per head. This may vary with the degree of risk aversion of the key managers in the relevant countries. A good prospective return may attract as strongly as risk deters, but it is not difficult to show how risk influences the pattern of FDI (Ramcharran, 1999a, b; Shah and Slemrod, 1991).

The relevant countries can be grouped according to the level of country risk and the level of FDI inflow per head of population (Fan 2004). This was done for the years 1997, 1998 and 1999 with the relevant countries divided into three and five groups for each of the two variables. The countries are placed in the nine, or twenty five, boxes according to the combination of risk and FDI inflow. Rejection of the relationship is indicated by a completely random distribution of the countries between the relevant boxes. Empty boxes at the extremes, away from the diagonal line, and a tendency of countries to fall more often into those close to the diagonal, in other words a bunching, confirms a strong relationship. The results are unambiguous. The following matrix diagrams show that there is clearly a relationship between the size of inflow of FDI and the risk rating of different countries. The diagram shows a heavy bunching along the diagonal. Since there are other factors which influence the direction of flow, such as prospective return, the fit is not perfect. Broadly speaking, high risk is associated with a small inflow of FDI, low risk with a high inflow and an intermediate position for risk is linked with an intermediate position for the inflow of FDI. There are exceptional cases which lie off the diagonal, but only in adjacent boxes. Usually there are obvious special

Table 12.6   Level of country risk and FDI inflows (3 groups)

	>200 (N=28)	10–200 (N=65)	<=10 (N=49)
60–100	Australia (347.36)	Netherlands (1905.76)	Greece (81.64)
	Austria (412.66)	New Zealand (205.06)	Italy (67.67)
	Belgium & Luxembourg (1587.56)	Norway (1039.84)	Japan (50.45)
	Canada (643.88)	Portugal (199.15)	Kuwait (24.43)
	Denmark (1066.26)	Singapore (1792.17)	Slovenia (96.62)
	Finland (1118.02)	Spain (233.59)	United Arab Emirates (47.4)
	France (519.42)	Sweden (3405.77)	(N=6)
	Germany (240.00)	Switzerland (823.17)	
	Iceland (445.24)	United States (697.01)	
	Ireland (2650.64)	United Kingdom (1014.57)	
	Israel (319.31)	(N=21)	

33–66	>200 (N=28)	10–200 (N=65)		<=10 (N=49)	
	Argentina (353.02)	Azerbaijan (119.38)	Bulgaria (73.22)	China (34.1)	Bangladesh (1.59)
	Chile (427.95)	Bolivia (119.44)	Colombia (81.84)	Egypt (17.45)	Ghana (4.4)
	Croatia (206.69)	Brazil (161.65)	El Salvador (61.34)	Guatemala (27.88)	India (2.89)
	Czech Rep (295.81)	Costa Rica (141.1)	Kazakhstan (89.61)	Honduras (24.47)	Indonesia (2.01)
	Hungary (202.84)	Dominica Rep (100.56)	Lebanon (62.54)	Jordan (43.8)	Iran Islamic Rep (0.87)
	Panama (302.18)	Jamaica (142.67)	Paraguay (63.72)	Morocco (27.12)	Kenya (1.36)
	Saudi Arabia (203.34)	Korea Rep (133.37)	Peru (76.54)	Papua New Guinea (22.32)	Nepal (2.51)
	(N=7)	Latvia (169.09)	Romania (62.31)	Philippines (16.72)	Syrian Arab Rep (5.13)
		Lithuania (159.58)	Slovakia (71.66)	Senegal (11.2)	Uganda (8.96)
		Malaysia (192.56)	South Africa (45.59)	Sri Lanka (15.09)	Vanuatu (1.19)
		Mexico (119.43)	Thailand (93.88)	Turkey (13.29)	(N=10)
		Oman (32.73)	Tunisia (50.15)	Uruguay (49.6)	
		Poland (161.88)	Zimbabwe (16.84)	Vietnam (27.6)	
		Venezuela (180.73)		(N=40)	

Table 12.6 Level of country risk and FDI inflows (3 groups) – continued

228

>200 (N=28)	10–200 (N=65)		<=10 (N=49)		
Angola (90.88)	Cambodia (13.14)	Russian Federation (27.8)	Algeria (0.2)	Kyrgyzstan (5)	Tajikistan (3.56)
Lesotho (108.27)	CoteDIvoire (24.39)	TFYR Macedonia (26)	Benin (5.12)	Liberia (4.87)	Togo (7.56)
Ecuador (59.25)	Georgia (29.03)	Turkmenistan (25.24)	Bosnia & Herzegovina (2.19)	Madagascar (1.92)	United Rep Tanzania (5.4)
Nicaragua (45.32)	Laos (13.57)	Ukraine (12.26)	Burkina Faso (0.99)	Malawi (4.84)	Uzekistan (8.59)
Albania (12.64)	Moldova (16.93)	Zambia (18.81)	Cameroon (3.15)	Mali (4.70)	Afghanistan (0)
Armenia (37.25)	Mozambique (12.88)	Central African Rep (2.31)	Mauritania (0.66)	Burundi (0.11)	
Belarus (18.78)	Nigeria (12.51)	(N=19)	Chad (2.11)	Mongolia (9.97)	Congo Demo (0.01)
			Comoros (3.05)	Myanmar (7.36)	Iraq (0)
			Congo (2.17)	Niger (1.63)	Korea Demo (0)
			Cuba (1.74)	Pakistan (4.32)	Libyan Arab Jamahiray (–20.31)
			Ethiopia (1.87)	Rwanda (0.75)	Somalia (0)
			Guinea (2.5)	Sierra Leone (0.74)	Yemen (–9.74)
			Haiti (1.94)	Sudan (9.83)	Yugoslavia (0) (N=39)

0–33

Table 12.7 Country risk and FDI inflows (5 groups)

	>200 (N=28)	50–200 (N=33)	10–50 (N=32)	0–10 (N=40)	<=0.11 (N=9)
80–100	Australia (347.36) 0.06	Netherlands (1905.76) 0.03	Italy (67.67) 0.02		
	Austria (412.66) 0.02	New Zealand (205.06) 0.07	Japan (50.45) 0.04 (N=2)		
	Belgium & Luxembourg (1588) 0.03	Norway (1039.84) 0.03			
		Portugal (199.15) 0.06			
	Canada (643.88) 0.04	Singapore (1792.17) 0.05			
	Denmark (1066.26) 0.03	Spain (233.59) 0.04			
	Finland (1118.02) 0.03	Sweden (3405.77) 0.03			
	France (519.42) 0.02	Switzerland (823.17) 0.04			
	Germany (240.00) 0.05	United States (697.01) 0.04			
	Iceland (445.24) 0.07	United Kingdom (1014.57) 0.04			
	Ireland (2650.64) (N=20)				
60–80	Chile (427.95) 0.14		Korea Rep (133.37) 0.1	Kuwait (24.43) 0.27	
	Czech Rep (295.81) 0.15		Slovenia (96.62) 0.23	Oman (32.73) 0.09	

Table 12.7   Country risk and FDI inflows (5 groups) – *continued*

>200 (N=28)	50–200 (N=33)	10–50 (N=32)	0–10 (N=40)	<=0.11 (N=9)
Hungary (202.84) 0.09	Greece (81.64) 0.07 (N=3)		United Arab Emirates (47.4) 0.13 (N=3)	
Israel (319.31) 0.14				
Saudi Arabia (203.34) 0.11 (N=5)				
Argentina (353.02) 0.20	Brazil (161.65) 0.17	Colombia (82) 0.15	China (34.1) 0.15	India (2.89) 0.16
Croatia (206.69) 0.28	Costa Rica (141.1) 0.13	El Salvador (61) 0.26	Egypt (17.45) 0.17	Burkina Faso (0.99) 0.19 (N=2)
Panama (302.18) 0.22 (N=3)	Jamaica (142.67) 0.12	Lebanon (63) 0.39	Jordan (43.8) 0.22	
	Latvia (169.09) 0.33	Peru (76.54) 0.27	Morocco (27.12) 0.11	
	Lithuania (159.58) 0.33	Slovakia (72) 0.18	Philippines (16.72) 0.23	
	Malaysia (192.56) 0.18	South Africa (46) 0.13	Sri Lanka (15.09) 016	
	Mexico (119.43) 0.09	Thailand (94) 0.17	Turkey (13.29) 0.15	
	Poland (161.88) 0.2	Tunisia (50) 0.14	Uruguay (49.6) 0.12	
	Venezuela (181) 0.14	(N=17)	(N=8)	

40–60

Table 12.7   Country risk and FDI inflows (5 groups) – *continued*

>200 (N=28)	50–200 (N=33)	10–50 (N=32)	0–10 (N=40)		<=0.11 (N=9)		
	Azerbaijan (119) 0.36	Ecuador (59) 0.17	Armenia (37.25) 0.32	Nigeria (12.51) 0.16	Algeria (0.2) 0.15	Madagascar (1.92) 0.16	Yemen (–9.74) 0.23 (N=1)
	Bolivia (119.44) 0.15	Kazakhstan (90) 0.26	Belarus (18.78) 0.24	Papua Guinea (22) 0.15	Bangladesh (1.59) 0.2	Malawi (4.84) 0.27	
	Dominica Rep (101) 0.21	Nicaragua (45) 0.26	Cambodia (–3.14) 0.58	Russian Fed (28) 0.39	Benin (5.12) 0.36	Mali (4.70) 0.14	
	Lesotho (108.27) 0.23	Paraguay (64) 0.18	CoteDIvoire (24.39) 0.17	Senegal (11.2) 0.10	Bosnia & Herz (2.19) 0.03	Mauritania (0.66) 0.27	
	Angola (90.88) 0.18	Romania (62) 0.21	Georgia (29.03) 0.17	TFYR Macedonia (26) 0.25	Cameroon (3.15) 0.12	Mongolia (9.97) 0.27	
	Bulgaria (73.22) 0.19	(N=11)	Guatemala (27.83) 0.22	Turkmenistan (25.24) 0.3	Centl Afri Rep (2.31) 0.36	Nepal (2.51) 0.22	
			Honduras (24.47) 0.15	Ukraine (12.26) 0.19	Chad (2.11) 0.3	Niger (1.63) 0.22	
			Laos (13.57) 0.49	Vietnam (27.6) 0.49	Comoros (3.05) 0.06	Pakistan (4.32) 0.25	
			Moldova (16.93) 0.33	Zambia (18.81) 0.17	Congo (2.17) 0.18	Rwanda (0.75) 0.37	
			Mozambique (12.88) 0.23	Zimbabwe (16.84) 0.16	Ethiopia (1.87) 0.18	Syrian Ab Rp (5.13) 0.24	
				(N=20)	Ghana (4.4) 0.15	Tajikistan (3.56) 0.31	
					Guinea (2.5) 0.24	Togo (7.56) 0.17	

20–40

Table 12.7 Country risk and FDI inflows (5 groups) – *continued*

>200 (N=28)	50–200 (N=33)	10–50 (N=32)	0–10 (N=40)	<=0.11 (N=9)	
			Albania (12.64) 0.26 (N=1)		
			Haiti (1.94) 0.27	Uganda (8.96) 0.23	Afghanistan (0) 0	Korea Demo (0) 0.83
			Indonesia (2.01) 0.26	Ud Rp Tanzania (5.4) 0.18	Burundi (0.11) 0.14	Libyan
			IranIslac Rep (0.87) 0.19	Uzekistan (8.59) 0.26	Congo Dm (0.01) 0.51	(−20.31) 0.07
			Kenya (1.36) 0.14	Vanuatu (1.19) 0.29	Iraq (0) 0.66	Somalia (0) 0.47
			Kyrgyzstan (5) 0.18	(N=33)		Yugoslavia (0) 0.4
			Cuba (1.74) 0.53			(N=8)
			Liberia (4.87) 0.38			
			Myanmar (7.36) 0.45			
			Sierra Leone (0.74) 0.28			
			Sudan (9.83) 0.34	(N=5)		

0–20

circumstances which explain such a divergence. There are no countries in the boxes distant from the diagonal. The analysis confirms the existence of a close relationship between country risk and the inflow of FDI for most countries. The main hypothesis of a link between country risk and FDI inflow is confirmed at an aggregate level.

- Patterns of FDI reflect country risk indirectly, through the opposing influences of familiarity and ignorance. There is a pronounced clustering in the countries receiving FDI. The World Investment Review has noted a tendency to mega blocks (UNCTAD 2003: chapter 1). The clusters within these mega blocks are dominated by a triad centre – the receiving countries cluster around the USA, the EU and Japan (Buckley 1996: 109–111). Together over the period 1985–2002 these three centres have accounted for 80% of the outward stock of FDI and between 50 and 60% of the inward stock (UNCTAD 2003: 23), and more than 60% of the relevant flows, with the proportion rising in the downturn of the business cycle.

The clustering reflects membership of various economic unions, and both geography and history. It is reinforced by the concentration of bilateral investment treaties and double taxation treaties among the Triad member and their associates (UNCTAD 2003: 26). The USA invests largely in the Americas – Canada and Mexico within the North American Free Trade Area, but most countries in Latin America. Outside this area there are some attractors which have a particular connection with the USA, such as the Philippines, Pakistan and Bangladesh, and Saudi Arabia. European Union countries invest largely within the countries of Western and Central Europe but increasingly within Eastern Europe. Strong historical connections with countries elsewhere mean designate them as the destination for significant FDI – Ghana and Morocco in Africa, Brazil in Latin America, India, Sri Lanka and Vietnam in Asia. Japan is not the member of any particular economic grouping, but invests most in South Korea, China, South East Asia and Taiwan.

This continuing and strengthening clustering is reflected in the picture depicted below:

Australia, a small developed country outside the Triad, also illustrates such a clustering. Traditionally, it has been an importer of capital, but the gap between inflows of FDI and outflows has narrowed markedly in recent years, since, after deregulation of the financial sector, FDI outflows have grown about five times over the last twenty years. A survey of the largest Australian companies investing abroad shows a

Table 12.8   FDI stocks among Triad
members (US$bill)

1985

USA
238

89↓ 128↑   9↓   16↑
EU   → 5   Japan
305   7 ←   *44*

Total Outward Stocks of Triad: 587
Estimated share of stocks in Triad: 60%

2001

USA
1,382

641↓ 694↑   64↓ 191↑
EU   → 24   Japan
3,172   88 ←   *300*

Total Outward Stocks of Triad: 4,854
Estimated share of stock in Triad: 69%

Source: UNCTAD 2003: 24.

clear pattern (Fan 2004: 175–177). There are four groups of destination
economies. By far, the most important is the group of six developed
countries in the English speaking world – the USA and Canada, the UK
and Ireland, and South Africa and New Zealand, which share not only
language, but cultural and historical connections of the closest kind.
They are also generally notable for their low risk ratings. The next
group, accounting for just under the number of locations for the first
group, comprises other developed economies, notably the developed
Asian economies – most prominently, Singapore, Hong Kong and
Japan, plus nearly all the Western and Central European economies
and the small but rich Gulf states. All of these countries have low risk
ratings. In the next group, are mainly rapidly developing Asian economies, such as Indonesia, China, Thailand and Malaysia, plus a
number of neighbours, notably PNG and Fiji. Outside these three
groups is the rest of the world, including nearly all Africa, western Asia
and all Latin America, accounting for a very small proportion of locations of Australian FDI projects, as little as 16%. This conclusion is
confirmed by the official statistics on the main destinations for the
aggregate outward flows of Australian FDI, which show the United

Kingdom, the United States and New Zealand as the main destinations. The share of these three countries in the total FDI outward stock has risen steadily, from 68% in 1992, to 73% in 1997 and to 78% in 2001 (UNCTAD 2000).

The role of risk

Risk is a determinant of FDI which has been much neglected but which is at last beginning to attract the attention it deserves (Buckley 1996: chapter 13; Moosa 2002: chapter 5). Any reasonable investment appraisal should take account of all the sources of risk, including country risk, whether it involves a simple go ahead for a well-defined project, the choice among the variants of a project which differ in timing and in strategic role, or the choice of a mode of entry into international business.

Risk is one of the main determinants of the choice of a mode of entry into international business. Different modes of entry are associated with different types and levels of risk, and different returns. The degree to which FDI exposes an enterprise to risk has led to those analysing the mode of entry to wonder why any enterprise even considers investment as an option (Buckley 1996, Whittington 2001). There is no doubt that the division between domestic and foreign location is significantly influenced by risk.

The aggregate flows of FDI and their change over time reflects the influence of country risk. Since the flows over a period of time make up the stocks, this is also true of stocks. Any theory, or empirical work, dealing with FDI and its movement must consider risk as one of the most important determinants. It plays a very significant role in explaining the unexpectedly low level of FDI, the recent significant increase in FDI, the fluctuations of FDI inflows over time and the clustering of inflows between different countries. Familiarity reinforces the impact of risk in establishing such clusters of countries with interacting flows of investment.

13
Conclusion

Although many management scientists are reluctant to acknow-
ledge the fact, it is often true that their exact solution to the
approximate problem is not as good as the approximated
solution to the exact problem.

(Carter 1972 – quoted by Hull 1980: 127)

A theory is needed which justifies a clear decision rule for international
investments and validates the method of measuring the variables
which are inputs into a relevant valuation. There is also a need for a
simple, transparent and easily comprehensible formula for making
the necessary investment decisions. Neither exists: the more elegant
the theory, the more unrealistic it is and the less easy it is to use; the
simpler the formula and the easier it is to use, the less justified is its use
by theory. There are major weaknesses with both the CAPM and real
options models and serious problems with a naïve use of the present
value formula. Inevitably, the prescription in this book is therefore a
compromise. There is a decision rule but it is not as simple as might be
hoped, which inevitably means that enterprises will continue to use as
a back-up the target payback period method.

General appraisal criteria are normally based on a general equilibrium approach. Without an equilibrium approach it is impossible to
say that a decision is a good one. In its absence, all decisions are made
on ad hoc grounds. The use of an adjusted net current value formula
has a theoretical justification which is provided in the text. Like the
nature of behaviour in the real world, it is not elegant. This follows
partly from the fact that it is important to tailor any technique to the
nature of projects of foreign direct, rather than financial or portfolio,
investment: they are not the same. It is easy to oversimplify the evalu-

ation of investments projects, either ignoring risk completely or reducing uncertainty to a known probability distribution. As this book has shown, there are an increasing number of techniques used for taking account of risk or uncertainty.

This book began by making a critique of existing methods of measuring risk and appraising investment projects. It continued by introducing the role of risk in decision making and by putting the case for a significant level of home country bias in foreign investment, as in other activities. Next, it argued for an approach which adopted three perspectives – the financial, strategic and organisational, advancing three propositions. Understanding the sources of risk is a major first step to reducing total risk, and it is total risk which is relevant. Individual projects must be viewed in a strategic context. It is not the risk of the owners alone which should be the centre of the analysis, but that of all stakeholders. It then showed how the risk threatening an international investment project, both generic and specific but focusing on country risk, could be classified and how relevant measures of project risk might be made. It concluded by showing how a risk measure can be incorporated into the appraisal of an investment project, taking full account of the uniqueness of every project.

The recommended decision rule is still a positive net present value. There are two ways of incorporating risk into such an investment appraisal method. The first is to add terms to create an expanded net present value formula. The terms include those which value various options, notably those for flexibility and growth, a term for the impact of strategic risk and any other terms to take account of favourable treatment of a foreign investment for tax purposes or for cheap credit. The second way is to adjust the inputs into the formula. The cash streams are adjusted to reflect both the most likely scenario and other resulting project possibilities, and also learning of various kinds. It is sensible to include in the case streams as much of any non-systematic risk as possible. The discount rate is adjusted to take account of the level of generic country risk in the host country relative to the home country and the specific risk of the project relative to the generic host country risk. This could be likened to a double beta approach but it is better not to think of it in this way. The latter adjustment includes one for any diversification effects.

The book has distinguished between a generic measure of country risk and a measure specific to a particular project. The generic measure is both a vital part of the specific investment appraisal and of any later monitoring of the condition of an operating project. All projects, and the strategies in which they are embedded, are unique. The way in which the appraisal is carried out reflects this uniqueness. There must be a full in-depth qualitative assessment of any investment project which includes a full description of all the main characteristics. Such an assessment is supported by a quantitative analysis based on an estimation of an expanded net present value, with sensitivity tests of the influence of all the key variables. The quantitative decision rule is not the be-and-end-all, it is only part of the appraisal.

The approach needs to be widened, so that it is both strategic and organisational, as well as narrowly financial. It is impossible to extrapolate the threat environment of the future from that of the past. Reading the future, and making allowance for the worst case scenario, is an important part of any strategy for risk control. Scenario building involves considering the discrete paths characterised by the specific incidence of risk-generating events. Sensitivity tests can be carried out to see the impact of different scenarios on appraisal. This is a critical part of the exercise. Nor is it desirable to rely solely on market information for a number of reasons, prominent among which are poor development of relevant markets, the centrality of asymmetries of information and the need to look forward in time rather than back.

Any strategy is emergent in ways directly relevant to project evaluation. It involves learning of various kinds:

- Learning in which scenario is being realised.
- Gaining familiarity with different risk environments, notably the country environments.
- Predicting with accuracy the development of the technology and markets relevant to a particular project.
- Making strategy better suited to a changing environment with projects continually being reappraised.

In the process of learning, the relevant responses to a situation of significant risk include risk mitigation, an important source of competitive advantage. Such mitigation is conducted in the normal course of business. A reasonable decision might be to retain the risk. As one commentator has put it, risk control can be regarded as a core competency of all enterprises (Rogers 2002: 51). Only if this process of mitigation has been taken to its 'optimum' level, is it appropriate to manage the relevant risk. The ability of an enterprise to control risk makes certain investment projects worth considering in the first place.

Risk is already a major determinant of FDI and rightly so. The statistics for FDI flows and the estimates of country risk, albeit still crude, show a clear relationship. Given the range and level of risk types it is not surprising that there is considerable home country bias in investment worldwide.

Appendix 1

Parity conditions

There are three sets of international parity conditions which can be used in measuring the degree of market integration (all these conditions should hold ex ante).

Uncovered interest parity (UIP)

The requirement for uncovered interest parity (UIP) is:

$Fd - e = r(1) - r(2)$ where Fd is the forward exchange rate and e the spot rate, that is $Fd - e$ is the discount or premium on the exchange rate; $r(1)$ is the rate of interest in country 1 and $r(2)$ that in country 2.

In other words, the forward discount (premium) of the currency should be equal to the difference in interest rates.

Covered interest parity (CIP)

The requirement for covered interest parity (CIP) is stronger:

$Fd = Ee$, where Ee is the expected exchange rate.

In other words the expectation of the spot exchange rate is equal to the forward rate.

Real interest parity (RIP)

The requirement for real interest parity (RIP) is even stronger, involving the satisfaction of ex ante purchasing power parity. The requirement for PPP is:

$Ee - e = Ep(2) - Ep(2)$ where the Eps are the expected inflation rates in the two countries. In other words, exchange rates only change to accommodate differing expectations of movements in price levels.

This means that, where these conditions are not satisfied, $r(1) - r(2)$ can be broken into three separate components:

    1. $\{r(1) - r(2)\} - (Fd - e)$ the covered interest differential

The *political or country premium* (which, according to Frankel (1992: 192) 'captures all barriers to integration of financial markets across national boundaries: transaction costs, information costs, capital controls, tax laws that discriminate by country of residence, default risk, and risk of future capital controls.'

2. $(Fd - e) - (Ee - e)$ the exchange risk premium
3. $(Ee - e) - \{Ep(1) - Ep(2)\}$ the expected real change in the exchange rate

Together these constitute the *currency premium* which captures currency rather than country effects.

Appendix 2

A case study – the pharmaceutical industry

Let us consider as a specific example the development of a new drug or medical process. The first step is to recognise the nature of the option. The main feature of the development of any new drug is that there are discrete investments which make possible future investments and that there can be exit at any stage in the process of development. The initial investments clearly have a negative net present value since there are no returns until later in the process.

In this case as we can assume that the project requires an initial expenditure of 60 million to ready a new idea for trial and then further expenditures of 400 million and 800 million for different stages in clinical development and trial; the first simply keeps the project alive but the latter brings to fruition with approval by the appropriate regulatory authority. Future scenarios have a degree of volatility for values of income streams, which is difficult to estimate. In this case the assumption is 18.23%, which is on the rather low side.

The following shows a lattice of possible outcomes in terms of the present value of the hypothetical drug project. The values are those which would exist if the project were complete at the present. The binomial model is therefore based on a decision tree. Valuation works backwards creating a replicating portfolio which produces a risk-free return which is the same as the pay-off actually produced.

Possible outcomes

			Good, good, good (1,728)
		Good, Good (1,440)	
	Good (1,200)		Good, good, bad (1,200)
			Good, bad, good Bad, good, good
		Good, Bad (1,000)	
Start – 1,000		Bad, Good	
			Good, bad, bad Bad, good, bad (833) Bad, bad, good
	Bad (833)		
		Bad, Bad (694)	
			Bad, bad, bad (579)
T = 0	T = 1	T = 2	T = 3

242

The following diagram works through the values of the option to develop this drug, indicating at different stages whether it is appropriate to continue or to exit.

Options values and implied decisions

$$1,728 - 800 = 928$$
Invest 800

$$699 > (1440 - 800)$$
Keep open

$$514 - 400 = 114$$ $$1,200 - 800 = 400$$
Invest 400 *Invest 800*

$$71 > (321 - 400)$$ $$259 > (1,000 - 800)$$
Invest 60 *Keep open*

$$168 < 400$$ $$833 - 800 = 33$$
Don't invest *Invest 800*

$$21 > (694 - 800)$$
Keep open

$$579 < 800$$
Don't invest

The binomial method works backwards. We therefore start with the position in period 3. The 'call' value in period 3 is S − X. This gives a series of possible values (payoffs) which are as indicated in the diagram above – 928, 400, 33 and 0, since the last is minus 221 and a project cannot have a negative value. The positive values indicate that the enterprise should go ahead with the project.

In order to estimate the value of the option in the previous period, period 2, a tracking or replicating risk-free portfolio is devised which has the same call value (value outcome). The exercise is done in pairs for each of the possible outcomes after period 2. We illustrate with the top possibility:

$$(1,728 \times \Delta) - (1.08 \times B) = 928$$
$$(1,200 \times \Delta) - (1.08 \times B) = 400$$

where Δ is the proportion of the underlying asset in which an investment is made, i.e. the equivalent of a share investment in that asset, usually called the hedging ratio or delta, and B is the loan which is taken at the risk-free rate, i.c. the equivalent of the bonds issued. The tracking portfolio consists of the shares held and bonds issued.

The two simultaneous equations can be solved for Δ and B, which have the values 1 and 741. The call option in period two is worth (S × Δ) − B, that is the value of the project times the hedge ratio minus the loan taken. This is $1,440 \times 1 - 741 = 699$. Δ can also be calculated directly as the spread of option payoffs divided by the spread of asset prices – in this case 928 – 400/ 1,728 – 1,200, which equals, as shown already, 1. The larger the spread of option payoffs, the higher the hedge ratio.

The values of Δ and B will differ for each of the three outcomes in period 2, but the same method can be used to estimate the option value for each possible scenario.

As the diagram shows, the value of the option is positive and exceeds the value of immediate exercise of the option, that is the value of the project, in all three possible scenarios and therefore the option should be kept open. This is despite the fact that in the third case the project has a negative present value.

Following the same method as used in period 3, it is possible to estimate the option values in period 1, feeding in the option values for period 2 to re-estimate the relevant Δ and B necessary to make this estimate. This indicates whether the enterprise should invest the 400 or not. As the diagram shows, with the upside scenario it is worth making the investment, with the downside not. Finally, an option value for period 0 is estimated, which in this case is greater than the starting investment, indicating the desirability of making the starting investment.

The net present value of the overall project, estimated according to the simple formula set out earlier is a negative – 9: which is derived from the present value of the project 1,000 minus 1,009 which is the present value of the three investment outlays discounted at a rate for the industry of 10.83%, i.e. $60 + 400/(1 + 0.1083) + 800/(1 + 0.1083)$.[3] If the project were integrated and all the expenditures were incurred at the present the situation would be even worse, with a negative value of –260. However, this misrepresents the situation since the value of the option to wait is positive.

Notes

Chapter 2   A Review of Existing Theory Concerning Risk and the Foreign Investment Decision

1. The interest in risk became a significant practical issue only about a quarter of a century ago, although some of the theoretical issues were discussed much earlier. During the late 1970s and early 1980s, there took place a considerable debate about the nature of risk, both in general theoretical terms (Hirshleifer and Riley 1992) and specifically related to country risk (Krayenbuehl 1985; Calverley 1985; Mayer 1985; Ciarrapico 1992; Coplin and O'Leary 1994). When the level of international investment by private institutions suddenly rose in the 1970s, risk and risk control became a practical problem. The debate on country risk and its assessment began with the commercial banks as a consequence of the debt crisis of the early 1980s when private banks were faced by considerable sovereign risk in lending to the governments of developing countries. This crisis gave an impetus to the development of techniques of 'hard' risk management applied to the creditworthiness of both governments and enterprises. Many different approaches were tried. Most banks built such assessment into their normal activities in order to improve their capacity to avoid significant risk exposure (Friedman 1983; Miklos 1983; Coplin and O'Leary 1994; Shapiro 1999 and Tucker 1994). At that time, the focus of concern was very much portfolio rather than direct investment, dwelling on the operation of financial markets and the position of financial institutions of various kinds.

2. All market-based models have a very bad track record of prediction. This is scarcely surprising since they ignore bounded rationality in a world where the future does not reproduce the past. The portfolio approach has produced results no better than the average. Recently there has been interest in dropping linearity, considering a non-linear world in which there may be a sudden jump from one mode to another, involving very large changes in the market (Lim and Martin 2000). The whole problem of pricing options is based on the non-linearity of the future. New analytical techniques have the potential of extracting information from what are usually treated as error terms, to improve prediction, from a 50% or worse – it is better to toss a coin – to a much more respectable figure. They are in their early stages and as yet untested. The rationale of this approach is that the future must in some sense be inherent in the past.

3. For a period, there was a pronounced tendency for enterprises to seek to diversify but with results which were not positive. As a consequence, most enterprises now concentrate on their core business. 'Down-scoping' is now recommended as a sensible strategy.

4. Alternatively such developments arise as a result of the research and development investments of the enterprise. The fixing of the level of

investment in research and development reflects a very significant strategic uncertainty and often reflects a kind of kinked demand curve in which the level is fixed by competitors (Baumol 2002). Too low a level by an enterprise implies being out-competed in innovation. Too high a level implies imposing excessive costs on the relevant enterprise. The level is path dependent in that it is fixed by the past interaction between the main players.

5. The nature of the investment project at the international level is largely determined by the nature of the multinational enterprise itself. Broadly there are three types of MNE (Caves 1996: 2):

   - Those that involve producing the same good or service but in different markets, those that are horizontally integrated
   - Those that involve producing various goods or services which are inputs into the value adding chain which eventually results in a final consumer good, those that are vertically integrated
   - Those that involve a deliberate decision to diversify, sometimes in order to reduce the risk to which the enterprise is exposed, that is international conglomerates.

Chapter 3 Risk and Risk-generating Events

1. This is understandable since it makes risk amenable to the kind of general equilibrium analysis undertaken by Arrow (1964) and Hirschleifer and Riley (1992). One of the crowning achievements is reckoned to be the Arrow-Debreu general equilibrium model in which they demonstrated the efficiency of a complete system of contingent markets. If the probabilities are known, it is possible to define an equilibrium system with its implied prices for all future periods. Leonard Savage (1954) even argued that only subjective probability estimates were needed rather than objective estimates, an assertion contradicted by the work of Daniel Ellsberg (1961). It is just as important that a theory is descriptive of reality as that it is logically consistent. Even if it were possible to define a general equilibrium with its optimum choices it might bear no resemblance to the real world.

2. Two other interesting states are what Kobrin calls objective uncertainty and subjective uncertainty (Kobrin, 1979: 70). The first comprises perfect knowledge of all possible outcomes and the probabilities attached to these outcomes, either 'through calculation a priori or from statistics of past experience' (Knight, 1921: p. 233). Like certainty, objective uncertainty is an ideal construct which cannot exist since we cannot know all outcomes and the probability of their realisation. Since all relevant events and decisions are unique and occur within an environment which is also highly complex there must be a high degree of subjectivity in any creative imagining of possible future outcomes, in such future forecasting exercises as scenario building. The real issue is how close we can get to objective uncertainty. Again we can only approximate objective uncertainty in a situation in which relevant information is readily available, all feasible outcomes are known, and almost everyone is agreed on the likely probabilities of different scenarios unfolding.

Chapter 4   Home Country Bias in Foreign Direct Investment

1. Clearly an enterprise can create a natural hedge for significant elements of country risk by borrowing in the host country or raising capital on its capital market, but this is not usually taken into account. Clearly, one way of managing country risk is to adopt a suitable form of organisation, which avoids the transfer of investment funds through international, or even national, markets, but promotes the transfer of technical knowledge or organisational know-how.
2. There are numerous texts which deal with this area, including texts on finance in general (Madura 2001), texts which deal with FDI from a financial perspective (Moosa) or texts which deal with the finance, risk and the FDI link (Doherty 2000 or Culp 2001).
3. The broadening began with Coase and Williamson and has become the basis of the work of Buckley, Rugman and Casson.
4. The literature on market integration and home country bias is extremely technical. It is not for the faint hearted. The present chapter seeks to offer references which clearly flag what the writer is doing. Unfortunately some of the relevant work is cryptic to a degree which impedes understanding of the relevant arguments.
5. There are two methodological arguments which should be pointed out. The first is the Friedman argument, that the assumptions of a model do not matter provided it can predict accurately. Secondly, there is the argument advanced by Doherty that where a model shows the irrelevance of an issue, e.g. risk control by managers, relaxing the assumptions of the model will reveal the reasons why the issue is not irrelevant.
6. However there are some who have argued the opposite (Moosa).

Part II   Different Perspectives on Investment Appraisal

1. It might also be possible to take an accounting perspective in viewing a project but this book does not consider all the relevant accounting considerations, mainly because they differ from country to country.

Chapter 5   The Investment Process and Decision Making: the Financial Perspective

1. If the distinction between systematic and unsystematic risk is regarded as important then it might be possible to combine the two adjustments. The systematic risk should be considered through adjustment of the discount rate, specifically using market based betas as a basis for the relevant risk premium, where this is possible, and the unsystematic risk taken into account through adjustment of the cash flows (Aven 2003: 36).
2. There is no separate information strategy for opportunities and threats. Both risk control and relevant information strategies need to be integrated into the general process of strategy making. In Culp's terminology the focus is the efficiency enhancement role of risk management, including enterprise wide risk management, rather than just risk control (Culp 2001: chap. 10).

3. Buckley (1996) gives a full account of the differences between capital budgeting for an international and for a domestic project. A more concise version is included in Moosa (2002), chapter 4.
4. The second approach is to use the well-known Black-Scholes equation which rests on a lognormal distribution of returns and a continuous pricing process. There are very restrictive assumptions for the BS formula. It is applicable to European type options when the option can be exercised only at maturity. In that sense, it is not really appropriate for real options. Nor can it accommodate compound options. It can only deal with one significant source of uncertainty, a known stochastic process for the underlying asset, a constant variance and a constant exercise price.

The formula, which looks rather more complex than it actually is, is:

Value of a call option = $Se^{(b-r)T}N(d_1) - Xe^{-rT}N(d_2)$

Where $d_1 = \ln(S/X) + (b + \sigma^2/2)T/\sigma\sqrt{T}$
and $d_2 = d_1 - \sigma\sqrt{T}$

N is the cumulative normal distribution function.

The two terms in the Black-Scholes equation represent the usual two parts to the tracking portfolio, the assumption that the option is 'in the money', i.e. that S > X (Vonnegut 2000 and Cox, Ross and Rubinstein 1979).

- The first is the present value of the share of the underlying asset which needs to be held in the tracking portfolio, with account taken in this case of any leakage of value (the b in the equation).
- The second term includes two components, the present value of the cost of the investment, but modified to take account of the risk-neutral probability of the option finishing 'in the money'.

The usual present value formula is a special case of the Black-Scholes formula. If S is very large relative to X, then both N(d)s converge on 1 and C = S – Xe – rt. Moreover the value of waiting converges on zero at maturity. At maturity, the value of such an option is therefore equivalent to the usual estimate of net present value, S – X. The value of an option at maturity is S – X, since when t = 0, the terms, R_f and σ^2, cannot affect the value of the call option.
5. Even if it is impossible to say with certainty whether a decision is optimal, then it might be possible to define procedures which make likely a good decision. Are the decision rules adopted appropriate for the relevant enterprise? Are the measurement systems capable of yielding an accurate indication of the values to be attached to the variables relevant to the decision rules?

Chapter 7   The Investment Process and Decision Making: The Organisational Perspective

1. There is a recent literature critical of the impact on efficiency of both legal arrangements. Some commentators have gone as far as to advocate the ex

ante development of individual contracts to establish liability and/or ex post bargaining in the event of a disaster, a situation which it is argued would ensure efficient decisions. However, there is one major impediment to both. the relevant transactions costs of both procedures would be enormously high. The present arrangements help keep those costs low.

Chapter 11   Responses to Risk

1. Those purchasing an option may place a subjective value on the option which reflects their assessment of the probabilities of the different outcomes and is different from the risk-neutral value, fixed in an equilibrium market in which no arbitrage opportunities can exist unexploited. If it is greater, then it means that the purchaser is risk averse; if it is smaller, then the individual will not purchase since he/she is a risk-taker. This shows that, if there is an influence from subjective probabilities and from risk tolerances, it is indirect, through the value of the underlying asset. In competitive markets where the individuals are price takers, it is assumed that this influence is imperceptible.

Bibliography

A Risk Management Standard (AIRMIC, ALARM and IRM: 2002).

Aaker, D. A. and Jacobson, R. 'The risk of marketing: the role of systematic, uncontrollable, and controllable unsystematic, and downside risk' in Bettis, R. A. and Thomas, H. (ed.) *Risk, Strategy and Management* (JAI Press, London: 1990): 137–60.

Adler, M. and Dumas, B. 'International portfolio choice and corporation finance: a synthesis', *Journal of Finance*, vol. XXXVIII, no. 3, June 1983.

Akerlof, G. A. 'The market for "lemons": quality uncertainty and the market mechanism', *Quarterly Journal of Economics*, vol. 84, no. 3, August 1970: 488–500.

Alon, I. and Martin, M. A. 'A normative model of macro political risk assessment', *Multinational Business Review*, vol. 6, no. 2, 1998.

Amram, M. and Kulatilaka, N. *Real Options: managing strategic investment in an uncertain world* (Harvard Business School Press, Boston, Mass.: 1999).

Anderson, J. E. and van Wincorp, E. 'Trade costs', vol. XLII, no. 3, Sept. 2004: 691–711.

Arrow, K. J. 'Uncertainty and the Welfare Economics of Medical Care', *American Economic Review*, vol. 53, no. 5, December 1963: 941–73.

Arrow, K. J. The role of securities in the optimal allocation of risk-bearing. *Review of Economic Studies*, vol. 31, no. 2, April 1964: 91–6.

Arthur, W. B. 'Competing technologies, increasing returns, and lock-in by historical events', *Economic Journal*, vol. 97, 1989: 642–65.

Atkins, J., Mazzi, S. and Ramlogan, C. A Study of the Vulnerability of Developing and Island States: a composite index (Commonwealth Secretariat, London: August 1998).

Aven, T. *Foundations of Risk Analysis: a knowledge and decision-oriented perspective* (John Wiley and Sons, Chichester, England: 2003).

Baird, I. S. and Thomas, H. 'Toward a contingency model of strategic risk taking', *Academy of Management Review*, vol. 10, no. 2, 1985: 230–43.

Baumol, W. J. *The Free-Market Innovation Machine: analysing the growth miracle of capitalism* (Princeton University Press, Princeton, N.J. and Oxford: 2002).

Baxter, M. and Jermann, U. J. 'The international diversification puzzle is worse than you think', *The American Economic Review*, vol. 87, no. 1, March 1997: 170–80.

Ben-Porath, Y. 'The F-connection: families, friends, and firms and the organisation of exchange', *Population Development Review*, vol. 6, 1980: 1–30.

Bernstein. P. L. *Against the Gods: the remarkable story of risk* (John Wiley and Sons, New York: 1996).

Bettis, R. A. 'Modern financial theory, corporate strategy and public policy: three conundrums', *Academy of Management Review*, vol. 8, no. 3, 1983: 406–13.

Black, F. and Scholes, M. 'The pricing of options and corporate liabilities', *Journal of Political Economy*, vol. 81, 1973: 637–54.

Boddewyn, J. and Cracco, E. F. The Political Game in World Business, *Management Review*, vol. 61, no. 4, 1972a: 244–8.

Boddewyn, J. and Cracco, E. F. The Political Game in World Business, *Columbia Journal of World Business*, vol. 7, no. 1, 1972b: 45–57.

Bodie, Z. and Merton, R. C. 'The information role of asset prices: the case of implied volatility', chapter 6 in *The Global Financial System: a functional perspective* (Harvard Business School Press, Boston, Mass.: 1995).

Bowman, E. H. 'A risk/return paradox for strategic management', *Sloan Management Review*, Spring 1980: 17–31.

Bowman, E. H. 'Risk seeking in troubled firms', *Sloan Management Review*, Summer 1982: 33–42.

Bowman, E. H. and Hurry, D. 'Strategy through the options lens: an integrated view of resource investments and the incremental-choice process', *Academy of Management Review*, vol. 18, no. 4, 1993: 760–82.

Bradley, D. G. 'Managing against expropriation', *Harvard Business Review*, 1977.

Brewer, T. L. Political risk assessment for foreign direct investment decisions: Better methods for better results. *Columbia Journal of World Business*, vol. 16, no. 1, 1981: 5.

Brewer, T. L. 'Politics, risks, and international business' in Brewer, T. L. *Political Risk in International Business* (Praeger, New York: 1985).

Briguglio, L. Alternative Economic Vulnerability Indices for Developing Countries. Report prepared for the Expert Group on Vulnerability Index. (UN(DESA): December 1997).

Brouthers, K. D. 'The influence of international risk on entry mode strategy in the computer software industry', *Management International Review*, vol. 35, 1995/6: 7–28.

Bryan, D. and Rafferty, M. *The Global Economy in Australia: global integration and national economic policy* (Allen and Unwin, St Leonards, Australia: 1999).

Buckley, A. *International Capital Budgeting* (Prentice Hall, Hemel Hempstead: 1996).

Burgelman, R. A. 'Corporate entrepreneurship and strategic management: insights from a process study', *Management Science*, vol. 29, 1983: 1349–1364.

Burgelman, R. A. 'Managing the new venture division: research findings and implications for strategic management', *Strategic Management Journal*, vol. 6, 1985: 39–54.

Burgelman, R. A. *Strategy is Destiny* (The Free Press, New York: 2000).

Burgelman, R. A. and Grove, A. S. 'Strategic dissonance', *California Management Review*, winter 1996: 8–28.

Calverley, J. *Country Risk Analysis* (Butterworths, London: 1985).

Carter, E. E. 'What are the risks in risk analysis?', *Harvard Business Review*, July–August 1972: 72–82.

Caves, R. E. *Multinational Enterprise and Economic Analysis*, 2nd ed. (Cambridge University Press, Cambridge and New York: 1996).

Chander, R. *Measurement of the Vulnerability of Small States* (UN(DESA), Washington: 1996).

Characteristics and appraisal of major rating agencies, Summary of report of the Japan Centre for International Finance, January 2000.

Christensen, C. M. *The Innovator's Dilemma* (Harvard Business School Press, Boston: 1997).

Christensen, C. M. and Bower, J. 'Customer power, strategic investment and the failure of leading firms', *Strategic Management Journal*, March 1996: 197–218.

Christensen, C. M., Johnson, M. W. and Rigby, D. K. 'Foundations for growth: how to identify and build disruptive new businesses', *Sloan Management Review*, vol. 43, no. 3, 2002: 23–31.

Ciarrapico, A. M. *Country Risk: A theoretical framework of analysis* (Dartmouth, U.K.: 1992).

Clark, E. 'Valuing political risk', *Journal of International Money and Finance*, vol. 16, no. 3, 1997: 477–90.

Coakley, J., Kulasi, F. and Smith, R., 'Current account solvency and the Feldstein-Horioka puzzle', *The Economic Journal*, vol. 106, May 1996: 620–27.

Collier, P. and Gunning, J. W. 'Explaining African economic performance', *Journal of Economic Literature*, vol. XXXVII, March 1999: 64–111.

Collier, P. and Patillo, C. (eds) *Investment and Risk in Africa* (Macmillan, London: 1998).

Copeland, T. and Antikarov, V. *Real Options: a practitioner's guide* (Texere, New York: 2001).

Coplin, W. D. and O'Leary, M. K. *Political Risk Services: The Handbook of Country and Political Risk Analysis* (International Business Communications – Political Risk Services, East Syracuse, New York: 1994).

Courtney, H., Kirkland, J. and Viguerie, P. 'Strategy under uncertainty', *Harvard Business Review*, vol. 75, 1997: 66–79.

Cox, J. S., Ross, S. and Rubinstein, M. 'Option pricing: a simplified approach', *Journal of Financial Economics*, vol. 7, September 1979: 229–63.

Culp, C. L. *The Risk Management Process: business strategy and tactics* (John Wiley and Sons, New York: 2001).

Cyert, R. M. and March, J. G. *A Behavioural Theory of the Firm*, 2nd ed. (Blackwell, Malden, Mass.: 2001).

Damodaran, A. 'Measuring company exposure to country risk: theory and practice', Unpublished paper, September 2003.

David, P. A. 'Clio and the economics of QWERTY', *American Economic Review*, May 1985: 332–37.

Dimpfel, M., Habann, F. and Algesheimer, R. 'Real options theory, flexibility and the media industry', *International Journal of Media Management*, vol. 4, no. 4, 2002: 261– 72.

Dixit, A. K. and Pindyck, R. S. *Investment under Uncertainty* (Princeton University Press, Princeton, New Jersey: 1994).

Doherty, N. A. *Integrated Risk Management: techniques and strategies for reducing risk* (McGraw-Hill, New York: 2000).

Dowd, K. *Beyond Value at Risk: the new science of risk management* (Wiley, New York: 1998).

Dumas, B. 'Partial vs. general equilibrium: Models of the international capital Markets', NBER Working paper No. 4446, 1993.

Dumas, B. 'A test of the international CAPM using business cycle indicators as instrumental variables', in Frankel, J. (ed.), *The internationalization of Equity Markets* (University of Chicago Press, Chicago: 1994): 23–50.

Dunn, J. 'Country risk: Social and cultural aspects', in Herring, R.J. (ed.), *Managing International Risk* (Cambridge University Press, New York: 1983): 139–68.

Dunning, J. H. and Narula, R. (eds) *Foreign direct investment and governments* (Routledge, London and New York: 1996), chapter 1, 'The investment development path revisited: some emerging issues', Dunning and Narula: 1–41, and chapter 13, 'The investment development path: some conclusions', Lall, S.: 423–41.

Economist Intelligence Unit. Monthly updatings of country risk rating.

Ellsberg, D. 'Risk, ambiguity, and the Savage axioms', *Quarterly Journal of Economics*, vol. 75, no. 4, November 1961: 643–69.

Elton, E. J. and Gruber, M. J. *International Capital Markets* (North-Holland Publishing Company, US and Canada: 1975).

Erb, C. B., Harvey, C. R. and Viskanta, T. E. Country Risk in Global Financial Management, The Research Foundation of the Institute of Chartered Financial Analysts.

Erb, C. B., Harvey, C. R. and Viskanta, T. E. 'Forecasting international equity correlations', *Financial Analysts Journal*, Nov.–Dec. 1994: 32–45.

Erb, C. B., Harvey, C. R. and Viskanta, T. E. 'Political risk, economic risk and financial risk', *Financial Analysts Journal*, vol. 52, 1996a: 28–46.

Erb, C. B., Harvey, C. R. and Viskanta, T. E. 'Expected returns and volatility in 135 countries', *Journal of Portfolio Management*, Spring 1996b: 46–58.

Euromoney, published monthly with country risk ratings bi-annually.

Fama, E. F. 'Agency problems and the theory of the firm', *Journal of Political Economy*, vol. 47, no. 2, 1980: 288–307.

Fama, E. F. and French, K. R. 'The cross-section of expected stock returns', *Journal of Finance*, vol. 47, no. 2, 1992: 427–65.

Fama, E. F. and French, K. R. The Equity Premium. The Centre for Research in Security Prices, Working Paper No. 522, Graduate School of Business, University of Chicago, 2001.

Fama, E. F. and Jensen, M. C. 'Separation of ownership and control', *Journal of Law and Economics*, vol. XXV1, June 1983: 301–25.

Fan, M. Country Risk and its Impact on the FDI Decision-making Process from an Australian Perspective, Unpublished PhD thesis Swinburne University of Technology 2004.

Fatehi-Sedah, K. and Safizadeh, M. H. 'The association between political instability and flow of foreign direct investment', *Management Investment Review*, vol. 29, no. 4, 1989: 4–13.

Feldstein, M. and Horioka, C. 'Domestic saving and international capital flows', *Economic Journal*, vol. 90, June 1980: 314–29.

Fitzpatrick, M. 'The definition and assessment of political risk in international business: A review of the literature', *Academy of Management Review*, vol. 8, no. 2, 1983: 249.

Fleming, D. and Bailyn, B. (eds) *Law in American History* (Little, Brown and Co., Boston and Toronto: 1971).

Foss, N. J. 'Real options and the theory of the firm', Unpublished paper, 1998.

Frankel, J. A. 'Measuring international capital mobility: a review', *American Economic Association*, vol. 82, no. 2, May 1992: 197–202.

Freeman, R. E. *Strategic Management: a stakeholder approach* (HarperCollins, Boston: 1984).

Fried, V. H. and Hisrich, R. D. 'Toward a model of venture capital investment decision making', *Financial Management*, vol. 23, Autumn 1994: 28–37.

Friedman, I. S. *The World Debt Dilemma: managing country risk* (Council for International Banking Studies and Robert Morris Associates, Washington D.C. and Philadelphia: 1983).

Friedman, M. and Savage, L. J. 'The utility analysis of choices involving risk', *Journal of Political Economy*, vol. 56, 1948: 279–304.

Froot, K. A., Scharfstein, D. S. and Stein, J. C. 'A framework for risk management', *Harvard Business Review*, Nov.–Dec. 1994: 91–102.

Gangemi, M., Brooks, R. D. and Faff, R. W. 'Modelling Australia's country risk: a country beta approach', *Journal of Economics and Business*, vol. 52, 2000: 259–76.

Glassman, D. A. and Riddick, L. A. 'What causes home asset bias and how should it be measured?', *Journal of Empirical Finance*, vol. 8, no. 1, March 2001: 35–54.

Goodman, L. S. 'Diversifiable risk in LDC lending: a 20/20 hindsight view', *Studies in Banking and Finance*, 1986: 249–262.

Gordon, R. H. and Bovernberg, A. L. 'Why is capital so immobile internationally? Possible explanations and implications for capital income taxation', *American Economic Review*, vol. 86, no. 5, Dec. 1996: 1057–75.

Graaff, J. D. *Theoretical Welfare Economics* (Cambridge University Press, Cambridge: 1963).

Green, R. T. 'Political Instability as a Determinant of U.S. Foreign Investment', Bureau of Business Research, Graduate School of Business, University of Texas, Austin: 1972.

Haner, F. T. 'Rating investment risks abroad', *Business Horizons*, vol. 22, no. 2, 1979: 18–23.

Haque, N. U., Mathieson, D. M and Mark, N. 'Rating the raters of country creditworthiness', *Finance and Development*, vol. 34, no. 1, March 1997: 10–13.

Hashmi, M. A. and Guvenli, T. 'Importance of political risk assessment function in multinational corporations', *Global Finance Journal*, vol. 3, no. 2, 1992: 137–44.

Helliwell, J. *How much do national borders matter?* (Brookings Institution Press, Washington D.C.: 1998).

Helliwell, J. and McKitrick, R. 'Comparing capital mobility across provincial and national borders', *Canadian Journal of Economics*, vol. 32, no. 5, Nov. 1999: 1164–73.

Hirshleifer, J. and Riley, J. G. *The Analytics of Uncertainty and Information* (Cambridge University Press, Cambridge: 1992).

Hofstede, G. *Cultures and Organizations* (McGraw-Hill, London: 1991).

Howell, D. and Chaddick, B. 'Models of political risk for foreign investment and trade', *Columbia Journal of World Business*, vol. 29, no. 3, 1994: 70–92.

Hull, J. C. *The Evaluation of Risk in Business Investment* (Pergamom Press, Oxford: 1980).

Huntingdon, S. *The Clash of Civilizations and the Remaking of the World Order* (Simon and Schuster, New York: 1996).

ISO/IEC Guide 73: 2002 Risk Management. Vocabulary. Guidelines for use in standards

Institutional Investor. Annual Country Risk Ratings: 1980–2003.

Jagannathan, R. and Meier, I. 'Do we need CAPM for capital budgeting?', NBER Working Papers, January, 2002.

Japan Centre for International Finance, Characteristics and Appraisal of Major Rating Agencies, Japan: 2001.

Jensen, M. C. and Meckling, W. H. 'Theory of the firm. managerial behaviour, agency cost and ownership structure', *Journal of Financial Economics*, vol. 3, 1976: 305–360.

Jones, E. L. *The European Miracle: environments, economies and geopolitics in the history of Europe and Asia*, 2nd ed. (Cambridge University Press, Cambridge: 1987).

Kaplan, R. S. and Norton, D. P. *The Balanced Scorecard: translating strategy into action* (Harvard Business School Press, Boston, Mass.: 1996).

Kasanen, E. 'Creating value by spawning investment opportunities', *Financial Management*, Autumn 1993: 251–58.

Kemna, A. G. Z. 'Case studies as real options', *Financial Management*, vol. 22, no. 3, Autumn 1993: 259–70.

Kennedy, C. R. Jr. *Political Risk Management: International Lending and Investing Under Environmental Uncertainty* (Quorum, New York: 1987).

Kim, W. C. and Mauborgne, R. *Blue Ocean Strategy: how to create uncontested market space and make the competition irrelevant* (Harvard Business School Press, Boston, Mass.: 2005).

Knight, F. H. *Risk, Uncertainty and Profit* (Chicago University Press, Chicago: 1921).

Knudsen, H. 'Explaining the national propensity to expropriate: an ecological approach', *Journal of International Studies*, vol. 5, no. 1, 1974.

Kobrin, S. J. 'Political risk: a review and reconsideration', *Journal of International Business Studies*, vol. 10, no. 1, 1979: 67.

Krayenbuehl, T. E. *Country Risk Assessment and Monitoring* (Woodhead-Faulkner, Cambridge: 1985).

Krugman, P. R. and Obstfeld, M. *International Economics: theory and practice*, 6th ed. (Addison Wesley, Boston: 2003).

Kunreuther, H. 'The pitfalls of an interdependent world', *Financial Times*, Aug 28, 2003: 11.

Kunreuther, H., Michel-Kerjan, E. and Porter, B. 'Assessing, Managing and Financing Extreme Events: dealing with terror' NBER Working Papers, No. 10179, December 2003.

Lee, T. J. and Caves, R. E. 'Uncertain outcomes of foreign investment: determinants of the dispersion of profits after large acquisitions', *Journal of International Business Studies*, vol. 29, no. 3, 1998: 563–80.

Lessard, D. R. 'Evaluating international projects: an adjusted present value approach' in Lessard, 1985, chapter 34: 570–84, or Crum, R. L and Derkinderen, F. G. J. (eds) *Capital Budgeting under Uncertainty* (Nijenrode Studies in Business, 5, Martinus Nijhoff, The Hague: 1981).

Lessard, D. R. (ed.) *International Financial Management: theory and applications*, 2nd ed. (John Wiley and Sons, New York: 1985).

Lessard, D. R. 'Incorporating country risk in the valuation of offshore projects', *Journal of Applied Corporate Finance*, vol. 9, no. 3, Fall 1996: 52–63.

Levi, M. D. *International Finance: the markets and financial management of multinational business*, 3rd ed. (McGraw-Hill, inc., New York and others: 1996).

Liebowitz, S. J. and Margolis, S. E. 'Path dependence, lock-in, and history', *Journal of Law, Economics, and Organization*, April 1995: 1–22.

Lim, G. and Martin, V. 'Forecasting large changes in exchange rates' in Abelson, P. and Joyeux, R. (eds) *Economic Forecasting* (Allen and Unwin, St Leonards, NSW: 2000): 255–76.

Lintner, J. 'The valuation of risk assets and the selection of risky investments in stock portfolios and capital budgets', *Review of Economics and Statistics*, vol. 47, 1965: 13–37.

Lipsey, R. G. and Lancaster, K. 'The general theory of the second best', *Review of Economic Studies*, vol. XXIV, 1955/6: 11–32.

Luehrmann, T. A. 'Investment opportunities as real options: getting started on the numbers', *Harvard Business School*, vol. 76, no. 4, 1998a: 51–61.

Luehrmann, T. A. 'Strategy as a portfolio of real options', *Harvard Business Review*, vol. 76, no. 5, 1998b: 89–99.

Madura, J. *Financial Markets and Institutions* (South-Western Publishing, Cincinatti: 2001)

Mandron, A. 'Project valuation: problem areas, theory and practice', *The Current State of Business Disciplines*, vol. 3, ed. Dahiya, S. B. (Spellbound Publications PVT-LTD, Rohtak, India: 2000).

Mariscal, J. O. and Lee, R. M. 'The valuation of Mexican stocks: and extension of the capital asset pricing model to emerging markets', *Investment Research*, Goldman Sachs, 1993.

Marris, R. L. *The Economic Theory of Managerial Capitalism* (Macmillan, London: 1964).

Mayer, E. *International Lending: Country risk analysis* (Reston Publishing, Virginia USA: 1985).

McGrath, R. G. 'Falling forward: real options reasoning and entrepreneurial failure', *Academy of Management Review*, vol. 24, no. 1, 1999: 13–30.

Merton, R. C. 'On the pricing of corporate debt: the risk structure of interest rates', *The Review of Financial Studies*, vol. 50, 1974: 53–86.

Meyer, S. and Qu, T. 'Place-specific determinants of FDI: the geographical perspective', Chap. 1 in Green, M. and McNaughton, R. (eds) *The Location of Foreign Direct Investment: geographic and business approaches*, 1995: 1–14.

Meldrum, D. H. 'Country risk and a quick look at Latin America', *Business Economics*, vol. 34, no. 3, 1999: 30–8.

Meldrum, D. H. 'Country risk and foreign direct investment', *Business Economics*, vol. 35, 2000: 33–40.

Miklos, J. C. 'Country risk analysis at Wells Fargo bank', *The World of Banking*, 1983.

Miller, K. D. 'A framework for integrated risk management in international business', *Journal of International Business Studies*, vol. 23, no. 2, 1992: 311–31.

Miller, K. D. 'Industry and country effects on managers' perceptions of environmental uncertainties', *Journal of International Business Studies*, vol. 24, no. 4, 1993.

Miller, K. D. 'Economic exposure and integrated risk management', *Strategic Management Journal*, vol. 19, 1998: 497–514.

Miller, K. D. and Bromiley, P. 'Strategic risk and corporate performance: an analysis of alternative risk measures', *Academy of Management Journal*, vol. 33, no. 4, 1990: 756–79.

Miller, K. D. and Reuer, J. J. 'Measuring organizational downside risk', *Strategic Management Journal*, vol. 17, Nov. 1996.

Mintzberg, H. D., Raisinghani, D. and Theoret, A. 'The structure of "unstructured decision" processes', *Administrative Science Quarterly*, vol. 21, no. 2, 1976: 246–75.

Modigliani, F. and Miller, M. H. 'The cost of capital, corporation finance and the theory of investment', *The American Economic Review*, vol. XLVIII, no. 3, June 1958: 261–97.

Moosa, I. *Foreign Direct Investment: theory, evidence and practice* (Palgrave, Houndsmill, Basingstoke: 2002).

Moran, T. H. *Managing International Political Risk* (Blackwell Publishers Ltd., Mass.: 1998).

Morrison, C. C. 'The nature of second best', *Southern Economic Journal*, vol. 32, no. 1, Jul 1965: 49–52.

Moss, D. A. *When All Else Fails: government as the ultimate risk manager* (Harvard University Press, Cambridge, Mass. and London, England: 2002).

Myers, S. 'Financial theory and financial strategy', vol. 14, Jan/Feb 1984: 126–37.

Nagy, P. J. Country Risk: how to assess, quantify and monitor it. (Euro-money, London: 1979).

Narula, R. *Multinational Investment and Economic Structure: globalization and competitiveness* (Routledge, London and New York: 1996), chapter 1, 'The dynamics of FDI and economic growth': 11– 36.

Nordal, K. B. 'Country risk, country risk indices, and valuation of FDI: a real options approach' *Emerging Markets Review*, vol. 2, no. 3, Sept. 2001: 197–217.

North American Industry Classification System: United States 1997 (Bernan Press, Lanham, V.A.: 1998).

OECD *Benchmark Definition of Foreign Direct Investment*, 3rd ed. (OECD, Paris: 1996).

Ojala, M. 'The dollar sign-using databases to determine political risk', *Database*, vol. 19, no. 2, 1996: 80–83.

Olsson, C. *Risk Management in Emerging Markets* (Financial Times and Prentice Hall, London: 2002).

Oxelheim, L. and Wihlborg, C.G. *Macroeconomic Uncertainty – International Risks and Opportunities for the Corporation* (John Wiley & Sons, Chichester: 1987).

Petry, G. H. and Sprow, J. 'The theory and practice of finance in the 1990s', *Quarterly Review of Economics and Finance*, vol. 33, no. 4, 1993: 359–81.

Pindyck, R. S. 'Irreversibility, uncertainty, and investment', *Journal of Economic Literature*, vol. XXIX, September 1991: 1110–48.

Poterba, J. M. and Summers, L. H. 'A CEO survey of U. S. companies' time horizons and hurdle rates', *Sloan Management Review*, Fall 1995: 43–53.

Quinn, J. B. *Intelligent Enterprise* (The Free Press, New York: 1992).

Ramcharran, H. 'International bank lending to developing countries: an empirical analysis of the impact of country risk', *Multinational Business Review*, vol. 7, no. 1, 1999a: 83.

Ramcharran, H. 'Foreign direct investment and country risk: further empirical evidence', *Global Economic Review*, vol. 28, no. 3, 1999b: 49–59.

Reisen, H. and von Maltzan, J. 'Sovereign credit ratings, emerging market risk and financial market volatility', *Intereconomics*, vol. 33, no. 2, March/April 1998: 73–62.

Reisen, H. and von Maltzan, J. 'Boom and bust and sovereign ratings', *International Finance*, vol. 2, no. 2, 1999: 273–94. ?? Not cited in text pls check

Ringlieb, A. H. and Wiggins, S. N. 'Liability and large-scale, long-term hazards', *Journal of Political Economy*, vol. 98, no. 3, 1990: 574–95.

Robock, S. H. 'Political risk: identification and assessment', *Columbia Journal of World Business*, vol. 6, no. 4, 1971: 6.

Roemer, E. 'Real options and the theory of the firm'. Unpublished paper.

Rogers, J. *Strategy, Value and Risk: the real options approach* (Palgrave Macmillan, Houndsmill, Basingstoke, England: 2002).

Roll, R. 'A critique of the asset pricing theory's tests – part 1: on past and potential testability of the theory', *Journal of Financial Economics*, vol. 4, no. 2, 1977: 129–76.

Root, F. R. 'Attitudes of American executives toward foreign governments and investment opportunities', *Economic and Business Bulletin*, January 1968.

Rugman, A. B. and Hodgetts, R. M. Chap. 13, Political risk and negotiation strategies, in *International Business: A Strategic Management Approach* (McGraw-Hill, New York: 1995).

Rumelt, R. P. 'Towards a strategic theory of the firm', in *Competitive Strategic Management*, ed. R. B. Lamb (Prentice Hall, Englewood Cliffs, N.J.: 1984).

Rummel, R. J. and Heenan, D. A. 'How multinationals analyse political risk', *Harvard Business School*, vol. 56, no. 1, 1978: 67.

Sandberg, W. T., Schweiger, D. M. and Hofer, C. W. 'The use of verbal protocols in determining venture capitalists' decision processes', *Entrepreneurship Theory and Practice*, Winter 1988: 8–20.

Saunders, A. *Financial Institutions in a Modern Perspective* (Irwin/McGraw, Boston: 2000).

Savage, L. J. *The Foundation of Statistics* (Wiley, New York: 1954).

Scheiber, H. N. 'The road to Munn: eminent domain and the concept of public purpose in the state courts', Fleming and Bailyn 1971: 329–402.

Scheiber, H. N. 'Government and the economy: studies of the "commonwealth" policy in nineteenth-century America', *Journal of Interdisciplinary History*, vol. 3, 1972–3: 135–51.

Scheiber, H. N. 'Property law, expropriation, and resource allocation by government: the United States, 1789–1910', *Journal of Economic History*, vol. 33, 1973: 232–51.

Scheiber, H. N. 'Instrumentalism and property rights: a reconsideration of American "styles of judicial reasoning" in the nineteenth century', *Wisconsin Law Review*, vol. 6, 1980: 1159–89.

Scheiber, H. N. 'Regulation, property rights and definition of "the market": law and the American economy', *Journal of Economic History*, vol. 41, 1981: 103–11.

Shrader, R. C., Oviatt, M. and McDougall, P. P. 'How new ventures exploit trade-offs among international risk factors: lessons for the accelerated internationalization of the 21st century', *Academy of Management Journal*, vol. 43, no. 6, 2000: 1227–47.

Schwartz, E. S. and Trigeorgis, L. *Real Options and Investment under Uncertainty* (The MIT Press, Cambridge, Mass. and London, England: 2001).

Shah, A. and Slemrod, J. 'Do taxes matter for foreign direct investment?', *World Bank Economic Review*, vol. 5, no. 3, 1991: 473–91.

Shapiro, A. C. 'Risk in international banking', *Journal of Financial and Quantitative Analysis*, vol. XVII, no. 5, 1982: 727–39.

Shapiro, A. C. 'Currency risk and country risk in international banking', *Journal of Finance*, vol. 40, no. 3, 1985a: 881.

Shapiro, A. C. 'International capital budgeting' in Lessard (ed.) 1985b: 548–69.

Shapiro, A. C. *Multinational Financial Management*, 6th ed. (John Wiley and Sons, New York: 1999).

Sharpe, W. F. 'Capital asset prices: a theory of market equilibrium under conditions of risk', *Journal of Finance*, vol. 19, no. 3, 1964: 425–42.

Simon, H. A. 'A behavioural model of rational choice', *Quarterly Journal of Economics*, vol. 6, no. 4, 1955: 99–111.

Simon, J. D. 'Political risk assessment: past trends and future prospects', *Columbia Journal of World Business*, vol. 17, no. 3, 1982: 62.

Simon, J. D. 'A theoretical perspective on political risk', *Journal of International Business Studies*, vol. 15, no. 3, 1984: 123.

Sinn, S. 'Saving-investment correlations and capital mobility: on the evidence from annual data', *Economic Journal*, vol. 102, Sept. 1992: 1162–70.

Smit, H. T. J. 'Investment analysis of offshore concessions in the Netherlands', *Financial Management*, vol. 26, no. 2, 1997: 5–17.

Smit, H. T. J. and Ankum, L. A. 'A real options and game-theoretic approach to corporate investment strategy under competition', *Financial Management*, vol. 22, no. 3, Autumn 1993: 241–50.

Smit, H. T. J. and Trigeorgis, L. *Strategic Investment: real options and games* (Princeton University Press, Princeton, New Jersey: 2004).

Solberg, R. L. *Country Risk Analysis: a handbook* (Routledge, London and New York: 1992).

Solnik, B. 'Why not diversify internationally rather than domestically?', *Financial Analysts' Journal*, July–Aug. 1974: 48–54.

Solnik, B. 'International arbitrage pricing theory', *Journal of Finance*, vol. XXXVIII, no. 2, May 1983: 449–57.

Smith, A. *An Inquiry into the Nature and Causes of the Wealth of Nations* (Clarendon Press, Oxford: 1976).

Standard Industrial Classification Manual (Prentice Hall Information Services, Paramus, N.J.: 1987).

Stein, J. C. Agency, Information and Corporate Investment NBER, Working Paper No. 8342, 2001.

Stevens, F. Y. 'Quantitative perspective on political risk analysis for direct foreign investment – a closer look', *Multinational Business Review*, vol. 5, no. 1, 1997: 77.

Stobaugh, R. B. Jr. 'How to analyse foreign investment climates', *Harvard Business Review* 1969.

Stulz, R. M. 'Rethinking risk management', *Journal of Applied Corporate Finance*, vol. 9, no. 3, 1996: 8–24.

Taylor, A. M. 'International capital mobility in history: purchasing-power parity in the long run', Working Paper 5742, 1996, National Bureau of Economic Research.

Teece, D. J., Pisano, G. and Shuen, A. 'Dynamic capabilities and strategic management', *Strategic Management Journal*, vol. 18, 1997: 509–34.

Thomsen, S. Investment patterns in a longer-term perspective. Working Papers on International Investment, no. 2000/2, Directorate for Financial, Fiscal and Enterprise Affairs, OECD, 2000.

Torre, J. D. L. and Neckar, D. H. 'Forecasting political risks for international operations', *International Journal of Forecasting*, vol. 4, 1988: 221–41.

Trigeorgis, L. *Real Options: managerial flexibility and strategy in resource allocation* (The MIT Press, Cambridge, Mass. and London, England: 1996).

Tucker, M.A. The assessment of country risk by Australian banks (Monash University Working Papers 1994).

Tversky, A. and Kahneman, D. 'Judgment under uncertainty: heuristics and biases', *Science*, vol. 185, 1974: 1124–31.

Tversky, A. and Kahneman, D. 'Prospect theory: an analysis of decision under risk', *Econometrica*, vol. 47, no. 2, March 1979.

Tversky, A. and Kahneman, D. 'The framing of decisions and the psychology of choice', *Science*, vol. 211, January 1981: 453–58.

United Nations Report of the Secretary-General on the Development of a Vulnerability Index for Small Island Developing States (Advance Unedited version to be submitted to the Commission for Sustainable Development, Sixth Session, April 1998, and to the Committee for Development Planning, May 1998).

United Nations Conference on Trade and Development (UNCTAD) (1994) World Investment Report: Transnational Corporations, Employment and the Workplace. United Nations Publication: New York.

United Nations Conference on Trade and Development (UNCTAD) (1995) World Investment Report: Transnational Corporations and Competitiveness. United Nations Publication: New York and Geneva.

United Nations Conference on Trade and Development (UNCTAD) (1996) World Investment Report: Investment, Trade and International Policy Arrangements. United Nations Publication: New York and Geneva.

United Nations Conference on Trade and Development (UNCTAD) (1997) World Investment Report: Transnational Corporations. United Nations Publication: New York and Geneva.

United Nations Conference on Trade and Development (UNCTAD) (1998) World Investment Report: Trends and Determinants. United Nations Publication: New York and Geneva.

United Nations Conference on Trade and Development (UNCTAD) (1999) World Investment Report: Foreign Direct Investment and Challenge of Development. United Nations Publication: New York and Geneva.

United Nations Conference on Trade and Development (UNCTAD) (2000) World Investment Report: Cross-board Mergers and Acquisition and Development. United Nations Publication: New York and Geneva

United Nations Conference on Trade and Development (UNCTAD) (2001) World Investment Report: Promoting Linkages. United Nations Publication: New York and Geneva.

United Nations Conference on Trade and Development (UNCTAD) (2002) Transnational Corporations and Export Competitiveness. United Nations Publications: New York and Geneva.

United Nations Conference on Trade and Development (UNCTAD) (2003) World Investment Report: FDI Policies for Development. United Nations Publication: New York.

Van Agtmael, A. 'How business has dealt with political risk', *Financial Executive*, 1976: 26–30.

Vonnegut, A. 'Real option theories and investment in emerging economies', *Emerging Markets Review*, vol. 1, 2000: 82–100.

Wafu, G. L. K. 'Political risk and foreign direct investment', Faculty of Economics and Statistics, University of Konstanz, Germany: 1998.

Werner, S. and Brouthers, E. 'International risk and perceived uncertainty: the dimensionality and internal consistency of Miller's measure', *Journal of International Business Studies*, vol. 27, no. 3, 1996: 571–88.

Wernerfelt, B. 'A resource-based view of the firm', *Strategic Management Journal*, vol. 5, 1984: 171–180.

White, C. M. *Russia and America: the roots of economic divergence* (Croom Helm, London: 1987).

White, M. J. 'The corporate bankruptcy decision', *Journal of Economic Perspectives*, vol. 3, no. 2, 1989: 129–51.

White, C. M. *Mastering Risk: Environments, markets and politics in Australian economic history* (Oxford University Press, Melbourne: 1992).

White, C. M. *Strategic Management* (Palgrave Macmillan, Houndsmill, Basingstoke: 2004).

White, C. M. and Fan, M. 'An integrated approach to risk as a determinant of foreign direct investment: i. developing a consistent terminology and theoretical framework, and ii. an empirical study'. Papers delivered at ABAS conferences in Bratislava and Tallinn, 2004.

Whittington, R. *What is Strategy and does it matter?*, 2nd ed. (Routledge, London: 2001).

Williamson, O. E. *The Economic Institutions of Capitalism: firms, markets, relational contracting* (The Free Press, New York: 1985).

Index